AT LEAST
WE LIVED

*The Unlikely Adventures of
an English Couple in World War II China*

E M M A   O X F O R D

BRANKSOME BOOKS

Book design by Cecelia Wong

Printed by CreateSpace

Available from Amazon.com, CreateSpace.com and other retail outlets

ISBN 10: 0615874851
ISBN 13: 978-0615874852

Branksome Books
atleastwelived@gmail.com

For Roxana and Gina

Contents

CHAPTER ONE

✧

Over the Hump
Leaving London 1943

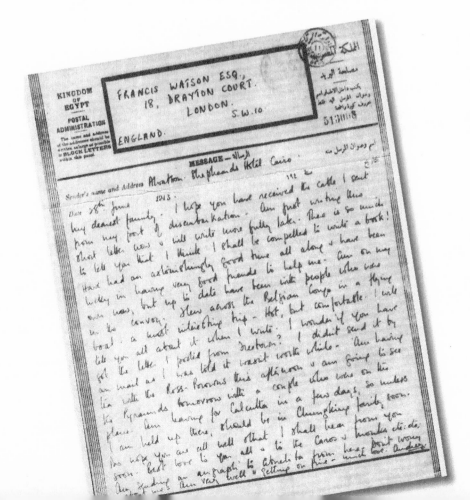

'There is so much to tell you that I think I shall be compelled to write a book!'
Audrey to her family, Shepheard's Hotel, Cairo, June 28, 1943.

She packed her trunk with great care – sprinkling mothballs around her winter woollens and tucking hand-stitched sachets of fragrant lavender among her blouses and dresses. She squeezed in a supply of cosmetics, her favourite books, and silver frames for the photos that would remind her of home; she would not be able to buy any of these precious items at her far-off destination – Chungking, the wartime capital of China. In blacked-out London she bid farewell to her widowed father, her two sisters and her close friends, with no idea when she would see them again. Alone with her luggage, she boarded a train for Liverpool – the northern port was more sheltered than the London docks from the ever present threat of German submarines. Finally on May 20, 1943, after one of the false starts typical of wartime transport, she embarked on a ship bound for the west coast of Africa, part of a convoy that sailed in formation for safety.

As her ship, the *Incomati*, steamed away from shore, she could scarcely imagine that her journey to China would last eight weeks and cover some 15,000 miles. It would take her halfway round a world at war, though her route, by land, sea and air, would zigzag through Africa, the Middle East and Asia to avoid the most dangerous battle zones. She wasn't in uniform and would travel as a lone civilian; she would have to figure out her own connections along the way.

Audrey Watson was more than ready for an adventure. A slender young woman of twenty-six, with fair, freckled skin and golden red hair, she was not the fragile English rose that she might appear. She had served in Britain's top-secret Special Operations Executive (SOE), working to support underground resistance to the Nazis. Now she was on her way to an equally sensitive post in China, a country of which she knew nothing, to work for a man she had never met. But she was not just eager for a new mission: she had reasons that she didn't admit to her family for leaving London that wartime summer of 1943.

Within days of leaving Liverpool, the gloom that had enveloped Audrey in the last few months lifted. She felt liberated, and didn't care that the sea voyage took her in quite the opposite direction from her ultimate destination – way out into the Atlantic and down the west coast of Africa. Her younger sister, Tottie, followed Audrey's progress – by coincidence, she was responsible for plotting the convoy's course from the naval base where she served in the Wrens. It was, Audrey would later write home, 'altogether the best holiday I've ever had'. After grey England, Audrey found the sea air and sunshine irresistible – a little too irresistible, since she got badly sunburned as she took part in exercises on deck. 'Felt exceedingly fit!' she wrote home.

After eighteen days at sea, the first port of call was Freetown in Sierra Leone. There the ship docked for four days and some of her companions disembarked, but Audrey continued to Lagos, and arrived in Nigeria's capital on June 18 to discover a whole new world of lights and luxury. A shipboard friend called Gerry Wormal, a dapper Cambridge-educated colonial service officer who seemed to know everyone in town, made sure Audrey had a fine time. Accommodation was impossibly scarce, but he found Audrey a hotel room – one with the unheard-of luxury of a private bathroom. She woke up at five o'clock most mornings to the unfamiliar sounds of local people gathering to gossip and draw water from the well under her window – despite the early hour, she enjoyed their chatter. 'They are a most cheery lot and always laughing,' she wrote home. 'Of all the natives I have met on this trip, I liked the ones from Lagos best.'

Gerry Wormal enjoyed the good life, and organised a full social calendar for Audrey and their shipmates. The first evening, he took them to dinner at the Ikoyi Club, a favourite haunt of the colonialists. After the dreary years of blackouts and food shortages in England, Audrey found this a joy. She had seen the lights of Freetown, but then the ship had been blacked out again going around the coast to Nigeria. Now to be able to sit out on a verandah with all the windows wide open and the lights blazing was simply wonderful. 'It was a very fine night and we sat out on the lawn and had drinks. They gave us an excellent dinner, and of course the fruit was super. You have bananas at every meal!' Audrey exclaimed with delight, as well she might: bananas had not been seen in England since the beginning of the war. The next night, it was back to the Club for a dance, and more novelty: 'I can't tell you how exciting it was to see everybody in evening clothes again, and the women using nail polish and perfume. I went around with my eyes popping out of my head.' There was more glamour to come. On Sunday, the party picnicked on a beach which looked straight out of a film set, with 'palm trees, white sand, breakers, native canoes, and really lovely native girls' carrying great baskets of bananas and coconuts on their heads.

After four days of fun in Lagos, Audrey parted from Gerry and most of her shipmates. She took off from the city before dawn on the next stage of her journey – an unforgettable four-day trip by flying boat over the heart of Africa. Stately flying boats, planes that could land on water, flew routes that had been opened up by Imperial Airways to link the far-flung outposts of the British Empire. Audrey could almost imagine the snaking line on a map, marking the stops this improbable plane took – first southeast from Lagos, crossing the equator, with overnight stops at Leopoldville and Stanleyville in the Belgian Congo, then north to Khartoum in the Sudan for another night stop, and on to Cairo. The route was published in the *Daily Telegraph*, so when she wrote home later Audrey saw no harm in telling her family about her journey:

> *The flying boat is exceedingly comfortable and they provide excellent food, either in lunch boxes, or at the places where you stop to refuel. The first place we stopped at [Libreville] was just north of the equator. It might have been a place out of a book – a shack built on sticks, with pigs and hens grubbing around underneath it. We had a lemonade here and then went on. Every time you stop to refuel it means getting out of the plane and having some sort of refreshment which is rather pleasant.*

Flying right over the Belgian Congo, Audrey saw nothing but miles and miles of impenetrable jungle, interrupted only by the deep waters of the Congo River. Then flying north through the Sudan and along the Nile, there was nothing but desert. Audrey had no idea there was so much uninhabitable land left in the world. Khartoum was quite the hottest place she had ever experienced. Everything she touched was burning hot – even the bed was scorching when she lay down on it.

Landing in Cairo on June 27, Audrey spent four nights staying at the famous Shepheard's Hotel, where she spotted General Montgomery surrounded by Allied troops, who only two weeks later would cross the Mediterranean from their bases in North Africa to take Sicily and begin the march through Italy. Amid this whirl of activity, Audrey waited patiently for transport that would get her across the Middle East and India to Calcutta, the gateway to China. Luckily, in Cairo she had an introduction to a couple called the Ross-Browns who were friends of her father. They took Audrey under their wing, entertaining her at their home and introducing her to an eligible young man over dinner at their club. That evening they went on to the cinema, but Audrey was so exhausted from the travel and the relentless heat that she fell asleep in the middle of the film. But she was wide awake on a day when she got a chance to see the Pyramids.

After a few days exploring the mosques and bazaars of Cairo, it was time for Audrey to leave the comforts of Shepheard's. The most challenging part of her journey was still to come. After departing Cairo for Calcutta, Audrey's plane twice had engine trouble. It landed on the Dead Sea to refuel, but could not take off again and passengers had to spend the night in Jerusalem, quite a diversion, but for Audrey an unexpected pleasure: she stayed at the King David Hotel, and had a chance to see biblical sights in the old city, and the Garden of Gethsemane. She was terribly impressed by Jerusalem, still under the control of the British mandate: 'What struck me more than anything was the cleanliness of the market in the city, after the filth and stench of Cairo.'

Eventually, the plane headed south again, touching down for the night in Basra at the top of the Persian Gulf. But the next day new engine trouble developed, and the party had to make an unscheduled night stop at Sharjah, a desert sheikdom with a tiny airstrip used by the RAF. 'It was supposed to be one of the hottest places on the Persian Gulf and altogether quite impossible.' Audrey wrote home. 'We drove miles into the desert from our landing point (saw several mirages) and the place where we had to spend the night was some sort of RAF camp. It was a great joke among the men, as I was supposed to be the only white woman for 700 miles that night! It was just the place for a murder or rebellion. Behind the rest house they had an open-air cinema – the seats consisting of upturned petrol cans. They took me to it and it is said I was the first woman of any colour to have graced the place. So apart from the suffocating heat and the fact that the sweat simply poured off one the whole time, and the sand and mosquitoes, it was an amusing episode. The sanitation of course, was practically non-existent.'

— • —

Making the best of non-existent sanitation in the desert, Audrey must have seemed to the RAF men in Sharjah as the epitome of a certain kind of plucky, well-bred English girl. But she had seen more of the world than most of the airmen. She came from a long line of adventurers. 'All my immediate ancestors were travellers,' she would write in her journal, many years later. 'Had I been a man I should like to have been an explorer. How marvellous to have been a member of one of the Polar expeditions – or of an expedition up the Amazon.'

She hadn't seen the Amazon, but it is hardly surprising that its mysteries appealed. For Audrey had been born and raised on the distant western coast of South America. Her paternal grandfather, Charles Watson, emigrated from England in the mid-nineteenth century, when the only way to get around was in a covered wagon. He married Mary Backus, an American descendant of early Quaker settlers in New England, and went into business with Henry Meiggs, Mary's uncle. Known in Latin America as the Yankee Pizarro, Meiggs was an engineer and speculator who built the railways that would open up the continent. Audrey's mother's side of the family was just as enterprising. Her maternal grandfather, Frederick Michael, traced his line back four generations to David Michael, an eighteenth-century refugee from Germany who was a founder of an early Jewish community in Swansea, Wales. Frederick, like Charles Watson, left Britain for South America in the nineteenth century, making his fortune in the mining industry in Chile and Peru, and marrying Charlotte Harvey, a strong-willed young woman from Cornwall.

Audrey was born on September 7 1916 in Iquique, a port in arid northern Chile, where her father Francis, known as Frank, pursued the family business of nitrate mining. In 1910 he had moved down from a mining camp in the high desert to the coastal town of Iquique where his career flourished. He soon fell in love with Frederick and Charlotte Michael's beautiful red-headed daughter, Dorothy. The couple were

Audrey spent her early childhood in Chile

married in January 1912, and had a family of three girls – Joan, Audrey and Daphne, known as Tottie.

By the time Audrey was nine, however, the nitrate industry was collapsing and Frank Watson shipped his wife and three young daughters across the Atlantic to England. Audrey attended Cheltenham Ladies' College, hating the strictures of the rigorous school after the relaxed ways of her Chilean childhood. She did not see eye to eye with the headmistress' ambitions for Cheltenham girls: when asked about her career goals, Audrey replied that she wanted to be a good wife and mother. And when she was sixteen, tragedy struck. Her mother Dorothy developed a chilblain on her toe during a cold English winter. Sep-

Audrey (right) at the English seaside with her sisters,
Joan (left) and Tottie (centre), 1931

ticaemia set in, and within days Dorothy had died, from a condition that only a few years later would have been easily treated with antibiotics. Adding to the girls' trauma, their father was away in Chile, trying in vain to rescue his failing business.

Frank returned to England and moved his family to London. The depression of the 1930s hit hard, and they lived a life of genteel poverty in a succession of rented homes in South Kensington. Frank teetered on the verge of bankruptcy, pawning the family jewellery until it was saved by a small inheritance – Joan and Audrey's earnings often provided the only steady income in the household. After Cheltenham, Audrey had persuaded her father to send her to college to study cooking and household management. Then Frank insisted that she add another arrow to her quiver – she trained as a secretary, and began her working life with a firm of stockbrokers in the City of London.

At the domestic science college, Audrey had met Dorothy Hutchison, a lively brunette with sparkling eyes who shared Audrey's sense of humour. They christened each other Watty and Hutch, and quickly realized how much they had in common. Born in Shanghai, Dorothy had spent her early years in an outpost of Britain's commercial empire, just as Audrey had done. In 1880, Dorothy's grandfather had founded J.D. Hutchison & Company, one of Hong Kong and Shanghai's foremost trading houses, and she had come to live in England only when her father sold his share of the family business in the 1920s.

Audrey, living in a household with only sisters and a widowed father for company, was drawn to the gregarious Hutchison family – Dorothy had two sisters and three brothers. Audrey often spent weekends at their welcoming home in Surrey, and it was through Dorothy that Audrey's wartime work began. After war with Germany broke out in 1939, Audrey took her best friend's place as a civilian secretary to a Royal Air Force commander in Farnborough, south of London – Dorothy had resigned to get married.

Soon Audrey witnessed up close the bravery of the pilots in the Battle of Britain – the fierce air war in the skies over southern England, which Hitler saw as the prelude to a ground invasion. Audrey spent her twenty-fourth birthday on September 7 1940 visiting her family in South Kensington. The weather was fine, with a cloudless blue sky, and for the first time German bombers launched a major attack on the capital in broad daylight: the Watson sisters and their friends watched from the roof of their building as the docklands some miles to the east went up in flames. That day alone, over 300 Londoners were killed and 1,300 were seriously injured.

Audrey was now living close to her job at RAF Farnborough. She shared a neat, suburban house with Dorothy and her sister, Helen, both married to army officers who were away at war, leaving their brides to cope with the babies that had quickly come along. Despite the hardships and the devastating losses of those days, the trio of friends found that companionship and shared laughter got them through. Much later, hearing a favourite wartime radio programme reminded Audrey of the extraordinary intensity of those years:

We were all so close then – laughed at such simple things – led such a monotonous and yet such a dynamic life. Every moment might have been our last – and so it seemed, as if we derived more pleasure in our leisure than we do now, when time might be endless. Everything was urgent. A friend home for a fortnight might never be seen again. We would sit up all night so as not to miss a second of the precious time...It was as if we all understood each other then. We worked towards a common end – that the war might end and we might have our lives to ourselves again. We played to the same purpose. To enjoy those friends who appeared and disappeared again as suddenly.

Laughter was especially poignant:

The humour in a parcel Eric sent to Dorothy – in which the tea and sugar had become inextricably mixed with the sealing wax – we sifted the tea from the sugar and boiled the sugar with the sealing wax, taking the wax off the top with a spoon. The butter which was rancid, but could not be wasted. So we beat it up and decorated a cake – and had near-hysterics as the cream-cheese like butter oozed from our improvised funnel...We did enjoy ourselves in some ways – we worked hard – we were often sad – we lost friends and yet made new ones – I think I learned more than those who did not share those hardships and had not the opportunity of seeing the English in their England at that time. Journal, June 30, 1949.

Audrey treasured those moments, but after two years in Farnborough she was anxious to rejoin her father and sisters, who had narrowly survived the Blitz but were coping with the daily stresses of life in the bombed-out capital. One night before Audrey's return, Drayton Gardens – the family's street in South Kensington – was strafed with incendiary bombs, which completely destroyed the building next door and the cinema opposite their flat. 'That was adjacent' said Frank phlegmatically, as he, Joan and Tottie woke up covered with shattered glass and debris. The Watsons, like countless other Londoners, picked themselves up, moving across the hallway to rooms left vacant by evacuees, and carried on as best they could.

In 1942, Audrey got the chance to return home for a job in central London. Her RAF boss recommended her for a transfer to a position with the SOE, the spy agency that Churchill had set up to conduct clandestine warfare against the Axis powers throughout the world. Audrey

Audrey (left) with Dorothy Hutchison (centre) on a hard-earned skiing holiday in Villars, Switzerland, 1938

was appointed a secretary in the French section, supporting agents of the resistance in occupied France. She moved back in with her family, never telling them exactly what she did at the agency's Baker Street headquarters, though in later years she joked that when she was sent out to buy lunchtime sandwiches for the supposedly anonymous office, the caterer would shout out for all to hear, "Six ham and cheese for the spies."

At night Audrey took her turn on firewatch duty on the roof of the South Kensington flats, watching for blazes sparked by incendiary bombs: when her family was on duty, they would light a big, cheering fire in their living room to see them through the night. Taking the pre-dawn shift was always the hardest. She did a lot of reading – Shakespeare and the Dictionary of Quotations were favourite companions during the dull and lonely watches.

Audrey took a lifelong pride in having worked at the SOE, and in having served her share of long hours on fire duty. But something was missing. Marriage and motherhood hadn't come as easily to Audrey as to her girlfriends, though there was nothing she wanted more. She had had one lightning romance with an army officer home on leave with a car and money in his pockets. Audrey confided in her elder sister, Joan, that they might get engaged when he returned from a posting to India, but it was not to be. Then she fell hard for a naval officer called Freddie, a man haunted by being pilloried in the press (though absolved in the official inquiry) for the sinking of HMS Thetis, a submarine disaster that had taken the lives of 99 sailors and civilians in 1939. Audrey's heart was broken when Freddie went off and married another woman. It was only many years later, in her journal, that Audrey admitted: 'Had my love for Freddie not been hopeless, I should never have gone to Chungking.'

But go she did. In the spring of 1943 Jack Hutchison, Dorothy's uncle, sent word that he was looking for a new secretary for confidential work at the British Embassy in Chungking, where he was the Commercial Counsellor. Audrey leapt at the chance. Nearly four years of war had drained her – the cold, the rationing, the bombs, the lonely nighttime fire watches, the deaths of friends – and, more than anything, her hopeless romances. Whatever the hazards and hardships of an assignment on the other side of the world, she was eager to escape.

— • —

By the time she got to the RAF base on the edge of the desert at Sharjah, she was half way there. The last leg of her journey to China would be the toughest yet. After leaving the Gulf, her plane turned east for India, stopping in Karachi for the night. The next day, Audrey finally landed in Calcutta, where she hoped to find a flight into China. But on reaching the city, she found herself completely alone – no longer a passenger of the British Overseas Airways Corporation (BOAC), who had looked after her up until that point. She had nowhere to stay, no local currency, could not speak the local language, and was suffering badly from sinus trouble. There were no hotel rooms to be had, but a friend in England had given Audrey an introduction to a Dr Nairn and his wife. She rang the couple in desperation, and they took pity on her, finding her a room with friends and showing her around the bustling city. The climate was unbearably hot and humid – 'you can't leave cigarettes out of a tin, and matches are so damp you can't strike them' – but Audrey began to discover the compensations of life in the Empire, reminiscing in later years about 'the perfect service, exotic foods, quiet luxury, the leisure – all so different from the 1943 England I had left.'

Calcutta offered a rare refuge amidst the turmoil of war in the Pacific. India was the only British colony in Asia that had escaped invasion in Japan's march through the region following Pearl Harbor. Calcutta became the headquarters for the Allied command in the Far East, and the city was teeming with soldiers and spies. Audrey began to learn first-hand about the war against Japan, which up until then had been more remote to her than the war in Europe.

Of course, back in England eighteen months earlier, she had followed the news of Japan's attacks on Pearl Harbor and on the British possession of Hong Kong. The British were dismayed by the fall of the colony on Christmas Day, 1941, and there was worse to come. The disaster of Hong Kong was quickly followed by the more shocking collapse of Malaya, a much larger colony. The supposedly impregnable island fortress of Singapore fell in mid-February, 1942. Even at the time this seemed to some like the beginning of the end of Empire. Burma was next on Japan's agenda that spring. In April the Burma Road, a tortuous mountain route connecting southwest China to Lashio in Burma, was closed. That cut off Free China – the inland part of the country not under Japanese control – from contact with the outside world by land or sea. The only lifeline of China's ruler, the Nationalist Generalissimo Chiang Kai-shek, was the air link over 'the Hump' of the Himalayas to India.

Audrey must have quickly grasped that Calcutta was the vital supply base for China at the Indian end of the Hump. A huge airlift of men and matériel was underway over the mountains. The United States, and to a lesser extent Britain, were pouring aid into China, despite reservations about Chiang's leadership, and suspicions that he was keener to suppress his Communist rivals than to defeat the Japanese enemy.

As a junior member of Britain's diplomatic staff, Audrey was a low priority for transport, and she had to wait ten days in Calcutta for a scarce spot on one of the small planes that flew the Hump route. She used the time to sort out formalities with the China Relations Office, the British liaison office for China operations. And she had some new clothes made by Calcutta's nimble tailors, having heard that this would be impossibly expensive in Chungking. She dined at the Saturday Club, a gracious colonial haunt in the heart of the city. Dr Nairn was able to treat her sinus infection before she flew – saving her from certain agony going over the Hump at an altitude that was at the limit of an unpressurized plane.

In the clubs of Calcutta, Audrey surely heard stories of the path into China. Intrepid pilots of the China National Aviation Corporation (CNAC), a Chinese-American joint venture, had opened up the Hump

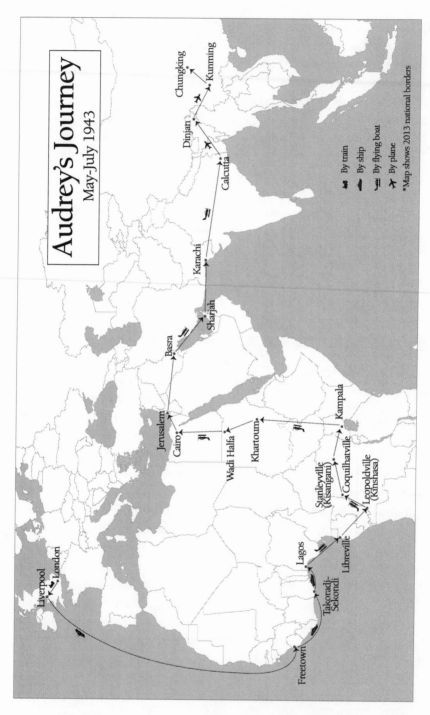

route in 1941. Flights in barebones twin-engine planes, mostly DC-3s or their military equivalent, C-47s, were both dangerous and extremely uncomfortable. The unpressurized planes could not climb high enough to fly over the highest mountains of the eastern Himalayas, so the pilots picked their way between rather than over the snow-covered peaks. At the dizzy altitudes, cabins became very cold, passengers piled on their warmest clothes, and – if they were lucky – pulled down oxygen masks. In the early days, only the pilots had these, and would have to lend them to passengers in distress.

The point and priority of the Hump airlift was to transport cargo, so seats were rudimentary or non-existent. Passengers sat on the floor, or on hard benches along each side of the cabin. They prayed for good weather, but there were always risks of unpredictable conditions – storms, strong winds, very poor visibility, turbulence at high altitude or wind shears at low altitude. And, of course, there were no emergency landing spots in the middle of the mountains. At best the ride was bumpy, and at worst it was deadly: there were many fatal accidents, not to mention Japanese attacks. Over three years of operating an airlift into China, over 500 military and civil planes came down along the Hump route – an astonishing number – and over 1,000 pilots and passengers lost their lives. It was said that on clear days pilots used the gleaming wreckage of crashed aircraft as navigational aids along what came to be called 'Aluminium Valley'.

Eventually, it was Audrey's turn to fly the route that was already a legend. She boarded at dawn for the twelve-hour journey from Calcutta to Dinjan airfield in Assam and on to make the breathtaking crossing of the snow-covered Himalayas. She soon had her first glimpse of China as CNAC flew her over the high peaks and valleys of Yunnan province into Kunming, a lakeside city on a high plateau, and the hub at the Hump's China end. After a brief stop, Audrey continued north over rolling hills and paddy fields, touching down at Chungking's makeshift airfield as the sun set on July 14, eight weeks after her departure. Wartime England – with all its camaraderie and friendship, with its blackouts and night watches, its hopeless love affairs, its rancid butter – was very far away.

CHAPTER TWO

Cabbage Patch Days
Chungking 1943

Audrey in Chungking, 1943

'Chungking is fascinating, filthy, fearfully expensive, primitive, picturesque, but altogether I like it.'

Audrey to her family, July 18, 1943.

A udrey stepped off the plane into the humid cauldron of heat that passed for summer in Chungking. Jack Hutchison, Counsellor to the British Embassy, was there to greet his new personal assistant. With her fair colouring and shy smile, Audrey must have looked as though she would melt in Chungking's torrid climate. But Mr. Hutchison knew that his latest recruit was much tougher than she seemed – that she had come straight out of the SOE, and that travel was in the family genes. The Watsons had that in common with his own family, the prominent Shanghai traders. Jack, now in his early fifties, had made his career as a diplomat, staying in China after the family business was sold.

Mr. Hutchison – as Audrey would call her new boss – had arranged for her to be billeted in one of the Embassy messes on the south side of the Yangtze River. From there, she gazed across at the ancient city of Chungking which was wedged into a peninsula rising from the north bank, a spit of land narrowing to a point where the Jialing River flowed into the mighty Yangtze. Jack Hutchison explained that the British Embassy was perched on the hillside in the cramped old town on the north side, but that it was safer and more comfortable to lodge on the south bank. Living quarters there were more airy, and more sheltered from the Japanese bombing raids that had plagued Chungking since Chiang Kai-shek retreated from the invaders in 1938 and made the Sichuan city his capital. The south bank was home to the first foreign merchants to steam up the Yangtze fifty years earlier, and Audrey soon noticed the grand European-style mansions that lined the waterfront, built by an Englishman, Archibald Little, and other early traders.

Audrey now joined a much larger influx of Westerners sucked in by war in Asia to serve in the remote city in the clouds. For all its obvious differences, Chungking must have felt a bit like Cairo, where Audrey

23

had stopped a few weeks earlier – a magnet for diplomats, soldiers and reporters drawn from all corners of the globe. The cosmopolitan buzz that Audrey would quickly discover was quite new to Chungking. Just a few years before, it had been an obscure city in southwest China – it was not even the capital of its enormous province, Sichuan. But Japan's advance had forced Chiang to retreat to the mountains. Chungking, his chosen headquarters, lay high up the Yangtze some 1,400 miles from the sea, well beyond the river's deep gorges. It was in a desperately poor and undeveloped region, a land of peasant farmers. But the arrival of Chiang's Nationalist government in 1938 opened a unique chapter in the history of the medieval city.

For eight years, Chungking would be the nerve centre of political and military operations in the China theatre of war. Officials of the Nationalist party (also called Kuomintang or KMT), representatives of Mao Zedong's Communists – supposedly allied with the Kuomintang in a united front against Japan – the diplomatic and military missions of all the Allied powers, and a whole caravan of journalists and advisers descended on the dank spot. Thousands of factories from the coastal region were literally dismantled and shipped up the Yangtze to bring some semblance of modern industry to the new capital. Scores of universities relocated from occupied eastern China, bringing thousands of students to the heartland. Chungking's population ballooned from around 300,000 in 1934 to over a million. Yet neither distance nor the encircling mountains had saved the city from horrific Japanese air raids – Audrey was amazed to discover that before Pearl Harbor Chungking was more frequently bombed than any other city in the world. By 1943 the air raids had eased up, but the damage was done: bombing had flattened almost half of the rickety old town, whose wood and bamboo lodgings clung to the rocky peninsula between the rivers. Nearly 12,000 civilians had been killed in the raids and the oxygen-sucking firestorms that raged in their wake.

Audrey witnessed the devastation on her first morning's commute to her new office at the Embassy. After taking just one day to settle in at her lodgings, she reported for duty. She and her roommates from the mess had to walk down hundreds of steps to the nearest pier on the south bank. The Yangtze was in full flood with summer rains, and they crossed the vast, swirling river in a small, wooden sampan – 'a most amusing, exhilarating and sometimes hair-raising trip,' Audrey told her family in a letter home – as the boatman struggled with strong currents to keep on course. The Embassy staff landed at a broad stone jetty by the ancient Chuqimen gate to the once-walled city on the north bank. From the gate, the staffers had to hike up another few hundred steps, often slick with mud (and worse), to reach the nearest road. There an Embassy truck would drive them the rest of the way to the office. If Audrey had to work late, she would miss the return truck and have to walk all the way down to the dock, through the ruins and the rat-infested, stinking alleys of the old town.

It was a city of steps: 'In fact there are roads which aren't composed of steps,' she soon wrote home, 'but this is not the general rule.' Chinese workers would race up and down steps all day, carrying heavy loads in wooden buckets hanging from bamboo poles balanced across their shoulders, while others pulled rickshaws or sedan chairs along dirt paths for those able to afford the fare. To be sure, the city was slowly modernising: the years of bombing had at least cleared the ground for construction, and by the time Audrey arrived there were a few roads for cars and more brick buildings. But the stench of open sewers was still overwhelming.

Chungking, with its intrigue, its cosmopolitan crowd, its primitive living conditions, its atrocious climate, and its backdrop of stunning scenery, instantly captivated and confused Audrey. After just a few days, she gave her verdict, writing her first letter home since Cairo: 'Chungking is fascinating, filthy, fearfully expensive, primitive, picturesque, but altogether I like it.'

— • —

Audrey wished she had a family letter to reply to: she had not heard any news since leaving Liverpool. No mail had reached Audrey en route, and she was terribly disappointed to find none awaiting her arrival at the Embassy. It was another agonizing month before news from England made its slow way to her. Meanwhile she threw herself into her new life, and at least once a week sat down with a pad of thin blue airmail paper to write to 'my dearest family', in long letters describing her impressions of China. At least Audrey had one link with home, since Jack Hutchison was Dorothy's uncle. On her very first weekend,

PHOTO COURTESY OF MICHAEL SULLIVAN

Chungking was devastated by Japanese air raids

he invited the new arrival to join a house party in the hills above her mess. Audrey's lodgings on the south side, though just across the Yangtze from the overcrowded city, were on the edge of spectacular countryside. Several ranges of green hills rose up into the distance behind the mess, and the Embassy kept a staffed bungalow on the first range, for the use of their diplomats at weekends. Jack Hutchison took Audrey up to the bungalow on foot – 'a long but really lovely walk' into the hills, she wrote home. The veteran China hand would take an avuncular interest in Audrey as she settled in, showing her around Chungking, introducing her to the strange delights of Chinese cuisine, and to many of his Chinese friends. He was an expert guide.

Born in China, like the rest of his family, Jack Hutchison had first-hand experience of the conflict with Japan. He had joined the China branch of the British diplomatic service after graduating from Cambridge, and married a formidable lady named Dora Evans, the first woman to have owned a car in Shanghai: they had a daughter, Mary, and a younger son. Hutchison was serving at the Shanghai Consulate at the time of Pearl Harbor. When the Japanese occupied the city's foreign concessions, the family and other diplomats were marched at bayonet point down the Bund, Shanghai's celebrated river promenade, and then corralled in the Cathay Mansions Hotel for several weeks before being evacuated on a Japanese ship, in an exchange with Japanese civilians who were on a British ship. The Hutchisons disembarked in Lourenço Marques in Portuguese East Africa, where Mary, then twenty and a skilled code-breaker, remained to continue her war work, whilst Dora and son took refuge in South Africa. Jack Hutchison, invaluable for his China expertise and fluency in Mandarin, was soon sent back to Asia to take up the post of Commercial Counsellor in Chungking. Separated from his family, he must have appreciated the company of a young Englishwoman who was not much older than his daughter.

Audrey certainly enjoyed her first weekend at the bungalow, writing home:

> Anybody from the Embassy can go and stay there free, except that you pay for the food, which was excellent when we were there. There is a most wonderful view up there, right down to the river. The hills are covered in pine trees and the whole set up is most romantic. You know what I mean, the bungalow on top of a hill, miles from anywhere, buried in a pine forest! We went up on Saturday evening. It was pouring with rain but this makes very little difference in the hot weather, because you are always wet anyway.

On Sunday, some Embassy colleagues came up for lunch – including Beth Thompson and Pat Sedgwick, a couple of around Audrey's age who would become great friends. In the afternoon they showed the newcomer an ancient walled Buddhist temple on the next hill, whose quiet beauty impressed her very much.

Trips to the hills were a welcome escape from the oppressive heat. On July 26, Audrey explained to her family why she was typing, rather than hand-writing, her letters home:

> I tried writing a letter last night and the perspiration just dripped off my brow on to the paper and made a horrible mess. In a way it is lovely to wake up and see the sun shining every morning, and the sky so blue, but on the other hand it is uncomfortable to be in a perpetual pool of sweat. You remember that summer a couple of years ago when we thought it was so terribly hot? That's rather what it is like here now, except that it is a damper heat in that you do drip the entire time.

Most of the men carried sweat rags around their necks, and wore shorts all the time – even the Ambassador. 'Am sick to death of this sea of knees you see everywhere', said Audrey in September.

Men outnumbered women at Audrey's lodgings – and throughout the foreign community. Her housemates were three other girls (as she called them), and half a dozen men. There was little privacy, and few comforts: she shared a room right up on the roof with one other girl. It had a verandah, but no chairs and got so hot at night that sometimes she could hardly sleep. She was not fazed by the mess's primitive bathroom – a thunder box, and a huge earthenware tub for a bath – though she admitted that 'a push-and-pull [a flushing toilet], which you sometimes see in other people's houses, is a great joy'. But the frequent power cuts, and the lack of anywhere to sit and relax were tiresome. She liked her roommates' company up to a point, but soon tired of their girlish escapades, writing one day:

> Must get dressed. The other girls are out at the moment so it is reasonably quiet. The other Sunday I was lying down before dinner (quite the thing to do), when they came along and wanted me to play hide and seek or murder! I suppose they were bored (the lights were out that night) but I felt a bit annoyed at

being woken up for that! Didn't play so they thought I must be ill. They are really all nice but rather frivolous. You know how decorous I am.

She made that last comment tongue-in-cheek: Audrey was regarded as the lively firebrand of the family. But even at twenty-six she was perhaps older than the other single girls, and her recent experiences had made her more reflective; not only her doomed romances, but also the four years of relentless war in Europe, which she had seen up close with the RAF and the SOE.

Writing one sweat-drenched letter, Audrey told her family that the mess had been without electricity for three days, which meant that the only fan in the house was off, there was no refrigeration and you could not see to read in the evenings. Many years later, thinking back to Chungking while writing her journal, she remembered what it was like:

The weather was never good. There was a day in which I rejoiced because it was fine and dry and I was able to do some washing and get it properly aired. Often things hung for days and were as damp as they had been on removal from the wash-basin. The lights were so dim we couldn't see to read or write – often we had only smelly, unsatisfactory candles – the heat from which seemed unbearable in that humid hot climate.

Perhaps I will never forget waiting for the wind on the roof that night, not so long after my arrival. It was to be a sign, and it came, quietly and gently, as if it were just a small wind just for me, so that I should know – down through the valley behind the house and from the first range. It was quite dark, and there were all those noises which were so essentially Chungking – the dogs, drums, calls – general exciting noise – and the lights of the North Bank – across that wide, wicked river. Perhaps the image is engraved on my mind. Journal, October 8, 1949.

A small wind, just for her, and what did it portend? She was on the verge of a momentous few months. There was so much to learn, and Audrey had to rely on her quick wits and natural curiosity. Chelten-ham Ladies' College had given her a good traditional education, and equipped her with all the social graces, but she hadn't had the chance to go on to university (nor had anyone in her family). Although her father was at one time honorary British consul in Iquique, this new world of high-flying diplomats with degrees from Oxford and Cambridge was quite unfamiliar – and sometimes a little daunting.

But before long Audrey found herself in the thick of things, in great demand in the heavily male foreign community. Within days of her arrival, the Ambassador and his wife, Sir Horace and Lady Seymour, invited her to a dinner party. Audrey must have been apprehensive: she was very short of smart clothes because her carefully packed trunk had not arrived when she did. She improvised by wearing a long cotton 'housecoat' that her hostess in Calcutta had given her – not very dressy, but casually elegant.

The Seymours put her at ease: although all the ladies wore long dresses, 'it was not a smart affair at all', she wrote home. The Ambassador's residence was a hilltop villa, with an upswept roof of green tiles, set in tranquil gardens. The villa, 'Feige', or flying pavilion, had a history: it was built as a guesthouse for Chiang Kai-shek, but he had lent it to Sir Horace's predecessor after the Embassy was badly bombed earlier in the war. 'They gave us a very good dinner and their place is right up on a hill at the back of the city and it was comparatively cool', Audrey told her family with some relief.

Sir Horace Seymour was a distinguished looking man with aquiline features, a moustache, and a penchant for bow ties. He had been Britain's envoy to China for over a year, succeeding Sir Archibald Clark Kerr, who had had the task of moving the mission from Nanking to Chungking, following Chiang's government. Sir Horace was a quieter, more restrained man than his predecessor and much less familiar with China. Lady Violet more than made up for her husband's reticence. She had recently joined him in the posting, tearing herself away from a son at school in England. Lady Seymour was a more outgoing and forceful personality, and essential to the social life of the Embassy. She kept a kindly eye on Audrey in the months to come.

Apart from Jack Hutchison, Sir Horace was supported by two other senior diplomats who knew China well, and were personally respected by its leaders: Berkeley Gage and Sir Eric Teichman. Both travelled out from London with the new ambassador in early 1942, forging a bond

View of Chungking rooftops and the southern hills from the Embassy quarter

that would serve them well. Sir Eric, known as 'Tei', had been summoned out of retirement to be Political Counsellor. A career China diplomat, he spoke Mandarin fluently and had travelled the length and breadth of the country, much of it on foot. He had the best sense of humour in the Embassy, according to his colleague Berkeley Gage.

Gage, First Secretary and Head of Chancery, was on his second tour of duty in China, and was close to Madame Chiang Kai-shek. They had become friendly during Gage's earlier posting, when she had agreed to be godmother to the Gages' son, born in London. Berkeley Gage was a large man with a booming voice. Unashamedly gregarious, he revelled in establishing dining clubs and organizing social events in every city he served in, happier in the field than in the office. 'I had no intellectual pretensions… only a sense of humour, some common sense and a human touch', he recalled in an aptly-titled memoir: *It's Been a Marvellous Party*. He was in Chungking without his family, and in his memoir bemoaned the absence of wives and the shortage of sex: 'From under our cold morning showers, we felt like monks looking down on the unemployed'. Innocently or not, he quickly befriended Audrey, taking her out to drinks and inviting her to his famous parties.

Then there were the military people, some of whom served as attachés to the diplomatic missions. Audrey very soon met a member of the Air Attaché's Office, Squadron Leader Gidley Baird. He was one of the men Berkeley envied: Gidley's wife, Pamela, was with him in Chungking as secretary to the head of the British Military Mission (BMM). The couple lived in a bungalow a little way below Audrey's mess. The house was shared with the senior Air Attaché, Group Captain James Warburton, and it was one of the more comfortable residences in the diplomatic community. Audrey fell into the habit of dropping by for tea on her way home. 'They have jam and butter – neither of which we ever see in our Mess – and as they have a wireless you can listen to the news', she said. And Audrey often dined with the Gidley Bairds, enjoying the ease of their company and of going out on her own side of the river. When she spent the evening on the north bank, she would typically stay overnight at a friend's lodging – a common arrangement given the hazards of crossing the river late at night. Audrey explained to her questioning family that the motto in Chungking was "where you dine, you sleep". With a blossoming social life, Audrey found herself doing this quite often.

In late August, Audrey heard from her younger sister, Tottie, that she was engaged to be married to Buffy Hebeler, a vet in Somerset. Audrey was delighted, but sad to be missing the wedding:

> I do wish I was home for it all. Unfortunately everything here is so exorbitantly expensive that the only thing I can think of in the way of a wedding present is to get the Army & Navy Stores in Calcutta to send home a food parcel for three months running. There is a girl going down there tomorrow from here and I have asked her to try and arrange to send home butter, jam, dried fruit, sugar or anything she can get in the way of food.

Food parcels being sent from India to England – this was truly a sign of Britain's wartime deprivations. Audrey felt guilty that the food in Chungking was good and plentiful, and about much more besides:

> It really pains me when I eat two eggs for breakfast and think

of you at home hardly ever getting them. In fact a great deal pains me when I think of what you are putting up with at home and the easy life we live out here. I was never aggressively patriotic before, but when I am asked "What do you think of Chungking?" or when people ask what on earth induced me to come to a God-forsaken place like this I really get annoyed. I consider that four years of war at home with people working long hours and having hardly any leisure, and no servants, not to mention rationing – for however good, it is enough to turn a housewife's hair grey – and suffering all the petty annoyances of queuing for buses etc., the people who are here <u>now</u> simply don't know what it can be like.... Perhaps when I have been here as long as some of these people though, I may too feel like grumbling. I admit the heat is trying and it is very annoying if the electricity fails, but the country is lovely and I am still enough of a tripper to be fascinated by everything I see...We are all so afraid of "defeatist" talk at home that people abroad imagine you are all living in a semi-paradise. Or perhaps the truth is that after some years abroad home <u>is</u> a paradise, no matter what.

So, after grey, depressed England, life in Chungking seemed pretty easy. There were problems and dangers of course – including the threat of air raids. But Audrey assured her family that the air raid shelters were wonderful – 'exactly like the caves at Hastings'. Since the onset of bombing four years earlier, the Chinese had hollowed out these cavernous shelters from the bedrock of the city. Audrey had heard that on one tragic occasion in 1941, during a particularly prolonged raid, nearly 1,000 people had suffocated in one of the caves, but in the main the shelters saved countless lives. Luckily, by now there was a well-developed early warning system, thanks to US Army Air Force Colonel Claire Chennault, who was based in Kunming, and Audrey would not often have to retreat to the caves.

The obvious dangers of war aside, Audrey's biggest headache was the extraordinarily high cost of living, caused by unbridled inflation, and an artificially fixed rate of exchange imposed by the weak Nationalist government. She, like all diplomats and soldiers, found it almost impossible to manage on a modest government salary, set in distant

England without much regard to ever-spiralling prices. Major General G.E. Grimsdale, head of the British Military Mission, said in an unpublished memoir that the unmanageable cost of living was a perennial issue. He reported in 1942, for example, that a seat at a local cinema cost a soldier several days' pay.

As soon as Audrey began work, she realized that her salary was totally inadequate. Jack Hutchison took up the issue on her behalf, but it was never really resolved, and the best she could hope for was that her board and lodging would be covered – at least, as she'd said, the food was plentiful and there were servants to help with the chores. She would have just a small cash salary on top, woefully little to meet all her other needs.

On August 28, Audrey was invited to a rare expatriate wedding – the marriage of Pat Sedgwick and Beth Thompson, the Embassy couple whom she had met on her first weekend. Beth was an Australian, and Pat was in economic intelligence. Her choice of wedding gift was revealing: she settled on giving the bride a pot of Yardley's Cold Cream, because anything more would bankrupt her.

The couple caused something of a stir, Audrey told her family, by getting engaged after they had known each other only three weeks:

> But then possibly there is something about this place, because I got a proposal the other day, after having known the chap five weeks! You may be glad to hear that I am not doing anything foolhardy though, and have refused.

It was still early days, and Audrey had no intention of giving up her independence too easily. In September, the oppressive summer heat lifted, and the 'social season' got into full swing. Audrey now truly appreciated the cosmopolitan buzz of Chungking, writing home on the 25th that the gregarious Berkeley Gage had taken to giving tea parties every Saturday afternoon on the Embassy lawn. Two courts were marked out, one for deck tennis and one for badminton, and lots of people came along for the fun. Audrey invariably saw some new faces: 'There are of course masses of people in Chungking, and every nationality under the sun. So far have met Australians, Canadians, Poles, Russians, Americans, Free French, Dutch, a Mexican, Indians, and of course many Chinese. It really is very interesting.'

That night, the British Other Ranks (BORs, or enlisted men) gave the opening dance of the season at their mess. Audrey quickly discovered that their Saturday night dances were the wildest parties in town, getting underway late in the evening and carrying on into the small hours to non-stop music from a couple of gramophones. 'A girl is kept on her feet for five hours straight, and becomes a trifle foot-sore by two o'clock in the morning', complained Audrey after experiencing a few BOR marathons.

Audrey enjoyed the dances up to a point. But she found the dinner parties beforehand more glamorous. At one, she met General Pechkoff, the Free French representative in China, and a much-decorated veteran of World War I. He was at the party with his colonel and captain:

> *The General was absolutely wonderful – he is very short, one armed, and has four rows of ribbon. Somehow it seems a double tragedy that a <u>Frenchman</u> should be one armed – but even with that one arm his gestures were most expressive.*

At the end of the party, Audrey watched in admiration as Pechkoff and his captain waited patiently for the colonel to disentangle himself from a beautiful Polish girl – 'the glamour queen of this place' – how very French, thought Audrey, for a General to let romance take precedence over his own convenience.

In October, Audrey was a dinner guest at the French Military Mission, and again admired French manners:

> *Enjoyed it tremendously, despite the fact they talked French the whole time. It was a very quiet affair, but their conversation (yes, I did understand it, so there) was so polished and amusing…Why is it the French can talk so much better than the English? We only had a cocktail before dinner and everyone was very gay, whilst the English drink gallons, become very stupid and dull, and eventually pass out.*

Audrey loved being invited to dinner with other foreign delegations – the Australians were famous for having a good cook, the Americans for giving a great Halloween party, and the Mexicans and Poles for being

Embassy staff worked in temporary offices like these

wonderfully entertaining. The irrepressible Berkeley Gage had instituted another regular social fixture on the British calendar: the North-South Club dances. The club was founded, Gage explained in his memoir, to get around a prohibition on dancing in public (a stricture of the Chiangs' New Life Movement, launched in 1934), and was conveniently housed in the home of a charming Chinese lady over the wall from the Embassy compound. It was perhaps there that Audrey learned to let her hair down, figuratively speaking: she would claim in later life that she had happily danced on tables without needing a drink to lose her inhibitions.

Another popular distraction was going to the movies – though the quality of projection and of the reels themselves, which had travelled thousands of miles in rough conditions to be screened in Chungking, could bitterly disappoint the audience. The first time Audrey watched a long-awaited film she could hear nothing but the noise of the projector.

Audrey had a string of dates with various admirers – lunches, dinners and country walks. John Munro, the suitor whose premature proposal she had rejected, did not give up, and he continued to court Audrey, once bringing her a welcome pot of honey from a trip down south. In October, Ben Ellis, doctor to the Military Mission, charmed his way into Audrey's affections by plying her with hot rum and orange when she was suffering from a bad cold, and sending a note to her boss excusing her from work for the rest of the day. She fell asleep in front of a log fire in the doctor's room, while he went out on a call, missing the truck down to the ferry and then waiting in the chilly evening air for a later ferry – the warming effects of the toddy quite dissipated.

But a sick day was a rare occurrence – Audrey worked conscientiously and discreetly at her job as aide to Jack Hutchison. His role was to promote commerce between China and Britain, even more important in wartime than in peacetime. Foreign trade was crucial to China as a channel for military supplies, and Chungking had industrialized fast. Factories turned out silk, textiles and hog bristles for export, as well as cement, iron and steel for domestic consumption. The city was also China's chief producer of armaments, with 14 ordnance factories. To facilitate trade, Hutchison developed extensive contacts with Chinese businessmen, and travelled frequently around the region, sometimes taking Audrey with him to inspect factories or dine with business contacts. As a fluent Mandarin speaker, he must also have been a valuable conduit of more sensitive information for his government. But letters home were censored, and Audrey could say nothing about the intelligence aspect of their work.

Instead she described the daily routine of life at the Embassy. The stately British mission stood high on a hill in the old city, overlooking the Yangtze. It was next to the American Embassy and opposite the French, off Lingshi Xiang, or Consulate Alley. The bombing of the British Embassy compound early in the war, coupled with the expanding numbers of diplomats working in the capital, meant that many offices were housed in temporary huts erected on grounds that cascaded down the steep hillside in terraces. Audrey worked in one row of huts, across a piece of ground known as the 'Cabbage Patch' from another row. The makeshift huts were quite comfortable: they had shaded balconies, and were surrounded by greenery. Audrey said that the two sets of offices exchanged notes constantly and sent each other a tray of tea and biscuits in the morning and afternoon. The staff of the Military Mission lived in a mess just behind the Embassy, and would sometimes invite Audrey and the other girls up to lunch in their rooms – 'a happy release from the interminable sandwiches', she noted.

Audrey was nicely busy at her job. The hours were officially from 9am to 5pm, but quite often she would stay later to finish her work or to type her letters home, or because she was going out on the north bank in the evening. When Hutchison travelled, he entrusted her to deal with his work too, so life was seldom dull. Outside office hours, Audrey had plenty of leisure – it helped that servants at the mess cooked and did the laundry for residents, an unaccustomed luxury for Audrey, who had been at times the cook and housekeeper for her family in England.

— • —

Audrey was eager to get outside the diplomatic bubble and learn about the customs and culture of China, but she felt painfully ignorant of the exotic country she had landed in. She became friendly with an English girl called Perle Longman, the daughter of missionaries who had spent most of her life in China, and (unusually) was engaged to a young Chinese. One day in September a visit to Perle's lodgings took Audrey into an unfamiliar neighbourhood. Perle lived in a tiny room, above a Chinese family. Looking out of the window, Audrey was depressed to see rats leaping up and down out of the gutters along the narrow alley below. Practically every house in the city was infested with rats, she told her family. They would cavort wildly around your rooms at night and eat your soap and candles. She was glad that her mess on the healthier south bank attracted only cockroaches.

The following month, she attended Perle's wedding. She thought it was the saddest event she had ever been to: the couple were married in a tiny, bleak Mission church, and the bride had a long, pink dress but had to make do with a crumpled veil full of holes, kept for girls getting married from the Mission. It looked, said Audrey, like an old curtain, and was tied up with a white bootlace. Neither bride nor groom had family or close friends in Chungking, but because of the importance of 'face' for the Chinese, they had to splash out on a reception for office colleagues and acquaintances at a foreign hotel, which they could ill afford. It was all in stark contrast to the very small wedding of the diplomats Pat Sedgwick and Beth Thompson, which Audrey had attended in August.

Venturing out to Chinese restaurants was also a novel experience, one she could seldom afford:

*It's terribly expensive feeding out, but great fun now and then.
When I say "restaurant", I mean a shop where you go upstairs
and sit in a filthy room (they throw the bones and uneatable bits
on the floor) where the boys who dish the food ("waiter" would
give you the wrong impression) shout at each other and dump
the food down on the tables, and you sit on hard stools round a
round table. Then it is every man for himself, and let the worst
man starve. If you are at all adept with the chopsticks, you come
away more than replete. Need I add that I became as adept as I
could in the shortest possible time?*

Poverty and squalor were all around – on the streets of the city, and
out in the country. On one trip outside the city, Audrey watched the
primitive industry of extracting tung oil from trees:

*The room was terribly dark and poky and in the middle were
a couple of oxen, blindfolded, going round and round in circles,
grinding up the seeds or whatever it is. In another corner of the
room was a terribly old man – blind – supported on a cross-bar
by his arms, working some kind of a trundle with his feet. It
seemed rather like Hell to me – wondered how long he had spent
moving his legs up and down – probably his whole life.*

Of course, it was a land of contrasts, and Audrey loved the plentiful
fresh produce, coming from a country that had not seen an orange in
years. In November, she wrote home:

*The streets are now full of oranges, tangerines and peanuts!
The tangerines are reasonably cheap, so we eat a lot – they are
delicious. It's rather pretty walking down a street and seeing
these baskets of bright fruit.*

By late September, the non-arrival of Audrey's trunk was making her
desperate. It had gone missing somewhere along her route from Lagos, and she began to dream of unpacking all her things, smelling the
mothballs and lavender sachets, putting out her books and bits and
pieces, but would wake to find her room as bare as ever, without any

homely touches. The weather was getting cooler, and nearly all her winter clothes were in the trunk. Given the impossibility of buying replacements in Chungking, this was a serious problem. Wires were sent from Calcutta in an effort to trace the missing luggage, and Audrey enlisted the help of her shipboard friend, Gerry Wormal, in Lagos. It was not until the middle of November that she heard the trunk had been located – in Cairo. The word went out from the Embassy that it must have the highest air priority (it never did), for Miss Watson was 'acutely embarrassed by lack of warm clothing'.

At the same time, Audrey received the news from home that her former beau Freddie had become a father. This must have unsettled her, and her letters hinted at sadness. Her English life seemed very re-mote, but writing and receiving letters was all the more important for that. The arrival of the weekly Foreign Office bag was a big event for everyone. Somebody usually stayed late at the office the day the plane from the south was expected, to bring the mail across to the mess. It was a gloomy week for the whole community when there was no bag. Communications with home were painfully slow and unpredictable, as Audrey had discovered in her early weeks in China. She found it dif-ficult writing into the void, without letters to answer, but did sit down regularly to write the long, vivid accounts of her new life that her elder sister carefully saved. She was always thrilled to hear from her grand-mother Charlotte – the matriarch of the family, fondly called 'Abuelita' – her father, Frank, and her two sisters, Joan and Tottie, writing on September 25 after receiving several long letters:

> ...*everything is so very foreign that unless you hear from home and people you know, it is easy to lose your perspective, and feel that you are being swallowed up in some vast continent, miles from civilization.*

News was often a bit stale – as was the piece of cake from her sister Tottie's wedding, when it reached her six weeks after the happy event – but savoured nonetheless. Tottie's account of her celebrations, enjoying lobster and Pimms, had made her sister particularly nostalgic for Eng-land – when the only drinks available in Chungking were rice wines or gut-rotting gin. 'When people are feeling homesick', said Audrey, 'they always talk of beer – this is a thing to dream about. Whisky of course is simply a thing of the past as far as we are concerned.' For Audrey, a wonderful cook, talk of food conjured up vivid memories:

> *Joan, when you talk about making a fish pie for Tom, Bertie and Daddy, it brings back the old kitchen so clearly that I can even feel the spoon digging into my palm as I mash the potatoes: and can just see the cheese sauce bubbling in the saucepan. And what is worse I can see the* <u>*beautiful*</u> *cider and taste the darned stuff too!*

Waves of homesickness could catch Audrey off-guard. Writing home in October, she admitted that going to meet an incoming plane was fatal:

> *It made me so homesick to see it taxi in though, that I won't ever go down to the aerodrome again until it is time for me to get a plane to go home. It reminded me terribly of Farnborough. Here you occasionally see a plane flying about, but to see one near to again was quite upsetting.*

During the summer the Yangtze was high and swift, swollen with rain and snowmelt, and almost a mile wide. It looked very different in the drier autumn and winter seasons. The subsiding waters exposed wide mud flats on either side of the channel. The river banks looked naked, where before houses came right down to the edge of the water. One large sandbank in the middle of the expanse of mud flats was used as the seasonal airfield. It was conveniently close to the old city, but the approach was unnerving. Pilots had to follow the course of the river to avoid the hills on either side, and make an awkward turn at a bend just as they descended to land.

Audrey did not know it, on her October visit to the airfield, but she would soon have reason both to take a close interest in aeronautical matters, and to forget her homesickness.

CHAPTER THREE

❦

The Mists of Love
Chungking 1943 and Hong Kong 1940

From 1936-38
Max flew for
Imperial Airways

'Had the most marvellous weekend at Pei P'ei....Quite like peacetime weekends!'

Audrey to her family, November 15, 1943.

As winter approached, a damp cold replaced the summer heat. The rains eased up, but the city seemed perpetually shrouded in fog. A sunny day was a rarity in Chungking – so rare, it was said, that dogs barked crazily when they saw the sun. The foreign community's constant partying helped to keep Audrey's spirits up, but by the end of October she was beginning to tire of the social round. Writing home on November 1st, she complained:

> *One party after another. They begin to pall after a time. It's fun dancing, but with such a shortage of girls, it is [...] exhausting. Also find the string of extravagant and equally worthless compliments rather nauseating. Married men sighing for their freedom, and single men giving you "sheep's-eyes" as they say! If one person paid you court, you might take it seriously, but when every other person does it, it is more than annoying. But still, one can always laugh it off!*

That Saturday she had gone to a birthday party for her doctor friend Ben Ellis – 'I have taken to drinking water, the local drink is so poisonous' – where she had danced well into the small hours. On Sunday evening, she was out again, at a Halloween party at the American mess next to her own, going home early since she was so tired.

But the highlight of her week, she said, was Sunday afternoon. Irene Ward, a British parliamentarian, was in town. China's first lady, Madame Chiang Kai-shek had invited the distinguished visitor to tea at the leaders' secluded compound in the pine-covered hills to the south of the city. The gathering was at Madame's private villa, which lay a short walk uphill from the Generalissimo's separate establishment. She had extended the tea invitation to Audrey and two other secretaries from the Embassy, wanting to 'meet some British women'. This was a rare honour.

Meiling Soong, who had married the Nationalist leader in 1927, was at the apogee of her power. Audrey knew that the American-educated Meiling, youngest of China's three famous Soong sisters, wielded enormous influence as interpreter and adviser for the non-English speaking Generalissimo. But Audrey couldn't have known quite what a mesmerizing effect Madame had on some VIP visitors. One who fell under her spell was Wendell Willkie. In 1942, President Roosevelt had sent his Republican challenger in the 1940 election on a world tour. The Generalissimo and his elegant wife gave Willkie an elaborate welcome to Chungking, and a highly stage-managed tour of the war zones. He took home a rose-tinted impression of the Chinese fighting spirit. According to his travelling companion, Gardner Cowles, publisher of *Look* magazine, he nearly took home Madame Chiang herself. He was captivated by her charms, and was even rumoured to have had a one-night fling with her, much to the fury of the Generalissimo.

Though he came to his senses quickly enough, Willkie did pave the way for a ground-breaking visit to the United States that Madame embarked on in November 1942. Ostensibly, she travelled to New York for medical treatment, but her stay developed into a prolonged rallying cry for support for China in the struggle against Japan. Madame was hosted by the Roosevelts at the White House, and honoured as the first Asian (and only the second woman) ever invited to address Congress. For war-weary Americans, China's courageous and glamorous first lady had incredible allure. Although her royal airs sorely tested the patience of the President (and British Prime Minister Churchill), Madame attracted adoring crowds wherever she went, and her barnstorming tour culminated in an extravaganza for thirty thousand people staged by David Selznick in the Hollywood Bowl.

Another eminent American, Henry Luce, played a major role in promoting Madame Chiang's cause, putting her on the cover of *Time* magazine after her masterful address to Congress. Luce, the co-founder of *Time*, had been born in China, the son of Presbyterian missionary parents. He led a lifelong crusade for American support for Nationalist China, unashamedly using the pages of his publications as a vehicle to prop up Chiang Kai-shek. After a ten day visit to China in 1941, he declared the Generalissimo the greatest leader Asia had seen for 250 years – a view that put him at loggerheads with his own Chungking correspondent, Theodore (Teddy) White, who could see the reality on the ground more clearly. The day would come when events such as a horrific famine in Henan province, first reported in the West by White, would cause many American diplomats to reassess their support for the Chiangs.

But Madame's aura was still very much intact when Audrey met her at Halloween 1943. Writing home the next day, she described in some awe her afternoon in the first lady's wood-panelled sitting room:

> Sir Horace and Lady Seymour also went, Berkeley Gage (he is First Secretary here), and another Air Attaché – also the Red Cross Commissioner who has just arrived out here. The American and Australian Ambassadors were there too, and a few other people. Anyway, we all got there and sat around for a few minutes, (in a smallish sitting room, with a coal fire which was pleasant) when Madame Chiang came in and shook hands all around. She looked stunning in an olive green Chinese dress, with a terribly smart red jacket, finger nails and shoes. She really is very good to look at.
>
> A few minutes later the Generalissimo turned up too and was introduced all round. He doesn't speak English of course, so has somebody interpreting. He spoke to all the Ambassadors in turn, whilst Madame spoke to all us women in turn. She sat on a sofa and we went up in strict rotation and had a chat with her. It was really very interesting. He is a tiny little man, but has such a pleasant face. It was, incidentally, his birthday.

The occasion was auspicious not just for the Generalissimo's fifty-sixth birthday, but also because for the first time Audrey noticed 'another Air Attaché'. This was Wing Commander Max Oxford, Assistant Air Attaché at the Embassy since January 1942. Audrey had heard of him: their mutual friends Gidley Baird and Berkeley Gage had doubtless talked about the urbane bachelor with a heroic past. But Max had returned only at 3am the previous day from a six-week trip to India. So even in Chungking's tight-knit diplomatic circles, it was hardly surprising that Max and Audrey's paths had not crossed earlier.

*Madame Chiang Kai-shek's villa, with a framed copy of her
cover portrait in Time magazine. Photo taken in 2005*

Soon the two Embassy staffers would have an opportunity to get to
know each other better. Audrey closed her letter by telling her family
that her next weekend would be a long one, and she was going up river
for a house party to a beauty spot called Pei P'ei (now Beibei). 'Am ter-
rified', she said nervously, 'they will play bridge! So far have escaped
getting entangled with the bridge fiends.' She need not have worried:
her next letter home enthused about the trip:

> *Had the most marvellous weekend at Pei P'ei. There were
> seven of us altogether and we drove up on Friday morning. The
> scenery going up is lovely, and the other girl in the party said it
> reminded her of Norway in bits.*

Over the rough roads of the time, Pei P'ei was half a day's drive from
the city, but a wonderful weekend retreat. The resort lay on the Jialing
River, just where it passed through a stunning gorge. High above the
west bank of the river, natural hot springs bubbled out of the rocks into
a pool that was enjoyed for its therapeutic qualities by Chinese and

foreigners alike. A winding road climbed on beyond the hot springs through bright green paddy fields and a pine forest until it reached the summit of the mountain. Here, perched on the very top of a ridge amongst aromatic pines, hundreds of feet above the gorge, lay the party's weekend destination. Their host, Alan Bell, was a British business-man whose gruff manner belied a heart of gold. He often entertained in the spacious house, which belonged to his company. That weekend Alan had invited six guests: Audrey, her girlfriend Iris Appleton, a Chinese friend TS Miao, the Air Attaché James Warburton, and that 'other air attaché' – Max Oxford. Audrey loved the relaxing atmosphere:

> We arrived in time for lunch, and fed ourselves so well that we all had a snooze until cocktail time. As there were 7 of us, I wasn't inveigled into playing bridge after all. The others played most of the time and I knitted or read, or had a quiet (and generally profitable) game of crap with whoever was dummy.

On Saturday morning everybody went for a walk in the hills before lunch. It was a foggy winter's day, and years later on her thirty-seventh birthday, an early morning mist in Kuala Lumpur would transport Audrey back to Pei P'ei. She remembered it in her journal:

> The amah [in Kuala Lumpur] was wearing a new bright blue suit, somehow it looked warmer that her usual dress, and I was reminded of wearing thicker clothes as the winter came on, with this same mist enveloping everything around – sounds muffled and yet surprisingly clear – the intimacy of a mist, which shuts off the whole world except for that vacuum in which we move. Here the sun has now come and dispelled Chungking…I am not <u>there</u> as I was for a moment this morning – there on that ridge, past the girls' school chanting the staccato National Anthem, walking towards Alan's house, perched on the very top of the ridge amongst pines.
> Such a welcoming house always – with log fires and trays of drinks – books and comfortable chairs. Bridge and dice – excellent food with so many of us at the table – walks in the steep hills – eucalyptus and mimosa – cherry blossoms – stark

branches, heavy blossom and bright blue sky, the emerald paddy, shady trees, steps leading up and up to lovely temples – drinking smoky tea with the monks. It would get hot as we walked, and we would strip off our cardigans, which had been so necessary at the start in the cold damp mist, and carry them on a stick across our shoulders, or tie them knotted by the sleeves around our hips. A friendly warm hand put on your shoulder or back to give a push up the steep places – sitting down on the hard earth, slippery with pine needles, for a rest. Horrid dogs that snap and growl – cowards all, but nasty to have at your heels as you pass their houses. Journal, September 7, 1953.

That November weekend, the British troops were out in Pei P'ei for a Sunday football game against the students of Fudan University. This was one of the universities that had relocated from eastern China to the war capital, and was now based in a campus surrounded by hills on the opposite side of the Jialing. Alan Bell and his guests threw a party for the BORs at the house on Saturday night, and then on Sunday took a sampan down river to watch the game. Audrey found this quite exciting: it was a twenty minute trip through the narrow gorge, but an hour's trip up river against a strong current to get back. The game was fun: the BORs lost 3-1, but were entertaining: 'One of our men lost his shoe three times (they play in gym shoes) much to the delight of the students.'

The weekend ended all too soon, with the house party dispersing on Monday morning. Audrey never forgot the long drive back to the city over muddy, slippery, broken-up roads. The sights and sounds of the countryside were vivid: she remembered pigs being carried to market in wicker baskets; peasants dressed in oft-patched jackets in every shade of blue; men with strong, muscular legs wearing straw sandals and trousers rolled up to their knees. Small boys drove water buffalo through the flooded rice paddies, the animals sometimes sinking up to their necks in water. The boys could get the buffalo to change direction with a single, sharp whistle. Even the buffalo were shod in straw sandals to get a purchase on the ubiquitous black mud.

Back in Chungking, the mud got everywhere too, with the onset of winter bringing rain once more. The streets of steps were dreadfully slippery and mucky, and Audrey found the walk up to her mess had become 'an absolute death-trap', especially on dark winter nights. Crossing the Yangtze to and from work was also even worse in winter. The water level was much lower than in the summer, exposing rocks and sand banks. Often a thick mist lay over the river early in the morning, and the ferry would not run until it lifted. 'You can take a crowded sampan' explained Audrey, 'but most of the Europeans won't take the risk. There have been several accidents. It's easy to lose all sense of direction apparently, and sometimes a sampan lands up again on the same side from which it started! When there is this thick mist, you have people beating drums, to guide the craft.' Drumbeats were a sound that would forever conjure up memories of Chungking in winter.

Pei P'ei, Audrey admitted in a letter, had been an extraordinarily pleasant interlude, quite like peacetime weekends. She did not mention that, among the convivial group, one man had made a great impression. Max Oxford intrigued her: here was a good-looking air force officer in his thirties, with elegant manners and entertaining conversation. He knew how to charm a lady, sitting next to her at dinner and plying her with fresh walnuts that he shelled into two perfect halves with his bare hands. Yet he didn't seem the usual Oxbridge-educated type. There was no hint of a wife back home, though there was Embassy gossip about love affairs. His past was a bit of a mystery. It was one that Audrey found herself keen to unravel. Soon, she heard his tale.

— • —

When war broke out in Europe and Audrey went to work for the RAF at Farnborough, on the other side of the world Max Oxford donned his RAF uniform, returning to active duty with the service for which he had last flown as a fighter pilot in Iraq eight years earlier. In 1939, Britain was not yet at war in Asia and in the colony of Hong Kong, where Max was based, he was assigned to air intelligence as a staff officer. For now he and his friends still had the leisure to enjoy a good party. Audrey would later read a wry account of one that Max hosted at his Kowloon home in the spring of 1940; it was memorialized in a best-selling book written by Emily Hahn, the New Yorker's free-thinking China correspondent.

Max Oxford, said Hahn, had a precise drawl that sounded just like his name. Recently arrived in Hong Kong, she was an uninvited guest at Max's cocktails, but he was far too diplomatic to let her feel unwelcome. Many of his guests had come by ferry across the harbour from Hong Kong Island, home to most of the Europeans in the British colony. But for Max the burgeoning town of Kowloon, on the Chinese mainland, was conveniently close to his prewar job at Hong Kong's airfield. Max lived in a brand new villa at 45, Kadoorie Avenue, an elegant white stucco house, with the curved Art Deco lines fashionable in the inter-war years. After years of globe-trotting, he revelled in the luxury of having a home of his own – taking pleasure both in hours spent alone, reading poetry in his favourite arm chair, and in evenings when he could throw open the French windows from his living room, encouraging a party to spill out onto the lawn.

Max was the perfect host – he had honed his social skills in years as principal aide to a colonial Governor in Africa. He welcomed his guests with a cocktail in one hand and a cigarette in an ivory holder in the other. He made a point of talking to women as much as men, and indeed looked an attractive catch – still a bachelor at the age of 34, he was not by any means tall, but women found the slim and witty aviator quite appealing. With neat features and the 'precise drawl' that Emily Hahn noticed, he seemed the English gentleman through and through.

At the time of Max's cocktails, Europe was in the bleakest war and Japan was ravaging China, but the lights were still bright in Hong Kong. True, the colony was uneasy. The Japanese had captured Canton, the south China city just a hundred miles from Hong Kong's border. Refugees from the war in China were flooding into Hong Kong, and many Europeans had left the territory, but others, like Max and his friends, remained there on active service in the military or the colonial government.

Max had arrived in Hong Kong in 1938 to manage the colony's fledgling air services. His base was the small airfield of Kai Tak, which had been carved out of a sliver of land immediately below the rolling hills – known to the Chinese as the nine dragons – that gave Kowloon its name. The approach to landing at Kai Tak was already notorious: aircraft had to bank sharply between the dragon hills before homing in on the short runway that hugged the shore. But many passengers commented that the sight of Hong Kong Island rising out of the water across the harbour was spectacular. Emily Hahn remembered it clearly, arriving from a winter in Chungking where she was researching a book on the Soong sisters. Flying into Hong Kong after dark, she was immediately struck by the contrast between the glittering island in the South China Sea and the city in China's inaccessible hinterland:

> How lovely it looked! We had not gone in for blackouts in Chungking as yet, but in retrospect I seemed to have been living in darkness. Hong Kong's red and blue neon lights and the brilliant yellow illumination all along the face of the Peak grew more and more beautiful as we circled around, lower and lower. It had been a foggy day but as soon as we dropped lower than the clouds the air seemed crystal-clear.

The night of Max's party, the glow of Hong Kong's lights suffused the sky above Kadoorie Avenue. Max's guests were an eclectic crowd, and included his closest colleagues in the military intelligence office: Flight Lieutenant Alf Bennett and Major Charles Boxer. Max enjoyed having a good time as much as the next man, but it must have been tough to keep up with Bennett and Boxer. These two were old buddies – both were fluent Japanese speakers, both hard-drinking, hard-partying characters, though each had a more intellectual side. Bennett was a larger-than-life figure with a handlebar moustache and a surprising love of poetry. Boxer, a graduate of the Royal Military Academy at Sandhurst, was also a man of paradoxes. He had perfected his Japanese in the early 1930s on a two-year attachment to the Japanese army. Posted to Hong Kong in 1936, he held the vital job of chief of military intelligence, and acted as liaison and interpreter between the British commanders and their Japanese counterparts in occupied China. He was something of a lady-killer and a cynic, but he was also a serious scholar, specializing in Dutch and Portuguese colonial history. In late 1939, he made an unlikely marriage, wedding a prim kindergarten teacher called Ursula Tulloh. She was renowned for her beauty, but by common consent was not an intellectual match for her brilliant husband.

Tensions were already surfacing in the Boxer marriage when Emily Hahn landed in February 1940, shortly before Max's party. Colonial Hong Kong society was wary of the unconventional American writer, who smoked cigars, kept a pet gibbon, and was quite public about hav-

Max at home, 45 Kadoorie Avenue, Kowloon, 1939

ing been addicted to opium and living as the concubine of a Chinese poet in her Shanghai years. Mickey, as friends called her, had first met Charles in that city back in 1937, and was intrigued by him. So it was no surprise that in Hong Kong she fell into the society of the Boxers, often making up a foursome with Alf Bennett. It was Charles who decided that she should join them at Max's cocktail party. "Old Max won't care. He invited everybody in town, anyway, and Alf's boss; Max won't dare object even if he wants to," said Charles.

In her 1944 memoir, *China to Me*, Emily Hahn remembered her evening at Max's villa:

> *His house in Kowloon was one of the new Spanish-style white stucco cottages that were growing up near the Kai Tak airfield; the Japs loved them later on, and squabbled bitterly over their shining newness, for each officer wanted a cute cottage all to himself. But this was back in 1940 when nobody dreamed of such a situation. The Empire stood solid and firm at Max's cocktail party.*

One stalwart representative of Empire was Albert Moss, Max's colonial service boss, who came to the party with his wife, May. Moss was a thin man – with a rather large wife. He had a sharp nose, a drooping moustache and practically no chin. He was an old-timer, in charge of Kai Tak since 1930, and Max may have been relieved not to be reporting to him now that he was back in the RAF. Other guests included naval officers, and 'willowy young girls', Mickey recalled. Then there were Helene and Gustav Canaval, an Austrian couple who had qualified as physicians in London in 1933 and set up a practice in Hong Kong – a pair of doctors that 'everyone was swearing by'. Although nobody dreamed of it that spring of 1940, to use Mickey's phrase, before too long many of Max's guests would be prisoners of the Japanese.

Charles Boxer, who was 'earnestly' drinking gin, had more foresight than most as he held forth on a favourite topic, the end of Empire. Mickey remembered his words:

> *"Don't you agree, Emily Hahn, that the day of the white man is done out here? Russia or no Russia, we're finished and we don't know it. All this is exactly like the merriment of Rome before the great fall. We are assisting in the death throes of capitalism. It's a very nice party too. Have another, Emily Hahn. Nonsense, you don't have to go yet."*

But Charles and Ursula ('smart and expensive in black') had to leave for a dinner party; Mickey and Alf Bennett adjourned to the Peninsula, the grande dame of Kowloon hotels, for a drunken dinner and dancing 'under the crystal chandeliers'. As Max bid farewell to his guests, another carefree Hong Kong evening drew to a close.

There may have been one guest who lingered, for Max was having an affair in Hong Kong with a woman he called Helen. All we know about the relationship is from his letters to his sister, who lived in South Africa: Helen was Chinese and a doctor – a rarity at the time. Max and Helen were deeply involved with each other, but her identity remains a mystery.

There were more mysteries in Max's life. Emily Hahn was one of the great reporters of her generation, but Max's accent had misled her. He was not at all a product of the upper class English public schools, like his friends Bennett and Boxer. His background was much more modest. But by seizing opportunities as a young man, he had had a series of unlikely adventures that had brought him to the shores of the South China Sea in his thirties, playing host at cocktails in Kowloon.

— • —

During the dark winter nights in Chungking, Max would find in Audrey a ready audience for his story.

Max Oxford was born in rural Dorset on May 3, 1905, the son of a master baker, William Oxford, and his wife Mary. Their firstborn son had died in infancy, and Max had one older sister, Margaret. William inherited his trade from his father and grandfather and never left the southwest of England, but Max would travel an immense distance from his roots.

His fascination with flying was sparked very early. In an unfinished memoir that he wrote in retirement, he said that his earliest memory was of meeting a pioneer aviator, the American 'Colonel' Sam Cody, who came to lodge at the Oxfords' house while on a tour of England, and impressed young Max with his stunts. But most of his youth was quite humdrum, and keeping the bakery business afloat was a constant struggle for the family, who lived above the shop in the hamlet of Ashfield, on the Broadlands estate near Romsey in Hampshire:

> There was an orchard behind the house and a field across the road. We kept a horse for the delivery van, a donkey, goats, chickens and ducks. The one employee was Sam. He and father made the bread, baked in wood heated ovens and we all served in the shop which appeared to be open continuously except Sundays. The sitting room led off from the shop so attending to customers was convenient.

The house had no electricity or bathroom, but Max's parents gave him and his sister the best education they could afford, at a private school in Eastleigh. Max spent most of his spare time as delivery boy for the bakery. He became the family mechanic, showing a practical bent that would lead to his future career. His parents were strict Methodists – a proud possession was a side table that Methodist founder, John

*Acting Pilot Officer MN Oxford at
No.3 Flight Training School, Grantham 1928*

Wesley, had preached from. Max took a pledge not to touch tobacco or alcohol until he was 21 – not a vow that he claimed to have honoured.

Chafing at the bit, Max left school in 1922 when he was just 17, and was sent to an uncle in the northern industrial city of Manchester, where he became a mechanic with a small engineering business. Searching for companionship, Max joined a Christian fellowship group called Toc H, which had been founded in Belgium during World War I as a rest centre for soldiers fighting in the trenches. He was soon recruited to work for the organization, first in Sheffield and then in 1926 at the London headquarters. He travelled around England as aide to Toc H founder, the Rev. PD 'Tubby' Clayton, and also became youth representative on the London Public Morality Committee, which acted as a theatre censor. Max enjoyed the free seats at West End shows, but his inclinations were too liberal for Toc H. After a time, he later wrote, he fell out of favour since he found 'insufficient to condemn'. In truth he did not have much of a commitment to the moral mission of Toc H, and kept a healthy scepticism of religion throughout his life. Max remembered with more pleasure visits to the French coast with 'an exciting group of friends' he had made through a pianist he met in London – a bohemian woman called Constance Spencer who became a lifelong friend.

Max was now almost 23. He had already seen more of the world than the average baker's son, and was anxious to travel further afield. But he had little formal education and no social connections. He needed to break into something new, and in 1928 he made a move that would set a course for the rest of his professional life. He won a short service commission in the Royal Air Force, recalling in his memoir:

> I think I passed the Selection Board through saying my recreations were golf and bridge; I played a lot of both in the years up to the War. The Officers' Mess at dinner was real glamour to someone so unsophisticated. The mess silver, decanters and the officers' be-medalled uniforms made a great impression, and to know I was part of this was almost unbelievable.

The RAF was the ideal fit for Max. Formalities and social graces may have counted, but it was the youngest and the least hidebound of the armed forces. And it needed level-headed young men with technical aptitude. Formed only in 1918 from the shell of the Royal Flying Corps, whose officers and men were known for their gallantry during the Great War, the RAF continued to develop the reputation for bravery and skill that would reach its apogee in World War II. The earliest surviving photo of Max shows a trim young man, posing confidently in his dress uniform as he began training. Despite a medical scare over erratic blood pressure which almost disqualified him from flying, Max passed out of flight training school with distinction – winning the school's annual landing competition by trouncing an Oxford graduate who had more flying experience.

As a newly qualified fighter pilot, he was posted to No.25 (Fighter) Squadron at Hawkinge, Kent in April 1929. He performed his share of the daredevil stunts which pilots were known for. He fell in with 'an odd crowd of local people which led to a lot of wildish parties,' he later wrote:

> One morning I only just managed to get on parade, still wearing evening shoes, and within a few minutes had taken off in a Siskin. I revisited my friends' house, party in progress, and did some no doubt hazardous low flying. On landing the Commanding Officer said we would drive to a chicken farm as my aircraft had been reported low flying and causing distress to the hens. This behaviour was treated seriously by the Air Ministry and could quickly lead to dismissal from the service and I was apprehensive. The C.O. questioned the farmer particularly on the time of the incident and we drove away. He told me that I was on the ground at the time alleged (the farmer had been 5 minutes out) and there was no case against me, but let it be a warning.

It was, Max recognized, 'a most magnanimous act' on the part of his Commanding Officer.

After a year at Hawkinge, Max took a navigation course for flying boats – planes that could land on water were invaluable in the days when airstrips were scarce – and he volunteered to serve overseas. In August 1930, the 25-year-old Flying Officer was sent to Iraq as part of the British occupying force operating under a League of Nations mandate. The Kingdom of Iraq had been cobbled together from three disparate provinces, one Kurdish, one Sunni Muslim and another Shi'ite Muslim. By the time Max arrived, there was a sullen stalemate between the factions, foreshadowing later troubles. Max was soon piloting missions to bomb and strafe rebel Kurdish strongholds in the mountainous north of the country – a task whose justice he always questioned, though he would also insist that the RAF warned Kurdish villages they were coming by dropping leaflets advertising the fact in advance. Of course, in the grand scheme of things, the British period in Iraq was a catastrophe, but it provided Max with an opportunity to prove himself.

In 1931 Max managed to get selected for a staff job, as personal

Max enjoyed polo and pig-sticking while serving in Baghdad

*Max piloting a Gipsy Moth bi-plane, in which he made
a forced landing in the African bush, 1933*

assistant to the Air Officer Commanding, Air Vice Marshal Edgar Ludlow-Hewitt, who was acting as High Commissioner. He became the most junior officer in the Senior Officers' Mess in Baghdad, and moved into a fine house where Gertrude Bell – a British adventurer and linguist who was one of the founders of Iraq – had once lived. Max played polo on horseback, and drove Hewitt around in an open white Rolls Royce. Hewitt was a somewhat stern and formal man, but he was impressed by his aide and for the first time Max's potential was spotted: in his confidential report for 1931, Hewitt described Max as a most promising officer.

Major Hubert Young, an Arabist who had served with TE Lawrence in the Arabs' desert revolt against Turkish rule, succeeded Hewitt as acting High Commissioner, and he took Max with the job. 'I moved to his residence', Max would later remember, 'and a period of great interest and much entertainment began'. Young was a formidable but kind-hearted man, a scholar at Eton and a graduate of the Royal Military Academy at Sandhurst. He liked company, and he and his young aide seldom dined alone. Max met 'everyone in Baghdad', including King Feisal and Freya Stark, a pioneering explorer and travel writer, who lived in a house overlooking the Tigris.

Hubert Young, who was twenty years older than Max, became an important mentor and Max would work with him for four years. It was during this time in Baghdad that they first developed a close and easy relationship. In late 1932, Young was appointed Governor of the colony of Nyasaland (now Malawi), and invited Max to follow him to Africa as his aide-de-camp, or ADC. Max had learned that he was three months too old for a permanent commission in the RAF, so he accepted Young's offer with alacrity, resigning his short service commission and paying his own way back to London. He left Baghdad in the front seat of a taxi, an Arab family in the back, for a bone-shaking five hundred mile ride, mostly across desert, to Damascus, then continued by boat to Brindisi, Italy, and made his way north to Asolo, in the foothills of the Dolomites, where he spent a happy week at the villa of his adventurous friend, Freya Stark.

Back in London, Max equipped himself for Africa. He was now on the reserve of Air Force officers, and ordered a full dress uniform for state occasions – since no tropical edition of the serge blue existed, Max had the tunic copied in white. This was a break with convention that later caused raised eyebrows from senior officers amid the formality of Government House in Nyasaland. Max sailed on a slow Union Castle boat to Beira, on the coast of Mozambique, where the governor of the then Portuguese colony plied him with whisky for breakfast, thinking it a habit of the English. Sir Hubert had sent a car to drive his aide to Zomba, Nyasaland's capital, and so Max arrived in style at Government House, a majestic white mansion that would be his home for the next two years.

Max always spoke with pleasure of his time with Sir Hubert and Lady Young (as they now were). In Nyasaland, he enjoyed riding, as he had in Iraq, and kept a horse called Poconos, together with a spaniel named Tony. Life was interesting but sometimes too leisurely for an energetic governor and the ADC who accompanied him everywhere: 'We travelled long distances in the Governor's official car, a Rolls Royce, often playing chess on a peg board in the back.' Sir Hubert was a keen chess player, and, Max continued:

> We played a lot at home: sometimes if H.E. was bored with a dinner party he would direct me to accompany him to his study to deal with some important telegram, there we would have a game until 11pm when he would return to say goodbye to his guests.

Sir Hubert was regarded as a far-sighted governor, and both he and his wife were early promoters of the benefits of air travel for getting around tropical Africa. Lady Young was quite a pioneer, a qualified pilot and founder of a flying club for enthusiasts in the colony. She had her own Gipsy Moth, and Max, as a more experienced pilot, often accompanied her. They shared some comical scrapes, and one more serious episode.

In June 1933, Sir Hubert and a visiting Bank of England director left for England from Salisbury – now Harare, the capital of Zimbabwe – on an Imperial Airways airliner, the *Artemis*. But the plane lost its way and landed in a jungle clearing. Lady Young and Max set out, each flying a small bi-plane, to search for the missing *Artemis*. They were separated in a storm, and, with darkness approaching, Max had to find somewhere to land: 'I chose a "dombo", a grass covered area water-logged in the rains but now dry. One elephant appeared to be only ankle deep in grass but must have been standing on a hillock for on landing the aircraft turned over in 10ft high vegetation.' He was stranded overnight, and slept on the wing of his plane, surviving on a tin of pâté and some dry biscuits. At daybreak he set out along animal tracks through the tall grass towards a village, whose drums he had heard in the night. The villagers were alarmed to see a white stranger, but eventually three men volunteered to guide him to safety – a walk that took three days with night stops in mud huts and very little food or water.

Despite reports in the British press of an airman missing in the African jungle – ones that gave Max's parents some anxious days – all ended well. On the third afternoon, Max and his guides reached a remote mission house. The missionaries' only car was out of action, but the ever-practical Max was able to repair the fault, and the following day set off to return to Zomba. The Imperial Airways plane had been located after its forced landing, its distinguished passengers unharmed. Max's small plane was eventually dismantled and towed out of the jungle for rebuilding. Some months later when Max was on tour with Sir Hubert, he discovered that two of his guides were in prison for not paying head tax. He gladly settled his rescuers' debt.

In January 1935, Sir Hubert was promoted to be Governor of Northern Rhodesia (now Zambia) which, with its rich copper and lead deposits was one of the most important African colonies. Young asked Max to follow him, and he spent two happy years in Livingstone, entertaining visitors with trips to the nearby Victoria Falls and boat picnics on the Zambezi.

Still, Max was now over 30 and his prospects were uncertain. He did not have a career appointment in the colonial service, and would be overtaken by younger men recruited as fast-track cadets. Max must have felt it was time to move on, and in 1936 he joined Imperial Airways as a commercial pilot based in Croydon, London's first civil airport. Imperial – the forerunner of BOAC and British Airways – was created in 1924 to take commercial air travel beyond Europe into the far-flung territories of the Empire. Max flew Imperial's 38-seater Handley Page bi-plane on the London to Paris route. Then he had a shot at piloting the first monoplane used by Imperial – a four-engine Armstrong Whitworth XV Atalanta, a model developed to carry mail and passengers around the Empire, able to land on small airfields, in heat and high altitude. Max flew a sister plane of the *Artemis*, the plane he had hunted in Africa. This one was called the *Amalthea* – back then, each plane was christened. And this gave him his first taste of Asia, piloting the sleek *Amalthea* on a new long-haul route from Karachi to Calcutta and on to Singapore.

But Max evidently did not see commercial flying as the long-term career he sought. While with Imperial, he applied for a permanent appointment back in the colonial service. He was accepted in 1938, and was soon posted further east than he had ever travelled before.

That September Max arrived in Hong Kong to become assistant manager of Kai Tak airport. The airfield at the head of Kowloon Bay below the nine dragon hills opened in 1925, on land reclaimed from the sea. In the early years, Kai Tak was both a military base for Hong Kong's skeleton air force and a civil airport. Max's former employer, Imperial Airways, brought its first scheduled flight to Hong Kong just two years before his arrival in the colony. By 1938, four airlines operated scheduled services from Kai Tak, and about 10,000 passengers a year came and went. The runway was still a grass field, but many planes – including a weekly Pan Am clipper service, which came all the way from San Francisco – landed on the water, and passengers disembarked at a jetty next to the hangar. There was as yet no passenger terminal. Max and his boss, Albert Moss, would personally greet VIP passengers, such as the celebrated Soong sisters: Madame Chiang Kai-shek, Madame Kung, wife of the Nationalists' Finance Minister, HH Kung; and Madame Sun Yat-sen, widow of the revered father of the Chinese republic.

Kai Tak was on the northern side of the harbour, in the mainland area into which the original British settlement on Hong Kong Island, founded in 1841, had expanded in the second half of the century. From his office in the control tower, Max looked across Victoria Harbour to the green peaks of the magical island. In 1938, the harbour was twice as wide as it is today, and one of the busiest stretches of water in the world since Hong Kong was a leading entrepôt for the China trade, surpassed only by Shanghai to the north. Max gazed on a scene of perpetual motion, as passenger liners, merchant ships, naval vessels, russet-sailed junks, and tiny sampans plied their trade in the waters of the South

Arrival of the PanAm Clipper from San Francisco,
Kai Tak, 1939

Mme Chiang Kai-shek (centre) and her elder sister
Mme HH Kung leaving Kai Tak, 1939

China Sea. Behind the hills of Kowloon, the New Territories stretched out for miles. Britain held these on a lease from China, and they were still very largely agricultural, their ancient villages given over to rice farming and fishing. And beyond the border lay China proper – Guangdong province.

Whenever Max crossed over to the Island side, which he did frequently for meetings at government headquarters and social events, he had to do so by water: ferries ran a constant shuttle service for people, goods and cars. The city of Victoria, the government and business centre of Hong Kong, had grown up along the north shore of the Island. Hong Kong's shortage of flat land kept the downtown area remarkably compact, despite successive extensions into the harbour. The godowns of the 'hongs'–the trading houses such as Jardine Matheson and Butterfield & Swire–sat solidly along the harbour front, ready to receive their wares. Appropriately for this entrepreneurial city, the most imposing building was the new headquarters of the Hongkong and Shanghai Bank – its squarish tower was said to be the tallest building between Cairo and San Francisco. A pair of bronze lions guarded the entrance of 'the Bank', as it was universally known. It cast its shadow over the elegantly domed Supreme Court next door, which was topped off with the royal coat of arms. A few steps closer to the waterfront, the gloriously Italianate building of the Hong Kong Club was the gathering point for the colony's elite. In true English style, a cricket pitch took up prime space right next door to the Club.

Other focal points for colonial life included the colonnaded buildings of the Hong Kong and the Gloucester Hotels, with their restaurants and bars. Max may have regaled Audrey with tales of his 'drinking buddy' Ernest Hemingway, who held court in the lobby bar of the Hong Kong Hotel during a reporting trip to Asia in early 1941. Behind the hotels, the narrow cobblestone alleys and stone steps of the Chinese neighbourhoods were dense with street life. Rising above the business district were the headquarters of state, church and army: Government House, St John's Anglican Cathedral, and the garrison commander's headquarters at Flagstaff House. The residences of wealthy Europeans were dotted along the contours of Victoria Peak – at the time, Chinese were prohibited from owning property on the Peak itself. Less prominent officers and government officials lived halfway up, in the more prosaically named Mid-Levels. Victoria Peak was no mere hill, but a mountain rising sharply from the sea to a summit of some 1,800 feet. Its slopes were thickly covered with vegetation, falling away to barren rock on the sheerest aspects. To visit friends, Max would hop on the Peak Tram, a funicular railway that since 1888 had cut a swathe through the greenery to carry passengers from the city to Mid-Levels and the Peak.

Max grew to love Hong Kong in the halcyon days before the war. Living in the smart new villa on Kadoorie Avenue, his life was comfortable and full of diversions. At home he listened to music on his gramophone, collected books, especially volumes of poetry, and played chess, using a handsome Chinese-made ivory set, the 'black' pieces coloured a brilliant red. With friends, he hunted with the British-style Fanling hunt in the New Territories, sailed a yacht, and played golf at the Hong Kong Golf Club. He was the proud owner of a Ford motor car. And – as he may have admitted to Audrey – at some point he became involved with the Chinese doctor called Helen.

In Chungking, as Max's tales of his prewar life unfolded, Audrey saw that he had come a long way from a baker's shop in rural England. But his world was soon to be turned upside down, and the story of Hong Kong at war would be the most incredible chapter yet in the adventures he related.

CHAPTER FOUR

It's War

Hong Kong 1941

XXXXXXX
CHUNGKING.
8th May, 1942.

Sir,

I have to inform you that as a result of the fall of Hong Kong, where I was Air Liaison Officer attached to Air Headquarters Singapore, and my escape on the 25th December, 1941, I lost through enemy action the whole of my service equipment, uniform, motor car, personal and household effects, and camp kit.

2. I have asked Air Headquarters, India, to replace my service equipment.

3. I hereby claim compensation for uniform and camp kit. The cost of replacement from India was £86.

4. From the outbreak of hostilities my private motor car was taken into use as as staff car owing to the acute lack of R.A.F. transport at Army Headquarters and the total lack of service transport available to me. The car was used constantly on service duty until damaged beyond repair by shell fire while moving petrol to our Intelligence W/T station. The car was a 1939 Ford 10 "Prefect" (mileage 9000) and its market value was H.K.$ 3200. I therefore claim the sum of £200.

5. Please inform me whether I have any claim for household effects in view of the fact that my appointment necessitated my living out.

6. I shall be grateful if you will pay the sum due to my account with Lloyds Bank Ltd., 6 Pall Mall, S.W.1., as early as possible for the blocking of my accounts in Hong Kong has left me very short of funds.

    I am, Sir,

        Your obedient servant,

            Squadron Leader.

The Under Secretary of State for Air,
    Air Ministry, London.

'Of course it was hopeless from the start.'

Max to his sister, January 3, 1942.

In the weeks after the Pei P'ei house party, Audrey's life became deliciously complicated. It was the height of the social season. As well as the usual events, there was a round of farewell parties for Max's boss, Group Captain James Warburton. The Air Attaché, a Japanese speaker with a background in intelligence, had been at the Chungking Embassy since 1940 and was now being posted back to England. A scratched-out entry in Audrey's diary suggests that she cancelled a dinner date with Ben Ellis, one of her persistent suitors, in order to attend a party for Warburton: his deputy Max was becoming a bigger attraction. But she had not yet admitted this to anyone. She kept a full diary of lunches and dinners with Ben and her other beau, John Munro.

Max was equally busy with business and social engagements. Then, two weeks after the Pei P'ei weekend, he hosted a dinner party to which he invited a mix of Chinese and English guests – including Audrey. Under Chungking rules ("where you dine, you sleep") 'Audrey Watson stayed', noted Max in his diary. The following Sunday they spent the whole day together, going for a walk in a neighbourhood known as Fu Ta Kuan, and again, according to Max's diary, she stayed the night. They were falling in love, and began to spend every spare minute together: on Tuesday they lunched, and on Wednesday they dined. On Saturday, December 4 they again spent the day walking at Fu Ta Kuan, and Max came back for dinner at Audrey's mess on the south bank.

It was exactly two years since Max had spent his last peacetime weekend in Hong Kong. As he and Audrey became close, he told her the story of that momentous December, the events that led up to it, and the drama that brought him to Chungking.

When war broke out in Europe in September 1939, Max had spent just a year on Kai Tak's civilian side. Recalled to active duty with the RAF, he was sent to the Far East Command Centre in Singapore for a short flying refresher course. But his assignment would not be in the air, and he returned to Hong Kong in January 1940 as a staff officer for air intelligence.

The war against Hitler seemed very distant for Europeans in Hong Kong; the more immediate concern was the threat posed from the north. Japan had invaded China in 1937, after first annexing Manchuria, taking advantage of her great rival's internal turmoil. China's last imperial dynasty, the Qing, had collapsed in 1911 to be replaced by a republic whose first president was the founder of the Kuomintang party, Sun Yat-sen. There followed two chaotic decades of power struggles between regional warlords, the Nationalists, and the Communist party, led from the mid-1930s by Mao Zedong.

After Sun Yat-sen died in 1925, his military commander, Chiang Kai-shek – whom Audrey met at the Halloween tea party – rose to the leadership of the Nationalist government. Chiang led brutal campaigns against warlords and Communists in a quest for national dominance, driving Mao's supporters west onto the Long March. By 1937, the Generalissimo held a tenuous grip on the nation, but his armies were ill prepared for Japan's full-scale attack on the Chinese heartland that July. Shanghai, China's commercial capital, whose foreign concessions had long been home to European traders, fell that year. Then the Japanese advanced on the Nationalist government's capital, Nanking, whose fall was marked by the massacre of an estimated 300,000 Chinese civilians and the rape of 50,000 women, during weeks of atrocities that became known as the Rape of Nanking. The Chiangs had already fled the city, making a temporary headquarters at Wuhan, further up the Yangtze River. A few months later, the weakened Chinese government was forced to retreat much higher up the Yangtze, which is how it came to be located in Chungking in 1938. Meanwhile the Japanese advance continued southward, skirting Hong Kong. Canton, the capital of Guangdong province, just up the Pearl River estuary from the British possession, fell in October 1938.

The loss of China's eastern ports was a boon of sorts for Hong Kong. The colony became a haven for foreigners and Chinese fleeing chaos on the mainland: Europeans abandoning Shanghai, Nationalist apparatchiks, and more than half a million ordinary Chinese refugees. With the fall of Shanghai and Canton, Hong Kong businesses boomed. Over in Europe, facing the threat of Hitler and Mussolini, the last thing the

British government wanted was to be drawn into a war with Japan. So in 1938 Hong Kong was formally designated a neutral zone, though in the territory there was much covert support for the Chinese cause. For the most part, the colony sat on the sidelines while China was pummelled.

But Hong Kong could not stay out of the firing line forever. The military intelligence people, led by Max's buddy Charles Boxer, understood sooner than most that Hong Kong was in fact a target for Japan. Its agents had thoroughly staked out the territory, and forward units of Japan's army were massing across the border as early as 1940. Boxer assiduously cultivated Japanese officers, trying to keep information flowing.

Max's contribution was to collect intelligence on Japanese and Chinese air power. Emily Hahn made light of one of his attempts to do so. At a Chinese dinner hosted by Max in honour of Ed Pawley, an American who was in the aviation business in China, Mickey sat next to Charles. Max was pumping Pawley for information on just how much American aid was going into China in the form of aircraft equipment (the answer was: a lot). Charles gave Max a hard time, Mickey recalled:

> But every time he [Max] came near the ticklish subject, while Ed listened gravely and silently, Charles would call irreverently from our side of the table, "Got the old pump handle working, Max?"
>
> It was enough to discourage any earnest beginner in the art of snooping for King and country. Max glared at Charles; Charles toasted Max.

It didn't take much snooping to know that Charles and Emily Hahn would soon become lovers. Within weeks of Max's cocktail party, Ursula Boxer had decided to join the officially encouraged evacuation of British wives and children and left Hong Kong for Australia. The coast was clear for an affair between Mickey and Charles that would scandalize the colony. Max was witness to its beginning: in the summer of 1940, after another stay in Chungking where she was working on her biography of the Soong sisters, Mickey spent her first night back in Hong Kong with Charles and Max – with the latter (perhaps diplomatically) falling asleep over nightcaps at a geisha parlour while

Mickey and Charles talked, and fell in love. Max was not a man to be censorious – he continued to enjoy the illicit couple's company, good-humoured banter and all.

While Max learned the art of spying in Hong Kong, over in London the Chiefs of Staff concluded that if Japan attacked, the colony was indefensible. At one point, surrender without resistance was debated, but by late 1941 British Prime Minister Churchill had determined that Hong Kong 'could not be held but must be defended', as Dr Selwyn Selwyn-Clarke, the liberal Director of Medical Services in the colony nicely put it. Anticipating a Japanese attack in the Pacific, the US command urged Britain to reinforce the defences of Hong Kong. Two battalions were sent from Canada to supplement the four regular battalions and reservists of the Hong Kong garrison, giving the Allies some 10,000 troops in the territory. The Gin Drinkers' Line, a frivolous-sounding but vital chain of defence positions designed to hold back the enemy in the New Territories, was shored up after a period of neglect. Supplies were laid in for a three-month siege of the Island.

By now Max carried the rank of Squadron Leader – the air force equivalent of an army Major – and he continued to work with Charles Boxer, Alf Bennett and others in the intelligence office advising the top brass. He had moved out of his spacious Kowloon home and now lived on the Island side near military headquarters in a Mid-Levels flat over-looking the harbour, at 1c Robinson Road.

There were two key leadership changes in late 1941: in September, Max found himself working for a Governor Young for the second time in his career. Sir Mark Young – younger brother of Max's old boss Sir Hubert – arrived to take charge of the colony. An old Etonian like his brother, he had studied Classics at Cambridge, graduating with first class honours. He had two previous governorships under his belt by the time he was appointed to Hong Kong at the age of fifty-five. People found him highly intelligent and energetic, if somewhat austere. He was aided by a new garrison commander, Major-General Christopher Maltby, a soldier who had spent his career in the Indian Army. Neither man had previous experience of Hong Kong. The intelligence office briefed the newcomers that the question was not so much whether the Japanese would invade as when. Most senior officials thought war was unlikely before the spring of 1942. A major concern was the loyalty of

Still enjoying a party: Max (standing on right), WL Bond of CNAC
(fifth from right) and unidentified friends in prewar Hong Kong

the Chinese who made up ninety-eight percent of Hong Kong's population. The colonial government had done little to win their allegiance or to entrust them to fight alongside the British and there were well-founded doubts about their support in the event of war. Nonetheless, the new leaders and their staff followed Churchill's orders and prepared to brave the enemy.

In early December 1941, the social season was in full swing despite the ominous signs of war. Max was doubtless among the elite of Hong Kong who gathered at the splendid Peninsula Hotel in Kowloon on Saturday, December 6 for a charity ball sponsored by prominent Chinese in aid of war relief in Europe. The new Governor was guest of honour, and Chinese high society present included two of the Soong sisters, Mme Sun Yat-sen and Mrs Kung. Gwen Priestwood, an English guest, said that two huge ballrooms were packed with people dancing. Then the orchestra struck up an old favourite, *The Best Things in Life are Free.* 'For a minute or two we forgot the red clouds of war that now seemed to be gathering, and swayed over the polished dance floor', Priestwood would later write. Suddenly, the music stopped for an urgent announcement: all men from ships in the harbour were to report aboard for duty – at once. They were to take their ships out to sea for safety. The last dance that Hong Kong society would enjoy for four years was brought to an abrupt end.

The same Saturday, Far East Command in Singapore cabled General Maltby to warn of suspicious Japanese shipping movements in the region, and ordered the RAF in Hong Kong onto the highest state of alert. Scouts observed Japanese regiments massed only eight miles from the Hong Kong border. On Sunday morning, Maltby and his staff were worshipping in the tranquillity of St John's Cathedral when they were summoned from their pews to a meeting of the Defence Council at the nearby Government House. The Governor and Maltby agreed that war was imminent, and ordered the entire garrison to battle stations. Reservists in the Hong Kong Volunteer Defence Corps were called to their units.

Max may well have spent Sunday, the eve of war, with his friends Charles and Mickey, whose very public affair had produced a baby daughter that October while Charles was still married to the absent Ursula. That December Sunday, the unabashed couple invited friends to cocktails at Charles' house, which was just up the road from Max's flat, and the evening continued with a buffet supper. The guests left about midnight, but Mickey stayed and listened to the radio with Charles, who was monitoring a Japanese station, hearing nothing special before Mickey went home near daybreak to nurse the eight-week old Carola: 'I climbed the hill, holding my long skirt up out of the dew and watching the cracked stairs carefully in the dawning light'. Charles went down to the so-called Battle Box for night duty: Fortress HQ, the command's emergency headquarters, was deep in a bunker fifty feet under the Murray Barracks in the centre of Victoria. Mickey was feeding Carola when Charles rang at six to say: 'The balloon's gone up. It's come. War.'

— • —

By that time, hostilities were a few hours old. By Hong Kong time, the Japanese bombing of the American fleet at Pearl Harbor began about 2am on Monday – which was 8am on Sunday, December 7 in

Hawaii, on the other side of the international dateline. In a stunningly coordinated operation, the Japanese attacked three territories almost simultaneously – Hawaii, the Philippines, and the British colony of Malaya. Charles was monitoring Tokyo radio at 4:45 in the morning when he heard the Japanese send instructions in code to their nationals, telling them that war with Britain and America was underway. The Governor was immediately informed and the garrison alerted. General Maltby and his staff joined the duty officers in the Battle Box. At 5am, troops were ordered to demolish forward installations on the border; at 5:45, the garrison was formally told that Britain and Japan were at war.

The news was scarcely out when at 8am the city woke to the sound of an air-raid warning. It was a clear morning, and from the Mid-Levels Max's neighbours had an unobstructed view of Japanese planes circling over his familiar Kai Tak airport. A dozen bombers, escorted by a bevy of fighter planes, dive-bombed and machine-gunned the airfield. By 8:20, plumes of smoke and dust were rising from Kai Tak, and the sound of explosions filled the air. In an attack lasting no more than five minutes, the Japanese had wiped out the RAF's token air force of two flying boats and three ancient torpedo bombers, along with seven civil aircraft that were parked in the open air, and the PanAm Clipper which was about to take off from the water. 'It was one of those flawless December mornings,' David MacDougall, Ministry of Information chief in the colony, would write later, 'brilliant and still. The harbour was full of junks and sampans. Chinese everywhere went about their usual tasks. It was all utterly unreal.'

It soon became all too real. After the opening salvo from the air, the battle shifted to the ground. Japanese infantry of the 23rd Army began advancing across Hong Kong's northern border in the New Territories. General Maltby was dismayed at how swiftly and stealthily the battle-hardened Japanese moved, especially at night. His own far less experienced and nimble troops inflicted some damage, but within twenty-four hours the Japanese were at the Gin Drinkers' Line, which snaked through the hills of the New Territories, and quickly overwhelmed its defenders. The troops dropped back, attempting to slow the Japanese advance on Kowloon.

On December 10, Max went out with Charles Boxer to assess the situation on the front line, visiting a company of Punjabi troops. 'Little information to give them', noted their commander forlornly. The next day, Maltby decided to withdraw all troops from the mainland, save for one unit guarding the eastern entrance to the harbour. To deny vital facilities to the Japanese, the British blew up Kowloon's cement works, power station and dockyards, and scuttled the merchant ships still in the harbour. A sorry procession of troops and equipment retreated across the water to Hong Kong Island that night. The Japanese succeeded in cutting the communications cables linking Hong Kong to the outside world. As December 12 dawned, the Island was totally isolated.

So within four days of the initial attack, the British had been forced to abandon Kowloon and the New Territories. Almost all Europeans were evacuated to the Island side, but most Chinese were forbidden from following, and unsurprisingly there was widespread panic on the Kowloon side. Fifth columnists, including members of Triad gangs, engaged in sabotage of the British military effort, and stirred up civil unrest until there was a complete breakdown of law and order.

On December 13, the remaining unit on the Kowloon side was withdrawn. Lieutenant General Sakai Takashi, commander of the Japanese forces, chose this moment to make his first demand for the surrender of Hong Kong. He despatched a launch across the harbour with a white banner reading 'Peace Mission', using two European women (and their dogs) as hostages. Boxer went to receive the delegation, and he took Sakai's letter by staff car to the Governor. The Japanese demanded unconditional surrender. Charles returned an hour later with the Governor's reply; he had categorically rejected the surrender terms. Churchill signalled Young with a dose of bulldog spirit: 'Every day of your resistance brings nearer our certain victory.' But there was to be no rescue of the besieged island. The attack on Pearl Harbor, followed on December 10 by the sinking off Malaya of two British warships, the *Repulse* and the *Prince of Wales*, had left Japan dominant at sea and in the air throughout Southeast Asia. As Hong Kong prepared for the worst, the only glimmer of hope was word that Chiang Kai-shek was sending one of his armies to relieve the territory from the north.

With the rejection of surrender terms, the Japanese forces pounded the Island with long-range shells fired across the water from Kowloon. To add to the misery, aircraft dropped bombs on the hapless population. At first there was an air-raid warning system 'in a most beautiful dug-out' which worked well until it was ordered to be destroyed and disbanded – somewhat prematurely, in Max's view – 'in one of the many "flaps"'. A degree of exhaustion and despair set in among civilians and military alike, but the defenders of Hong Kong struggled on, even developing a routine of sorts. Max, as a senior staff officer based in the Battle Box military headquarters – 'an elaborate dug-out with electric light plant and forced ventilation' – was somewhat protected from bombs and shells. But though the Battle Box had its own power, telephone and ventilation systems, he found the mood at the underground bunker dispiriting: 'The staff I think stayed in it too long, the atmosphere was depressing, and one rapidly became a defeatist. I preferred the sunlight and perfect winter weather above ground', he would write to his sister after it was all over. After dark most people took shelter: moving about at night was highly dangerous, for troops and police fired first and asked questions afterwards, said Max: 'I remained indoors with a whisky and water'.

By his own admission, Max had 'a gentlemanly war, bathing and shaving each day and going to bed at night though in my clothes.' He stayed in his apartment on Robinson Road during the first week of the battle, housing as many as eight lodgers. Helen, his elusive lover, was among them. She had a vital role: she was a surgeon at a nearby emergency hospital. But the hospital (most likely the Canossa) was located so close to an anti-aircraft battery that it was badly damaged in the air raids. From then on Helen had to operate on the premises of (strangely enough) a Japanese school. Max's flat was hit too, when the sitting room took a shell through the roof. His water, electricity and telephone all failed, so Max de-camped to a boarding house that had become an officers' mess. But his Chinese cook loyally stayed in the apartment, and Max went back most days, as he put it, 'to cheer up my boy and have a decent meal'. At least food supplies held out until late in the siege, and the city's European hotels and restaurants remained open for business, serving basic meals. The prestigious Gloucester and Hong Kong Hotels were bursting at the seams as key personnel moved their offices to the solid buildings, and bunked down there at night.

Like Max, everyone sheltered the refugees who were streaming over from Kowloon. Under billeting plans many residents of the Mid-Levels vacated their homes and moved up to the Peak to lodge with families

The Hong Kong & Shanghai Bank dominates central Hong Kong, postwar photo

there. Mickey Hahn and baby Carola went to stay with the family of the Director of Medical Services, Dr. Selwyn-Clarke and his wife Hilda. Selwyn-Clarke was seldom home – he was tireless in his efforts to minister to the people of Hong Kong, and a true hero throughout the war. Charles Boxer and Max, out on one of their tours of inspection, visited Mickey on the Peak and were distressed to find the house was positioned between two anti-aircraft batteries and being shaken by shelling – but then so were most houses.

David MacDougall, the information chief, later wrote that he slept in his own bed for the first week, but that the road up to his house became increasingly dangerous from heavy fire, and the surface pockmarked with shell-holes and debris. One night, a car driving ahead of MacDougall took a direct hit: he took the hint and from then on slept in his clothes in his office on the third floor of the Gloucester Hotel, not taking a bath or changing for weeks. He had a lucky escape; his house was destroyed by shells the night after he left it, and all the family possessions were lost. He had to leave his new car in the garage, 'the first I have ever paid for fully and owned', he noted wistfully.

Max was also the proud owner of a car, a 1939 Ford Prefect, with just 9,000 miles on the clock. He put it to good use, transporting people, petrol, ammunition and medical supplies. The Ford lasted ten days, surviving a bomb falling within a few paces of it, but it was finally put out of action by shell fire. (Max later claimed the sum of £200 in compensation from the Air Ministry.) Somehow Max got hold of another car, but that was stolen on Christmas morning. Many civilian volunteers shared the dangerous work of driving supplies about, serving in food kitchens under fire and helping in emergency hospitals. Gwen Priestwood, who had been at the Peninsula ball, earned particular praise as a fearless supply truck driver.

Max had precious little 'air intelligence' to do during the siege. He could only watch as Japanese planes flew over Hong Kong daily, bombing military targets and sometimes just dropping propaganda leaflets. The defenders were sitting ducks: the RAF's few aircraft had been bombed out of existence on Day One, no other air support was available to the distant colony, and with only limited anti-aircraft guns there was no way to defend the skies.

But as the battle intensified, a new and critical role fell to the Squadron Leader. Charles Boxer had reassured Mickey Hahn early on: 'Nobody's going to get *me*. They protect staff officers.' But he was wrong. On December 20 Boxer was badly wounded while on a mission to interrogate Japanese soldiers reportedly held in a house on Shouson Hill, on the southern side of the island. He was shot in the chest, his life only saved by treatment at Queen Mary Hospital.

Max later told his sister that he lost all fear of being killed after the first few days of battle, but dreaded the thought of capture by the Japanese. Now, with his friend Charles out of action (along with at least two other staff intelligence officers), it fell to Max to play a part in one of the most delicate tasks remaining to the British in Hong Kong.

For Max now took on Boxer's job of 'keeping in contact with the Chinese intelligence, who were doing good work in keeping the lid on the Fifth Column elements and in guerrilla tactics'. The Chinese in charge of this vital effort was Admiral Chan Chak, a feisty, one-legged veteran of China's internal turmoil and president of the Southern Kuomintang.

Max took Boxer's place at daily liaison meetings with the tiny but ruthless Admiral. Chiang Kai-shek had sent Chan to Hong Kong well before the outbreak of war. The KMT was officially a proscribed organisation in the colony (as was the Communist party), but as its political and military representative, Chan was to quietly build up a Nationalist underground effort to support resistance to Japan. Now aged forty-six, he had the advantage of having lived in the territory as a young man, and when the Japanese invaded he pulled together thousands of tough operatives and a complex organization, almost a shadow government, to keep the million and a half Chinese population from rising up against the British. Early in the battle, they helped to head off a major uprising by Triad gangs on Hong Kong Island, preventing the sort of rioting that Kowloon had suffered. (Chan's vigilantes could have done much more in the fight against the Japanese, but despite the desperate need for reinforcements, the British command refused to arm the Chinese until the battle was all but lost.)

In return for this support, the British had a secret understanding with the Chinese government that, if Hong Kong fell, they would ensure that Chan and his deputy, Colonel SK Yee, were spirited off the Island. Chan, with his wooden leg, would be easily spotted, and the two Chinese would be sure targets for torture and execution if they were captured. So General Maltby asked FW 'Mike' Kendall, a mining engineer by profession, and head of Z Force, the local arm of Britain's SOE, to lay plans for an escape by senior Chinese and British officers. Kendall, described by Max as 'a Canadian adventurer I had known for some time' invited Max to join the breakout, and agreed to include two senior figures who had been brought into Hong Kong from India – Arthur Goring, an Indian army major, and Bill Robinson, an intelligence officer who was a superintendent in the Indian police.

Everyone knew that the end of the battle could not be far away once enemy troops made landfall on Hong Kong Island. This happened on the night of December 18, after the Governor had rejected the Japanese commander's second demand for surrender. Lt. General Sakai struck, not at the city of Victoria, where General Maltby had concentrated his forces, but at three points on the northeast shore, which were much more lightly defended. The Japanese plan was to skirt the enemy and take a crucial pass known as the Wong Nei Chung Gap in the mountainous centre of the Island, together with the high land to the east of it. That fateful night some 7,500 Japanese troops crossed the narrow Lei Yue Mun channel, at the eastern entrance to the harbour, aboard every vessel they could find, and began to fan out into the eastern half of the Island.

The fighting was fierce, both at sea and on land, with many casualties on both sides. By dawn on December 19 the Japanese held much of the east of the Island, and proceeded to take the high ground in the centre, killing one of Maltby's two field deputies, Brigadier JK Lawson. Maltby ordered a counter-attack on the Wong Nei Chung Gap, under the false impression that only two rather than six Japanese battalions were on the Island. A fierce battle followed, which continued through the night of December 19, leaving the dead, dying and wounded of both sides scattered over the hills. The struggle between the two armies went back and forth, with the Japanese gaining ground daily despite meeting more resistance than they had anticipated. By December 21, Sakai had driven a wedge between the British forces, and divided the Island. There were a number of atrocities. In one of the most horrific incidents, 53 Canadian and British POWs were massacred at Eucliffe Castle on the south shore, their bodies plunging to the bottom of a cliff. To this day Hong Kong people believe the site to be haunted.

Governor Young knew the game was up. His series of secret cables to the Admiralty in London make heartbreaking reading. On December 21, he described a desperate situation and requested permission to seek surrender terms. The Admiralty, in line with Churchill's orders, insisted that Hong Kong should resist to the end. The Governor's tortured cable of December 23 reflected back Churchill's admonitions:

> *Enemy has slightly improved his position in last 24 hours but lines hold generally as yesterday. Troops are very tired indeed but spirit generally good. It is understood that every day's resistance is of value to the allied cause.*

In other words, the lives of people in Hong Kong were being sacrificed for what London thought to be the greater good. By now gas and electricity supplies had been cut, the city was almost out of water and food supplies were running very low. Quite apart from the military losses, Young estimated that about 1,000 civilians had been killed, with thousands more wounded. Maltby advised surrender, but the Governor still felt it was his duty to struggle on.

By Christmas Day, the British only clung onto Victoria and the western tip of the Island. That morning two civilians held in the Repulse Bay Hotel on the south shore were taken across the island under Japanese orders to persuade the Governor to surrender – on their forced march, the hopelessness of the defenders' position was all too clear. The Japanese called a three-hour truce, but Young once again refused to give up. When the truce ended at midday, the Japanese fired everything they had at the remaining British positions. The line in Wanchai, to the east of Victoria, broke and the Japanese began to pour into the centre of the city. At 3:15 on Christmas afternoon Maltby advised the Governor that 'no further military resistance was possible'. Young finally accepted that it was all over, and ordered a ceasefire. At 6:30 in the evening he and Maltby gave themselves up to the nearest Japanese commander and were escorted across the harbour by motor boat to Sakai's headquarters in the Peninsula Hotel – the very place that less than three weeks before had been the scene of a glittering ball. There, by candlelight, Young signed a document of unconditional surrender, with Max's comrade Alf Bennett acting as interpreter. Bennett, Boxer, and nearly all of Max's surviving friends and colleagues would endure the rest of the war as prisoners of the Japanese.

CHAPTER FIVE

Escape to China
Hong Kong to Chungking 1941-42

*Max, in white sweater and plimsolls, was one of twelve survivors
from the Cornflower launch, 'the swimming party'*

*'There didn't seem much we could do except swim back
and surrender!'*

Max to his sister, January 3, 1942.

Audrey found Max's account of the battle for Hong Kong quite chilling. So many lives were needlessly lost; so many soldiers and civilians were still in captivity. Max had no time for heroic versions of the events: writing to his sister immediately after the disaster, he commented that the fall of Hong Kong was 'the inevitable result of badly conceived defence plans, lack of fighting spirit in the troops, no air support and a million civilian population who if not against the British were largely indifferent'. Max had estimated that Hong Kong could hold out for four days against a concentrated air attack, but in fact the Japanese air strikes were far from an all-out assault. Max judged it 'no credit to us that we fell apart in 17 days against a force not numerically greatly superior'. The difference in troop numbers may have been insignificant at the start of the battle, but what may not have been apparent in the fog of war was that the Japanese, unlike the beleaguered Allies, were able to bring in waves of fresh troops. By Christmas Day, after thousands were killed or wounded, just 8,000 exhausted men defended Hong Kong against around 20,000 Japanese.

Against these odds, Audrey must have wondered how Max escaped with his life and liberty, and ended up in Chungking. It was a dramatic tale that he now told. Before he had reached the Chinese capital two years earlier, he had begun a long letter to his sister, Margaret, who lived in Cape Town. It was one of the earliest accounts of the escape to reach the outside world: a South African newspaper published the story headlined: 'His Christmas Day' with extracts from Max's 'Letter from China'.

Mike Kendall, charged with smuggling out Admiral Chan, had planned an escape by sea to the coast of China: 'The plan', Max told his sister, 'was to take our two most prominent Chinese intelligence people [Chan and Yee] and join the Motor Torpedo Boats which were to be ordered to run for it when the moment came but not a minute before as they were doing very useful work.' After an audacious action in Hong Kong harbour on December 19, the Royal Navy had just five Motor Torpedo Boats (MTBs) left afloat, the remaining vessels of its 2nd Flotilla, under the command of Lt. Commander Horace Gandy. On December 20, the naval Commodore, Captain AC Collinson briefed Gandy to prepare to evacuate Chan. The flotilla was to stand by in hiding, ready for a 'desperate thrust through the enemy blockading line with a party consisting of the high officers of the Army, Navy and Air Force', as Chan put it later.

The MTBs had their shore base at the fishing village of Aberdeen on the west side of the Island. Aberdeen's deepwater harbour was sheltered from open waters by Ap Lei Chau (or Aberdeen Island), a precipitously steep small island that faced the port across a channel crowded with fishing junks and sampans. On December 21, Kendall quietly boarded Gandy's boat, *MTB 10*, at Aberdeen, leaving on shore his Chinese wife Betty. Two fellow SOE commandos, Colin McEwan, a Scottish educator, and Monia Talan, a White Russian from Shanghai, boarded other vessels in the flotilla. The plan was to pick up the Chinese leaders from Aberdeen Harbour when the end came, but this was a dangerous spot to wait for them. So on Christmas Day Gandy's fleet was hiding in more sheltered bays – three of the MTBs lay on the offshore side of Ap Lei Chau, and two were anchored in the Island's Telegraph Bay to the west of Aberdeen.

While Gandy positioned his fleet, back in the Battle Box Maltby was readying to surrender. Max was there: 'Things looked black on Christmas morning,' he wrote, 'and after a dash up to the Peak to evacuate some women and children I struck down to BHQ. I had already asked the General's permission to try and escape and at about 3pm he told me and three other Staff officers to go if we could.' Max, described as 'unflappable' by Maltby's ADC, Iain MacGregor, was ready to take his chance. As soon as the white flag of surrender was raised at 3:15pm, he surfaced from the Battle Box. He heard the sounds of gunfire from the approaching Japanese as he made his way half a mile across town to the Gloucester Hotel, where he and Bill Robinson, the Indian police intelligence superintendent, had been told to find Admiral Chan. Chan waited on the fourth floor with his immediate entourage – his deputy and intelligence chief, Colonel Yee, his young ADC Lt. Commander Henry Hsu Heng, and his bodyguard, Coxswain Yeung Chuen. David MacDougall, who was a long-time friend and key liaison to the Admiral in his role as secretary to the Far Eastern Bureau of the Ministry of Information, and his deputy Ted Ross, an athletic young Canadian, were nearby. They anxiously waited for the Colonial Secretary's blessing to go, then came up from their office on the third floor to join the group. Two of the staff officers who had, with Max, been given Maltby's permission to leave, turned up too: Captain Peter MacMillan, a bishop's son from the Royal Artillery and Oxford rowing blue, and Captain Freddie Guest, a blustering former cavalry officer. Now they were ten: a distinguished crew who all had good reason to stay out of the hands of the Japanese. And for practically the first time in the whole conflict British and Chinese worked together on a joint operation.

Just after 3:30pm, the ten men piled into two cars that were parked around the corner from the Gloucester by the King's Theatre – a big new Buick, driven by Ross, and a soft-top Austin, driven by Hsu. There was not a moment to lose as they headed out of town, away from the advancing Japanese forces. It was six dangerous and exposed miles to Aberdeen. They raced along the roller-coaster route, climbing out of Victoria to the west, cresting a ridge by the Queen Mary hospital (where Charles Boxer was recuperating) and descending along the snaking coast road into Aberdeen, which was still being shelled despite the ceasefire. There the large figure of Major Arthur Goring, a career soldier sent to Hong Kong from the Indian Army, appeared and joined the group. He had thought it his duty to stay with Maltby until the bitter end.

Max and his companions reached Aberdeen naval base at about 4pm. To the group's dismay, there were no MTBs in sight. 'Unfortunately they had been told to go at the same time as we had so were not [there]!' said Max. Commander Hugh Montague, the officer in charge of the base, explained that he had passed on orders from naval HQ for the MTB flotilla to head out to sea to save themselves from the enemy – an instruction that upended Kendall's plan. Chan's party would have to find an alternative, and fast, since the Japanese were advancing on Aberdeen, one of the few places on the Island that they had not yet overrun. At the waterfront the men found a twenty-five foot motor boat which could be made serviceable. It was the launch of a scuttled ship, *HMS Cornflower*, and though it was far too small to make the passage to the coast of China, it was their only chance to get away.

Montague came up with a Plan B: he expected to re-float a beached diesel tugboat at high tide, and told the Admiral's party to take the launch and wait at the western end of Ap Lei Chau, the island facing Aberdeen, out of range of Japanese fire. If they failed to see the MTBs, Montague would try to pick them up after dark. Max and his comrades conjured up petrol from the naval stores, and a supply of food, water, and rifles. They asked for volunteers to crew the launch, and five men stepped forward: Captain Alec Damsgaard and a merchant seaman cadet, Holger Christiansen (both Danish); D Harley (a Norwegian engineer), and two men from the naval volunteer reserve, William Morley Wright and John Jacob Forster.

The party of sixteen men got underway in the Cornflower launch 'in brilliant sunlight and a dead calm at about 6 knots', recalled Max. It was 1700 hours, Max reported: 'We could not afford to wait for darkness as the enemy was but a few hundred yards off and would be in Aberdeen as soon as resistance ended'. David MacDougall later explained to his wife Catherine 'it was a suicidal thing to do but anything seemed preferable to tamely waiting capture'.

'Of course, it was hopeless from the start', Max wrote to his sister. The flimsy wooden launch chugged away from Aberdeen dock by the east channel (the Channel route), believing that the alternative western channel (the Harbour route) was mined and more vulnerable. Fisher families lived on board their junks on the water, and the launch steered through them to curious stares. 'After ten minutes [some said less] we were greeted by rifle fire, followed by machine gunning, the engine was hit and there we lay between Hong Kong and Aberdeen Island with bullets ripping through the boat', said Max. The hail of fire came from the direction of Brick Hill, a peninsula south of Aberdeen, where the Japanese had seized a British defence position, pillbox number 12. The engine quickly caught fire, and the disabled and defenceless launch began to drift only 200 yards from the Japanese-occupied shore.

'We abandoned ship to swim for Aberdeen Island', said Max, 'We were machine gunned continuously whilst swimming about a quarter of a mile and while getting ashore on the rocks.' Damsgaard, at the helm, and Forster were shot and never made it out of the boat. Harley, the engineer, drowned 'noisily' after going overboard. Others were wounded before taking to the water – David MacDougall was hit in the shoulder, Chan Chak in the wrist, as he reached for a life-ring to give to his bodyguard, a non-swimmer. Henry Hsu helped the wounded Admiral to unstrap his wooden leg, which he left on the launch – along with tens of thousands of Hong Kong dollars stuffed inside it. Hsu was a Christian, and Chan vowed that he would himself convert, should he survive. They both headed into the water and Hsu, a champion swimmer, tried to carry the Admiral along, until his boss told him that it was every man for himself. Max wasn't sure what happened to Colonel Yee, a poor swimmer: 'He left the boat but was not seen again' Max reported. (Yee would reappear weeks later. He had actually stayed on the launch, and escaped with the help of local Chinese.)

The dozen swimmers spent about twenty-five minutes in the cold water, though some later said that it felt like an hour. One by one, they hauled themselves onto the unwelcoming, rocky shore of Ap Lei Chau, still being targeted by gunfire. Max landed alone, and lay exhausted behind a rock, 'with an occasional shot coming my way'. Once he'd caught his breath, he tried to get over the crest of the impossibly steep island, but found the journey too far and exposed, so sheltered again. He then ran into Arthur Goring, and together they made a dash for 'a low neck of land', most likely a narrow spit which connects Ap Lei Chau to its smaller sister, Ap Lei Pai. They could see some other men on this spot 'and some of us gathered there in the gratefully warm sunshine on the sheltered side from the enemy'. Shivering and clad only in shorts, 'there didn't seem much we could do except swim back and surrender!' lamented Max.

Meanwhile, the wounded MacDougall had struggled to swim to the island: he was losing blood, and had been unable to take off his shoes or unstrap his revolver, which weighed him down in the water. After several desperate attempts, he finally managed to discard his shoes, and reached the rocks completely exhausted. He tore the nails off his right hand trying to get a grip in the swell, and his left hand was useless because of his injury. Ted Ross helped to pull his boss out of the water, and then MacDougall crouched behind a rock for an hour 'while the sun went down in calm beauty', hallucinating about his own death, he would later tell his wife. He said he felt like Hemingway's hero at the end of *For Whom the Bell Tolls* – perhaps because the American author had made a big impression when he visited Hong Kong earlier that year.

As daylight faded, the ragged group of survivors despaired of rescue. But then, said Max, 'a new arrival brought the surprising news that he had seen three MTBs round the corner'. At last, there was hope. Max, Freddie Guest and a naval rating set out to investigate. 'It was tough going over the rocks, shoeless,' Max said. He and Guest at one point found a Carley float, or life raft, but it was too heavy for them to operate and they carried on walking. Then came a fresh volley of machine gun fire – 'we dropped to cover like rabbits; we were getting good at that; it was extremely discouraging to find the enemy in possession of our small island'. But this time it wasn't the enemy: as Max (who had lost touch with Guest) went down to the water's edge to try the life raft again, hallelujah, with his own eyes he saw one of the elusive MTBs quite close to shore, with one man swimming towards it and two others following.

The first swimmer was Holger Christiansen of the Cornflower crew, and as he struck out for the torpedo boat, its crew thought they heard him shout 'There are ten Japs following with machine guns' and duly began shooting at the figures on the island. In fact, Christiansen was saying: 'There are ten chaps following being machine-gunned'. Eventually, he made himself understood and *MTB 27* hauled him on board and drew closer to shore.

Max scrambled and slid over the rocks, in and out of the water towards the large camouflage-painted boat, swimming the last few yards. 'I only just made it, and was very grateful for the rope which dragged me in,' he said. Three MTBs were gathered on the seaward side of Ap Lei Chau, ready to receive their important passengers. But Chan was missing, and both he and MacDougall were reportedly too badly wounded to do any more swimming that night.

It was almost dark when Gandy sent out a dinghy from *MTB 10* to pick up MacDougall and Ross – Ross had gone back on 'a cruel journey over jagged rocks in his bare feet and clad only in his underwear', said a grateful MacDougall, to fetch his boss from the landward side of the island. Locating Admiral Chan was much more difficult. A rowboat took Hsu and Yeung back to shore to look for him. Earlier, the two aides had carried Chan, immobilized by the loss of his wooden leg and a bullet in his wrist, to a sheltered cave, Hsu, it was said, leaving his boss with a Bible and a gun. But Chan had managed to leave the hiding place. Hsu and Yeung couldn't find him anywhere, but Lt. Commander John Yorath (who had joined the MTBs from naval HQ) and Bill Robinson volunteered to make a second attempt, eventually locating the Admiral practically at the top of a hill. Somehow he had dragged himself to higher ground, probably on the smaller island, Ap Lei Pai. It was completely dark by the time the hardy Admiral was brought on board Gandy's ship. Kendall, according to Max, had refused to go without the Chinese as he considered them necessary for the journey into China – a fact that Gandy didn't dispute.

Max and his companions learned that Gandy had done them an enormous service. He had ignored the high-level command – one that according to military procedure had to be issued before the hour of surrender – that Montague had transmitted that afternoon to 'go' to save his fleet. Gandy had signalled the reply 'Propose go after dark must pick up two Chinese at Aberdeen dock'. In the event, it was impossible for his MTB to get into Aberdeen dock, but even when the command to leave was reiterated, Gandy had lingered nearby, off Ap Lei Chau. When it was all over, Gandy was commended for his judgement in showing 'commendable discretion in not precipitately obeying the order to "go at once"'.

During the search for Chan, Gandy signalled the rest of his flotilla to leave Telegraph Bay and join *MTBs 10* and *27* where they lay to the west of Ap Lei Chau. By 9:15pm the five vessels were assembled in the darkness. The twelve survivors of the Cornflower escape divided up among the boats. The wounded were bandaged up, with rough dressings that went unchanged for the next ten days. The sailors dug out dry clothes for the swimmers, and gave them each a warming tot of rum. Max borrowed a pair of flannel trousers, a white submarine sweater, and a naval officer's cap. Gandy lent the Admiral his spare uniform (and his only peaked cap), which he sported proudly throughout the coming journey.

Chan Chak, despite his injuries, had a clear head and was in no doubt about the route the escape should take: he determined that the flotilla should head for Mirs Bay to the northeast of Hong Kong, and then take a land route over the mountains and across Japanese lines into Free China. He would enlist the help of local guerrilla groups along the way.

At around 9:30pm the five boats revved up their powerful engines for the get-away. Heading out to sea through the East Lamma channel, the convoy made a wide circuit of Hong Kong Island. The men could only imagine the horrors facing those they had left behind. As the convoy rounded the Stanley peninsula explosions, bursts of gunfire and flames rising from burning buildings disturbed the night air.

Soon they were in open water. Lieutenant David P Legge of *MTB 11* later recalled: 'Fortunately the moon was not yet up. It was one of the most beautiful nights I remember. The sea was calm and the wind was warm.' The convoy settled into a rhythm, and the men's tension eased as they relished the peace of the night and the prospect of freedom. But they were far from being out of danger. After an hour or two of running at 22 knots they had a major scare. They saw the searchlights from a Japanese warship circling in the distance. A 'red rocket' was fired in their direction, but thankfully the warship was too far away to pick off the convoy.

Around midnight, the flotilla steamed into Mirs Bay, to the east of the New Territories, and approached Ping Chau, a tiny crescent-shaped island just off the coast of China, and a known staging post for smugglers. It was the most easterly point of Hong Kong's territory. The Z Force trio, Hsu, Yeung and a couple of others went ashore gingerly, under cover of the boats' guns, and brought the village headman out to see the Admiral. Chan learned that Leung Wingyuen, a man who had previously served under him in the Chinese navy and was now a guerrilla leader, controlled the coastal area. This was encouraging news. Chan was assured that there were no Japanese in the immediate vicinity. Armed with this local intelligence, the Admiral advised the convoy to pull into the fishing village of Nan'ao, which lay just opposite Ping Chau on the Guangdong coast, and was near the walled town of Dapeng where Leung had his headquarters.

It was about 2am on Boxing Day morning when the flotilla drew into Nan'ao. Villagers and guerrillas helped to scuttle the five MTBs while it was still dark, in order to cover the escape party's tracks. It was a wrench for the sailors to destroy the vessels they had lived aboard

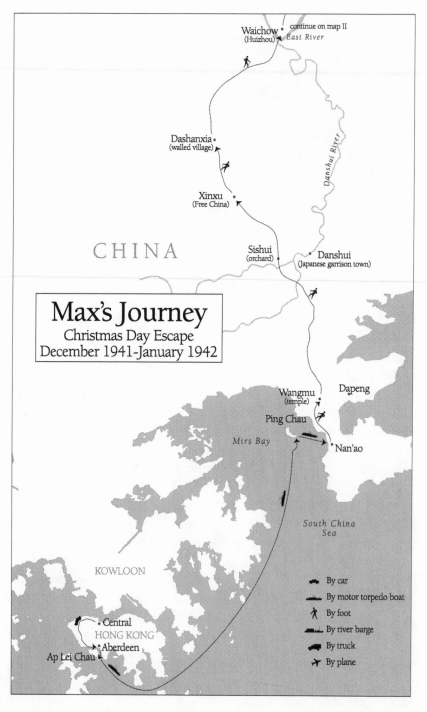

Max's Journey
Christmas Day Escape
December 1941–January 1942

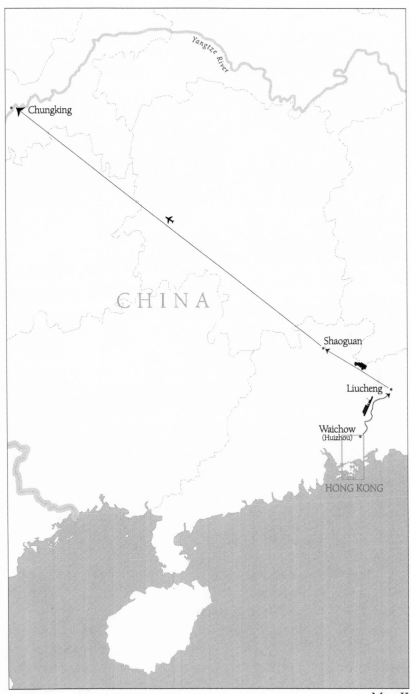

Map II

and it proved hard to sink them completely in the shallow water off Nan'ao – villagers had to pile rocks on the wreckage to weigh it down. The escape party unloaded all the provisions and weapons they could carry – Leung's guerrillas appropriated the radios and other heavier equipment. The men salvaged shoes, naval sweaters and other pieces of uniform to wear on the journey. Each was armed with a rifle and a revolver, and carried food, water and ammunition, preparing for a long and hazardous trek.

— • —

Their party had grown: Commander Montague and a crew of six had succeeded in re-floating the diesel tugboat at Aberdeen, and made their way independently to the coast of China. As luck would have it, the MTB party arrived just in time to help the tug, stranded on rocks at the entrance to Nan'ao.

With this addition, the company was 68 strong. The fifty-two year old Montague was the senior British officer, but Kendall and Chan were the undisputed leaders of the expedition, each with a distinct role to play. Max's official report paid tribute to both: '[Kendall – his name was blacked out] proved an outstanding leader and it is through his energy and foresight that the escape was successfully carried out.' Chan was a local hero, essential to persuading Leung to provide guerrilla escorts for the trek, and 'the presence of Admiral Chan Chak assured most hospitable treatment from the towns and villages en route'. Henry Hsu also won Max's praise as 'an admirable organizer', who did much for the comfort of the party. It would be a long and arduous journey inland on foot, along rough trails most often used by smugglers. The aim was to get across the Japanese-held coastal strip without being detected and to make it to Huizhou (then known as Waichow), the first sizeable town in unoccupied China, over 70 miles away.

Leung told the party it would not be safe to walk in daylight, so he led the weary men up into the hills above Nan'ao, heading a couple of miles inland to find shelter. Gratefully, they rested up for the day at a village known as Kow Tit, hiding in a rice storehouse. Stores from the scuttled boats provided quite a feast for dinner. 'That evening', said Max, 'we set out northwards carrying what kit we could and escorted by Chinese guerrilla troops.' Retracing their steps through Nan'ao, and then following the coastline north by moonlight, by midnight the company reached Wangmu – by now they had covered some 17 miles. Their arrival was expected – Max and the other headquarters staff (the 'odds and sods' group, as Gandy privately called them) slept in a village house, and the sailors slept on the straw-covered stone floor of the local temple.

Leung judged that the next stage of the march, over narrow hill paths, should be tackled in daylight, so the next morning, December 27, the party set off at 8am. 'We got coolies [to carry supplies] and marching in single file we formed a snake nearly a mile long' said Max. Chan, and now MacDougall too, were carried in makeshift sedan chairs. The path took them up and down over two ranges of hills and across two rivers. Men suffered from sore feet and heavy packs: Max didn't complain, though he walked most of the way in borrowed tennis shoes. They paused for lunch, and at 5pm for another meal to stoke up before crossing Japanese lines.

Under cover of darkness, they surreptitiously approached the enemy lines, crossing a heavily patrolled road west of Danshui, a Japanese garrison town. By some accounts Japanese patrols were seen, but the column of 68 men and their escorts made it through. 'Owing to the masterly scouting and screening of Mr. Leung's guerrillas we had crossed the Tah Shui (Danshui) – Shao To Kok road without being detected by the Japanese', said Montague in his official report. Locals advised them not to pause, and so they continued to march until midnight, covering a punishing 31 miles that day, and spending sixteen hours on the trail. They slept out in an orchard, but by 5am the bitter cold was unbearable and they set off again. On December 28, the company walked 16 miles through rolling hills, breaking their journey at Xinxu, the first outpost in Free China. 'Here we were within the lines of the Chinese regular forces, and owing to their kindness, were generously fed and comfortably housed', wrote Montague. The day ended at an old Hakka walled village, Dashanxia, where the staff officers spent a comfortable night – at last – in the local magistrate's family temple.

The men completed the trek of 70 miles on the fourth day, some riding the last stretch on rickety bicycles, arriving on the edge of the town of Huizhou on the afternoon of December 29. While they waited to make a ceremonial entrance into the town, escorted by Chinese soldiers and civic officials, they witnessed a procession of retreating troops from the army that Chiang had sent to relieve Hong Kong – but which had never materialized. That evening, the two senior Chinese army commanders in the area laid on an elaborate welcome banquet, and the men bedded down for some well-earned rest in an American mission hospital.

Early the next morning the bedraggled crew assembled in front of the hospital for a triumphant photo, later captioned to read: 'Admiral Chen Chak with British Officers and men whom his Excellency led through the Japanese lines after the fall of Hong Kong and arrived safely at Waichow.' Kendall and his fellow SOE agents, McEwan and Talan, opted to stay out of the photo to remain incognito. Soon they bid farewell and slipped off to continue their clandestine work in southern China. After the photo was taken (with the photographer's last glass plate) everyone enjoyed a hearty breakfast in the mission dining room – Max and a few other officers mucked in to serve and wash up. Later on, Max did another good deed – according to MacDougall, whose wound was festering from a clumsy attempt to remove the bullet, Max gave his friend a bottle of an antibacterial 'wonder drug' that he had found in a Chinese junk shop. When MacDougall finally had the bullet examined by surgeons in Chengdu the site was 'as clean as a whistle'.

— • —

The men were now in friendly territory, but their odyssey was far from over. Travel by road or rail was not possible from war-torn Huizhou, so at 6pm on New Year's Eve the company boarded barges to continue their journey by water. The party spent four days and nights going northeast on the broad East River in slow and overcrowded boats. It was, Max wrote: 'on the East River, between Waichow and Shuikwan' (now Huizhou and Shaoguan) that he began his long letter to his sister. He was on one barge with Chan and the rest of the Cornflower party, crammed in with some Chinese soldiers and guerrillas in a single large room, while most of the naval contingent was billeted on the other boats. Rations were meagre, consisting mainly of rice, and the barges' engines broke down frequently. The men were supposed to stay below deck to avoid being spotted by Japanese planes that occasionally flew overhead.

The restless men were relieved to reach Liucheng on January 4. There they were met by the tall figure of Lt. Col. Harry Owen-Hughes, a military liaison officer who had caught the last plane out of Hong Kong after the attack on Kai Tak. A fluent Cantonese speaker and head of a family trading firm, he had flown to Chungking to try and persuade Chiang to send an army to relieve Hong Kong – the one that never arrived. But now he was very glad to see Chan's party: he gave the grateful men Chinese army padded jackets to keep them warm in the wintry weather, and organized onward transport. The people of Liucheng slaughtered a cow for a banquet held in honour of the Admiral's party – one of many lavish welcomes that greeted them along the way.

At 6am the next morning the company hit the road again – this time in five trucks, together with a car for the injured Chan and MacDougall. The convoy drove for two days over mountainous terrain on bone-shaking, narrow roads. They headed northwest towards Shaoguan, which served as the provincial capital after the fall of Canton, stopping off at an ancient Buddhist monastery at Nanhua, and arrived at Shaoguan to great fanfare on January 6, the thirteenth day of the escape. Local girl guides gave the men 'hero' rosettes, and 'we were…given a banquet at which there were at least a dozen generals and yesterday a large tea party with speeches and not too much tea' wrote Max. 'In the town there were streamers across the street saying "Welcome to Admiral Chan Chak and the Defenders of Hong Kong"'.

The whole company was billeted on the 'Sea Palace', a large houseboat that normally had more colourful occupants – it was a floating brothel. Max found it 'overcrowded but otherwise pleasant'. He shared a cabin, or 'entertainment' cubicle, with Freddie Guest, and pronounced the conditions 'very tolerable'. At the town's Methodist Mission, an

The escape group in Huizhou, with Max (second row, third from left), December 30, 1941

Irish doctor Samuel Moore and his wife Jean showed the company un-
stinting hospitality. Max enjoyed his first European meal since having
porridge for breakfast on Christmas morning. He and other staff officers had walked over to the mission compound on January 7 to make
an important phone call. Using a military telephone line installed by
Owen-Hughes, the senior officers made their first report of the escape
to the British Embassy in Chungking, listing names and details of the
entire party. They learned that they were to be flown up to the war
capital for debriefing on the fall of Hong Kong and their escape through
China. Gandy was to lead the naval contingent out of China by road
and rail towards Burma – a land journey of some 2,500 miles. (They
would eventually reach Rangoon on February 14, shipping out shortly
before that city fell to the Japanese.)

Though the British command was keen to hear first-hand accounts
of the battle for Hong Kong, seats on planes to Chungking were scarce.
Max and his companions waited in Shaoguan for nine days, a time to
reflect on their blessings – and their losses. During the spell of enforced
leisure, Max wrote the second part of his letter to Margaret:

> *Shopping is difficult for there is little to buy and that of poor
> quality and very expensive. A pair of H.K. shoes costs Ch.N.
> $350 (about 70/-), a razor blade 1/-. My total worldly posses-
> sions are a pair of flannels, too long and with holes in the seat,
> 2 pairs of socks, 1 shirt (no collar), a submarine sweater and
> 1 Chinese vest and a pair of Chinese slippers. Rather different
> from a month ago with car, flat, radio, gramophone, saddling,
> golf clubs and masses of clothes!*

But it was, he commented, a cheap price for liberty. 'My most serious loss is Helen', he admitted, 'who I think loved me very much. As
a doctor she should be treated well but I am anxious and there is little
prospect of getting any news.'

Finally word came that a small plane would be available the night
of January 14. The six British 'high officers' who had begun their escape with the Chinese at the Gloucester Hotel twenty days earlier now
said goodbye to the sailors who rescued them, and to the Admiral
and his aide who had led them through China. Chan stayed on at the

Methodist Mission to recuperate from surgery to remove the bullet in his wrist. Arthur Goring, as on Christmas Day, would follow later – he was laid low with malaria. The six, with the addition of Montague, the senior naval officer, were taken by truck to a grass airstrip at Nanxiong, and at 9:15 that evening took off in a CNAC 14-seat Douglas DC-2. After a one-hour stop in Guilin, its expert American pilot landed the officers safely on Chungking's tricky sandbank airfield. 'Arrived Chungking by air at 4am today and shall wait c/o the British Embassy for orders', said Max.

'Going to have a drink with the Ambassador this evening,' Max wrote in closing his letter. 'Except for rice wine, my first since Hong Kong.' He had made it.

CHAPTER SIX

∾

Quite Perfect
Chungking 1942-44

*Max and the Office of the Air
Attaché, Chungking*

'Am getting married in my Utility Suit...and a pair of clod-hoppers – no hat or smart bag and gloves!'
Audrey to her family, January 3, 1944.

While the British Ambassador toasted Max and his companions that cold January night in 1942, the China correspondent of the London *Times* filed his report of the heroes' landing in Chungking 'dressed in an odd mixture of naval, civilian and Chinese clothing...all were looking very fit in spite of the hazards of their thrilling escape'. As Max told Audrey his story, she may have remembered reading about the breakout from Hong Kong over breakfast with her housemates in Farnborough – the Hutchison sisters' connections to China meant that they seldom missed news from that part of the world. And this had been a rare piece of good news during a winter that saw Britain's Asian colonies fall like dominoes to the Japanese.

Max now explained to Audrey that whilst his fellow officers left Chungking for new assignments outside China, he had been selected for a posting that would keep him in the war capital – Assistant Air Attaché to the British mission. He would have diplomatic status and build on his experience of air intelligence to carry out the sensitive role. His good relations with Chan and SK Yee, soon to reach Chungking themselves, gave him a head start with the shadowy world of the Kuomintang and Chinese military intelligence.

But before his appointment was announced to the Chinese, Max headed for India, headquarters of Far East Command, and a country that Max knew well from his days with Imperial Airways. On January 31 he left Chungking with Freddie Guest and Bill Robinson and took his first flight over the Hump to Calcutta, an awe-inspiring experience even for a veteran pilot. During a six-week stay in India, he briefed the top brass on the events in Hong Kong and was in turn prepared for his new assignment. He also enjoyed some well-earned rest and relaxation. As Audrey would find in her turn, colonial India offered plenty of opportunities for that. Max went to the Delhi Hunt Point to

Point and the Calcutta Paper Chase; and he joined the Saturday Club in Calcutta, swimming, lunching and dining there constantly. He picked up his old pursuits of riding and playing golf, and renewed a friendship with Chuck Sharp, a roguish Texan who managed CNAC's Hump operations from Calcutta's Dum Dum airport. Sharp and his wife Sylvia introduced their bachelor friend to a woman called Joyce Franklin. She enlivened his stay in Calcutta, and one way and another it seemed that he seldom ate alone.

After this welcome break, Max headed back to Chungking to settle into his new home, landing on the wintertime airstrip in the Yangtze on the night of March 13. Going ashore in the dark, he made his way up the steep cliffside and through the old town to his lodging at Jialing House, the only European-style hotel in the city. He had arrived just in time for a lunch given by the Sino-British cultural association, one of the capital's many international friendship societies, to welcome the new British Ambassador. During Max's absence, Sir Horace Seymour had arrived to succeed Sir Archibald Clark Kerr, the envoy who had greeted the escapees in January, and who went on to cap off a stellar career with postings to Moscow and Washington. Seymour quickly sensed that British prestige in the Far East was at a low ebb. His staff reported a change in Chinese attitudes after the humiliating losses of Hong Kong, Malaya and Singapore. John Keswick, taipan of Jardine Matheson, his family's trading firm, who now ran the China branch of the SOE from the Chungking Embassy, was a leading voice of British business in China. Keswick commented in April: 'It is only now that one realises how sad and how bitter is the feeling about Hong Kong where all the Chinese that count had their money, their wives and quite a few sweethearts.'

The loss of Hong Kong was just one factor in the complex politics of the region. The Americans really ran the show in the CBI – the China-Burma-India theatre of war – with the British playing a supporting role, and not always seeing eye-to-eye with their powerful cousins. The British and the Americans shared the primary goal of defeating Japan, but beyond that the Allies had distinctly different priorities in the Pacific War. Churchill made it plain that he wanted to take back Britain's occupied colonies after the war, which meant that he had to rebuff any Chinese claim to Hong Kong. Colonial rule was anathema to Roosevelt,

Allied officers and civilians in Chungking, including Max (centre)
and Admiral Yang (on Max's right)

and he favoured the return of Hong Kong to Chinese sovereignty at the end of the war.

And of course the US government had most of the financial, military and political clout: it was much the largest source of war aid to Chiang, propping up the Generalissimo as the best available defence against Japan. President Roosevelt had nominated an American, Lt. General Joseph Stilwell, to be chief of staff to the Chinese leader (an unprecedented move) and commander of all US forces in the CBI sector. It was a choice the President eventually came to regret: Stilwell spoke Mandarin fluently, but scarcely endeared himself to Chiang. His acid tongue earned him the nickname 'Vinegar Joe' and privately he called Chiang 'Peanut'. The two stubborn men were constantly at odds. In messages Stilwell sent from his imposing hilltop headquarters above the Jialing River, the General was blunt about Chiang's shortcomings, and less willing than his president to put faith in the Chinese autocrat. Despite the differing long-term goals of London and Washington, at least local British diplomats could sometimes help to calm the troubled waters of Chungking.

Max walked into this tricky situation when he took up his appointment in 1942. By the time that he met Audrey he was a veteran of negotiating the shoals of diplomacy, and fathoming the depths of Chungking's murky world. He had rubbed shoulders with many of its strong-willed leaders. He met Chiang and his wife for the first time in Lashio in northern Burma in April 1942, when they were on a visit to rally Chinese troops on the hard-pressed Burma front, and Max was returning from a second visit to India. He flew on the Chiangs' plane from Lashio to Kunming (the Allies' base in southern China) – two towns over 700 miles apart that were linked by the Burma Road until Japan completed its conquest of Burma later that April.

Max soon saw Madame Chiang again – this time with the Flying Tigers, the renowned band of American volunteer pilots who flew for China under contract and were credited with bringing down well over 100 Japanese planes in daring sorties over Burma and south China. Their commander, the swashbuckling Colonel Claire Chennault, was a favourite of Madame's, and when the Flying Tigers disbanded in July 1942, she threw a grand Chungking banquet in their honour. Max was present as Chennault paid tribute to his men; Chennault went on to command the US Fourteenth Air Force from Kunming, taking with him some of the American pilots who kept their trademark sharks' teeth insignia on their Air Force planes. Other Flying Tigers signed up as civilian pilots for CNAC, and Max often saw their familiar faces on his travels over the Hump and around China.

For he was seldom on the ground for long at a stretch: his work involved incessant travel around Free China, to gather intelligence, to consult with top Chinese and US officials, to visit air bases, to escort visiting delegations from Britain, and to check on the RAF's efforts to train the Chinese Air Force at Chengdu, Sichuan's capital a couple of hundred miles west of Chungking.

In late 1942 Max was promoted to the rank of Wing Commander, and for four months he was Acting Air Attaché in the absence on home leave of his boss, Group Captain James Warburton. He relished the extra responsibility, handling tricky situations such as a meeting with the irascible Stilwell in January 1943 over the forced landing of an RAF plane on the Salween, occupied Burma's longest river.

Max had an easier time of it building relationships with his colleagues and intelligence counterparts in the Chinese, American and

European missions. He grew close both to Warburton – the Air Attaché was just a year older than his deputy – and to a third senior member of the office, the jovial Air Staff Officer, Squadron Leader Gidley Baird. He celebrated the anniversary of his escape at Christmas 1942 with Gidley and his wife, Pamela, and went on to a tea party hosted by the Chiangs for the foreign community. Madame staged a nativity play and the Generalissimo handed the guests red silk ties embroidered with his monogram.

The Christmas cheer brightened up a winter that was particularly cold and damp – Max moved into new lodgings in Tennis Court Mansions, but noted in his diary on February 1 that the maximum temperature indoors was 51 degrees. A few days later it snowed and was only 42 in his room. Throwing a party was one way to warm up the place, and he and a colleague, Major Giles, hosted one in their rooms on January 30: 32 people came, consuming 10 bottles of gin at a cost of $1,380 in local currency, Max noted ruefully in his diary.

Like everybody, Max suffered from the horribly high cost of living – especially until 'Operation Remorse' kicked in. This was an ingenious clandestine scheme to trade imported diamonds and other high-value goods for Chinese currency at favourable black market rates. It was improbably run by agents of the SOE, led by Walter Fletcher, an outsize former rubber trader and later Member of Parliament. The operation was wildly successful, turning an enormous profit for the SOE, and for Embassy personnel like Max helping to make salaries go further.

In the complicated world of Chungking, where everyone was looking for an angle, currency schemes and propaganda were important tools in the Allied armoury. John Galvin and Stanley Smith, a pair of Australians who had been buddies since youthful days as jackaroos in Queensland, were both now serving British psychological warfare efforts: John Galvin was deputy head of the Far Eastern Bureau of the Ministry of Information, an agency which dealt in both 'white' and 'black' propaganda. He had been David MacDougall's regional boss until the fall of Hong Kong, and was present at the Chungking debriefing of the senior officers who had escaped on Christmas Day. Stanley Smith was Press Attaché and from mid-1942 the Ministry of Information chief for China, in charge of British propaganda efforts throughout the country. The pair were budding entrepreneurs and seemed to know

'Feige', the British Ambassador's wartime residence. Photo taken in 2008

a good deal about the hush-hush currency scheme. More innocuously, Smith produced a daily newspaper for Embassy staff printed on paper made from eucalyptus wood. 'Thus at breakfast-time we could read the news while simultaneously warding off colds by inhaling the fumes of eucalyptus rising from the newsprint', remembered the First Secretary, Berkeley Gage.

As he would later do in Audrey's company, Max enjoyed the foreign community's more leisurely pastimes: evenings playing bridge, weekends in the country outside the city, and walks in the hills. One weekend he entertained a famous escapee from Hong Kong: Gwen Priestwood. She had been at the eve-of-battle ball at the Peninsula and was the first woman to escape from the Hong Kong civilian internment camp at Stanley. Berkeley Gage remembered Priestwood presenting herself at the Embassy wearing trousers and in such a dirty, bedraggled state that he took her to be a man. But Max treated her like a lady – taking her to dinner, and out of the city for a weekend in the hills.

While Audrey was making her roundabout way to China in the summer of 1943, Max was on local leave, taking a six-week trip to Fujian, a coastal province, in the company of Berkeley Gage and Berkeley's manservant Wu, who was a native of the region. In an incident that made a good story for years to come, the governor of Fujian caused a major breach of protocol by giving precedence at a banquet to the manservant, the local hero, over Max, the unknown foreigner. The trio drove over 600 miles in an old Ford station wagon with worn out tyres, reaching the port of Fuzhou shortly before it was occupied by Japanese forces. It was a trip full of adventure: lunches with senior Chinese army officers, tea parties with British Consuls, cocktails with benighted foreign residents of Fuzhou and dinners aplenty. Along the way, Max and Berkeley were stranded by heavy flooding, and spent one night in a Buddhist temple and another at a Benedictine mission. They each gave speeches to business and military groups and made courtesy calls on local dignitaries.

In the city of Guilin they stayed with members of the British Army Aid Group (BAAG), an undercover outfit formed by Hong Kong academic, Colonel Lindsay Ride, in early 1942 to help prisoners escape from Hong Kong's internment camps, often using the trail that was blazed by the Christmas Day escapees. Waiting for a flight back to the capital, Max was dismayed to discover that he had been turned out of his room in Tennis Court Mansions – a common risk of an extended absence. Returning to Chungking on July 21, he moved in to share Berkeley's flat above the Chancery office at the Embassy. Berkeley and Max were from very different backgrounds – the former was an Eton and Cambridge man from a wealthy military family, while Max was a baker's son without a university education – but they were the same age and had become great friends, sharing a bachelor life in Chungking and the escapades along the road in Fujian.

Visiting the BAAG officers reminded Max that he was a very lucky man; whatever the hardships of wartime China, they were 'a cheap price for liberty', to paraphrase his letter to his sister after the escape. But everything in Chungking was impermanent – the lodgings, the work, the people who came and went. He surely missed Helen and had no hope of seeing her while Hong Kong was occupied. Occasionally he wrote, and once noted in his diary 'letter from Helen'. There was an alluring new woman in his life. In late 1942, Max began an intense affair with a Polish beauty called Maya Redevitch. She was something of a legend in the foreign community – a multilingual refugee from Shanghai, who worked as an interpreter for the Chinese. For many months, Max saw Maya constantly – for lunch or dinner, for picnics, for walks, and sometimes, after an official engagement, for late night trysts. But by the summer of 1943 the relationship seemed to be running into the sand. His diary noted 'goodbye from Maya' shortly before his return from Fujian, and it didn't help that it was a liaison frowned upon by the top of the Embassy. An English redhead from Cheltenham Ladies' College was a much more suitable catch.

— • —

So there were audible murmurs of approval when Max and Audrey's affair took off after the Pei P'ei house party. The forthright Lady Seymour made her views plain in a private letter to her husband (who was away in England), written on December 3: 'The Max Oxford-Audrey Watson affair is progressing well according to Berkeley. He is beginning to forget the Pole which is all to the good.' Audrey herself made no mention of a new beau in a stream of chatty letters to her family, but hinted that she was enjoying life: 'I have been home very little these past few weeks, as I have been out a lot on this side [the north side], and have been spending the night at various other people's Messes.' But the pace would slow down when, on December 5, Max had to leave town for ten days – an enforced pause for reflection. Max escorted Warburton's successor, Air Commodore Gilbert Bartholomew, on a tour of Chinese Air Force bases, while Audrey managed the office in *her* boss' absence in India.

The moment that Max returned on December 15, he invited Audrey to dinner. Three days later, they were to attend a major event on the diplomatic calendar: Lady Seymour and Sir Humphrey Prideaux-Brune (standing in for Sir Horace) were welcoming General Sir Adrian Carton de Wiart VC to Chungking. Churchill had sent Carton de Wiart, a much-decorated veteran of the Great War, to be his personal envoy to Chiang in the hope of improving relationships with the Chinese leader. (Sporting a black eye-patch, and missing an arm as well as an eye from war wounds, the charismatic General would do well at earning the respect both of Chiang and 'Vinegar Joe' Stilwell.)

Lady Seymour prepared the hilltop Ambassadorial villa for a large cocktail party, arranging her bedroom as an extra sitting room warmed with a charcoal brazier, she told her husband in a letter. Max and Audrey came to cocktails, and were among a more intimate group invited to stay for dinner with the General. Towards midnight, they went on together to one of the British troops' relentless Saturday night dances. As the sparkling evening drew to a close, Max asked Audrey to marry him. It was just six weeks since the weekend house party in Pei P'ei. Audrey knew in her heart that Max's proposal wasn't just another of the worthless offers that had plagued her, but she asked for a little time to think. On Sunday morning, she and Max drove back to Pei P'ei with Alan Bell, and a Mr. Main who was visiting from England. In the romantic spot where they had begun to get acquainted Max popped the question again.

Audrey did not leave her suitor in suspense for long. Over dinner on Monday, December 20, she joyfully agreed to be married. Far from family, Max and Audrey decided that the first person to learn their happy news should be the matriarch of the diplomatic tribe, Violet Seymour. On Tuesday morning, they shyly called the Ambassador's wife out of her office at the Embassy, and asked her to come up to the Chancery flat, which Max still shared with Berkeley, so that they could give her the news privately. As soon as Lady Seymour saw Max and Audrey together, she burst into congratulations, admitting that she and Berkeley had been hoping that the couple would make a match, even before their affair had begun. 'They are so happy that it is a delight to see them', wrote Lady Seymour to her absent husband, and 'she is very attractive and just the right sort to have for a wife.'

Audrey had still not mentioned Max in her cheery letters home – though she had talked about fending off someone else's offer of marriage – and so writing on December 21 she dropped the bombshell:

> *My darling family,*
>
> *Although I had the best mail I have received since being in Chungking this week (ten letters), am not going to answer them at the moment, because I have other matters to discuss! I am at last taking the plunge and getting married – I do hope you will be pleased. I am sure you would be if you knew the man in question. But there is a Mr. Main out here from the Ministry of Supply who is flying home soon, and I have asked him to get in*

touch with you and give you a first-hand account! But in the
mean time I will do my best to give you a few details.

To begin with, he is called Max Oxford and is Assistant Air
Attaché at the Embassy. He is 38 years old, no taller than I
am, quite nice looking, blue eyes, brown hair, very humorous;
intelligent; nicely-mannered; considerate – seems very fond of
me, as I am of him. Altogether he is a very good type for a hus-
band I feel. At the moment he is a Squadron Leader acting Wing
Commander. Before the war he was in the Hong Kong Colonial
Service, and may go back to it after the war. He was at one time
a pilot in B.O.A.C. and was also Aide to the Governor of Kenya
or Nairobi – not sure which. He has no private means but earns
enough to support me quite comfortably. Altogether I think the
financial side is O.K.

Audrey may have been hazy on Max's career in Africa, but she was
sure of her decision to marry. She explained that Max was due to go
home, but was volunteering for another year in China so that she could
see through her two-year contract. Over the next few days, Audrey gently dispatched her original suitor, 'which wasn't easy' she wrote home,
and Max broke the news to the effervescent Maya.

The coast was clear for a magical Christmas, the happiest that either
Max or Audrey had ever known. Audrey wracked her brains to find a
gift for her fiancé among her meagre belongings, and gave him the most
modest, but perhaps the most cherished present of their lives: 'an old
and not very good handkerchief', said Audrey in a note. 'I hope you will
keep it, since with it I send all my love, which, honey, will last long after
the handkerchief is worn out.' And even if the handkerchief did eventually wear out, Max treasured the handwritten note in his wallet all
his life. The blissful couple went to a cocktail party at the Air Attaché's
office on December 22, and at least three parties on Christmas Eve.
With the Ambassador still away, Lady Seymour hosted a lunch party for
about fifty guests on Christmas Day. There she took the opportunity to
announce the staffers' engagement – somewhat to Audrey's embarrass-
ment. On Boxing Day, Max drove Audrey to Pei P'ei for a festive house
party with Alan Bell, Berkeley Gage and other friends, three days that
must have felt very different from the long weekend in November when

Max impressed Audrey with his walnut-cracking skills.

On their return to the city, however, there was a disappointment in store that meant the engagement would be even shorter than the courtship. In one of those quirks of wartime deployment that must have blighted the lives of thousands, Max learned that the Air Ministry had turned down his request to have his tour of duty extended; he would be expected to return to England very soon. 'So, from being quite the happiest person am now more than somewhat despondent', wrote Audrey. Barely used to the idea of being engaged, but completely sure about taking the plunge, Max and Audrey resolved to get married as quickly as possible. Then if Max really were sent home, he would try to arrange for his wife to follow. The kindly Jack Hutchison was sympathetic to their plight and agreed to ask Whitehall for a replacement assistant – though Audrey was so good at her work that he hated the idea of losing her, Lady Seymour would tell Frank Watson. The couple braced for months of separation.

The race was on to plan a wedding early in the New Year. 'It's funny to think' said Audrey, 'I shall have no trousseau, or fuss and bother. It is really a great relief.' Then she had another thought. 'What would be nice,' she wrote, 'would be for my trunk to arrive.' The latest news was that the missing luggage was being sent, agonizingly slowly, by sea to India.

Canon Allen, the Embassy Chaplain, agreed to marry Max and Audrey on Saturday, January 8. The sympathetic minister dispensed with the customary three week posting of marriage banns, 'probably jeopardizing his whole career', thought the bride. Instead, their "banns" consisted of a typewritten notice pinned on a door at the Embassy. In this 'unholy haste' Audrey went around in a bit of a daze, and then there was another complication. Max had asked Berkeley to be best man, but on January 3 his friend came down with mumps. Audrey wrote home, more amused than alarmed: 'Since Max shares his flat, we are now just waiting for *him* to develop it – Max has moved out and is staying at another Mess until Saturday'. Luckily, Max didn't succumb to the dreaded illness, and Alan Bell, their generous host at Pei P'ei, stepped into the breach as best man.

The wedding invitations were typed on plain paper and sent out just four days before the event. It was to be a very simple affair, but Lady Seymour, who acted as mother-of-the-bride and hosted the reception, made sure that it was memorable. The guest list for the ceremony itself was short but distinguished: it included Lady Seymour, Sir Humphrey Prideaux-Brune and General Carton de Wiart, Churchill's newly appointed envoy, who had particularly asked to be included. Audrey found him 'an awfully nice man', and she and Max were flattered that he chose to come. Then there were the Gidley Bairds, who helped with the catering and the flowers, two of Audrey's girlfriends, Iris Appleton and Pamela Owen, Max's fellow officers Gilbert Bartholomew and Fraser Crawford, and a few military aides – sixteen guests in all.

The ceremony took place in the Embassy chapel, and Jack Hutchison, the next best thing to a father, walked Audrey down the aisle. A Chinese student violinist was roped in to play some music, and performed those traditional anthems, *Love Divine* and *Jerusalem*. Describing her eclectic wedding attire, Audrey told her family:

> I wore my Utility Suit, my old clod-hoppers, no hat, gloves or smart bag – Lady Seymour gave me the most lovely lace blouse which I wore, and also a very cunning pair of chiffon cami-knickers – neither of which were new, but she gave me a really pretty handkerchief which she hadn't used, so I should have <u>something</u> new! It had some blue embroidery on it, so I wore something old, new, borrowed and a touch of blue!

The borrowed item was, believe it or not, the wedding ring, which belonged to the best man. Max had ordered a platinum wedding band and a diamond engagement ring from Calcutta, sending down a typewriter spool for sizing. But the rings didn't arrive in time, and then were not exactly right – neither fitted and the bands were gold rather than platinum. Audrey didn't mind gold, and was happy to keep the engagement ring – 'a magnificent sapphire surrounded by diamonds' – that could be altered to fit. (Sadly, she lost it some years later, swimming in the sea off Hong Kong.)

Audrey had never set her heart on a white wedding, she reminded her family, and she relished the impromptu celebrations – though a few photos would have been nice. Straight after an 11:30am service, the wedding party strolled down from Consulate Alley to the Office of the Air Attaché at 15, Fang Niu Hang. There, in the mess on the upper floor of the simple grey brick house that served as wartime offices, over 120 guests toasted the happy couple at a buffet lunch reception.

Max and Audrey enjoyed their celebration 'immensely' wrote Audrey later, telling her family:

> We had all the British Military Mission, the Embassy, several of the Press people, some Chinese Generals and Admirals (who sent _the_ most magnificent floral tributes – most of them completely ruined by having a few odd paper flowers stuck amongst the most lovely yellow blossoms and yellow, red and white roses and gardenias), representatives of the Dutch, Russian, Polish, American, Canadian, French and every other Embassy or Military Mission – my Mexican friend – a few business contacts of mine and all sorts of other people.

Among this cosmopolitan crowd, there were some top Kuomintang officers that Max had got to know very well in his time in the Chinese capital. These included the powerful Admiral Yang Xuancheng, who was head of military intelligence and a Japan expert, who had recently accompanied the Generalissimo to the Cairo summit of the 'Big Four' Allied leaders. Max met with Yang frequently throughout his time in Chungking, and now introduced his bride to the Admiral, who presented the couple with a pair of exquisite Chinese scrolls. Then there was Admiral Chen Shaoguan, commander-in-chief of the Chinese navy, and an array of other senior officials.

Guests gave generous gifts despite the war conditions: wedding presents included silver ash trays from military colleagues, table linens from the Australian Ambassador, a vase from the Polish Ambassador and numerous gifts of money.

Violet Seymour, who had commented wryly to her absent husband that the reception would mean 'the death of another lot of champagne', nonetheless saw it as a good cause. She wrote immediately after the wedding to Audrey's father to describe the auspicious occasion, assuring him:

> You can be perfectly confident that Audrey is completely happy – indeed, it has given me the greatest pleasure to see her with

LADY SEYMOUR

requests the pleasure of the company of

Mr. W. J. S. Oxford

at the marriage of

WING COMMANDER MAX OXFORD and

MISS AUDREY WATSON

on

Saturday, 8th January 1944

at 11.30 o'clock

at the British Embassy,

and afterwards at a reception at

the Office of the Air Attache,

15 Fang Nui Hang.

British Embassy,
CHUNGKING.

Buffet luncheon.

COPY OF ASSOCIATED PRESS CABLE MESSAGE

BRITONS WED IN CHUNGKING

Chungking, Monday (delayed) - The first British Service romance in wartime Chungking culminated with the wedding today of Wing Commander Max Oxford, R.A.F. Assistant Air Attache, and Miss Audrey Watson, who flew from England last year to join the British Embassy.

Wing Commander Oxford comes from Bournemouth and is one of the heroes of the Christmas Day escape from Hongkong in 1941.

Miss Watson was born in Iquique, Chile, and is the daughter of Mr. Francis Watson who is connected with the nitrate industry.

Those present at the wedding included Admiral Chenshaokuan, C.-in-C. of the Chinese Navy, and Admiral Yangsuanchen, an expert on Japanese affairs who went with Generalissimo Chiang Kai-Shek to Cairo.

Associated Press 8.1.44.

Max...They are rather alike to look at and from the moment Audrey arrived here I thought that they would suit each other very well. I love Audrey – she has the greatest charm and much dependability and I know she will make a wonderful wife. It has been a great satisfaction to watch them together and to help them start out on their adventure together.

The newlyweds disappeared during the luncheon party, reported Lady Seymour, and went off to Pei P'ei, where Alan Bell was generously lending them his house for the honeymoon: 'They should be back in a week, which is a sensible length for a honeymoon, I think'.

Max had many friends among the foreign press in Chungking – no doubt they were adept at trading information with the Assistant Air Attaché, as well as being good company. Several came to the wedding, including Günther Stein of the Christian Science Monitor, an American who was sympathetic to the Communists and one of the first journalists to interview Mao Zedong; and Spencer Moosa of the Associated Press, who brought his wife, Nina. They did what journalists do everywhere, and got the news out: the Associated Press despatched a cable announcing "Britons Wed in Chungking":

The first British Service romance in wartime Chungking culminated with the wedding today of Wing Commander Max Oxford, RAF Assistant Air Attaché, and Miss Audrey Watson, who flew from England last year to join the British Embassy.

A mountain retreat was a chilly proposition in early January, but Max and Audrey were too much in love to care. Audrey later described their 'most wonderful honeymoon' in a long letter home. They were thrilled to be back in the welcoming house on top of the ridge, with the most magnificent view of the gorge below. Their host laid on champagne and turkey and also:

Alan arranged that the fire in the sitting room should be lit and as an extra extravagance we had a fire in the bedroom every evening. It is a comfortable little house and has upholstered furniture, not the cane chairs you see everywhere else, and plenty of books. Max took up his wireless which works off a battery so we were able to get the news. The food was excellent and the Boy used to give us four courses for lunch and dinner ending up with walnuts and tangerines.

Max and Audrey worked off the sumptuous meals with brisk walks and bathing in the hot springs. The river was beautifully clear at that time of year: 'an unbelievably lovely green and you can see the rocks on the bottom. One day we crossed the gorge by sampan and went for a walk up to the top of the hill overlooking it – must be about 7,000 ft.' Afterwards, they found the hot springs full of school children, so decided instead to take a plunge in the icy waters of the Jialing: 'I can't tell you how cold it was (said Audrey). Nearly died from shock and have never had such a quick bathe in my life. Just jumped in and came straight out again. Felt wonderful after it I must say.'

The whole week was quite perfect, said Audrey. And at last, in the mists and mountains of Sichuan, she and Max were alone together, ready to face whatever adventures married life held in store.

CHAPTER SEVEN

Joy and Sorrow
The Road Home 1944-45

24-hairpin bend road near Qinglong,
World War II photo

'I remember thinking that my child should be fearless and feel something of that freedom which those great expanses of uninhabited country gave me.'

Audrey writing in her journal, December 4, 1947.

Berkeley Gage's case of the mumps had prevented him from being Max's best man, but it had one unexpected benefit. The newly married couple was to share with Berkeley the flat above the Chancery, where Max had been living for some months. But after emerging from quarantine and throwing a splendid 'recovery party', the considerate First Secretary disappeared to the warmer climes of Kunming to recuperate. This gave Max and Audrey ten delicious days to pretend they had a home of their own, and to launch their career as party-givers. The first part of Audrey's schoolgirl dream of being a 'good wife and mother' was coming true. And Max could guide her in the protocol of entertaining; she said he was marvellous at it having been a Governor's aide. 'We keep on making out lists of "distinguished" guests, and arrange the parties very carefully. It really is great fun', she wrote home. They gave no less than three cocktail parties to repay the hospitality of the BORs, the British troops who hosted so many dances, but were too numerous to include in the wedding invitation. And they entertained friends at lively dinner parties, with Audrey noting the guest lists and the menus in her diary, a habit she would keep up for years to come: 'Duck orange salad, bread sauce, peas and chips' or the following week: 'Soup, omelette, chicken pie, chocolate pudding'.

The Chungking round of diplomatic receptions and dinners also continued, with Audrey able to relax and enjoy herself more fully now that she was reliably squired by her new husband. They were guests at a dinner given by the Seymours (Sir Horace was back from England, to his wife's great relief) to bid farewell to the departing Australian Ambassador, Sir Frederick Eggleston. At nearly 70, Eggleston was a respected elder statesman of the diplomatic community, who bore Chungking ('like living in a cellar', he said) with fortitude despite being afflicted by arthritis and gout. Copious quantities of wine at certain parties can't have helped him, or Audrey – when the Russian Embassy celebrated the anniversary of their revolution with lengthy toasts, she was left 'incapable of doing any work' that afternoon.

But there were also sobering experiences. One freezing February weekend Max and Audrey went up into the mountains to visit Gordon King, a Scottish doctor known to Max from Hong Kong, who was in charge of one of the medical schools evacuated from the East Coast. In the evening, Dr King showed them around the 'terribly primitive and rather depressing hospital', which had no light except oil lamps, and no heat. 'The wards were distinctly smelly,' said Audrey 'and apparently they are troubled considerably with rats':

> If they have to do an emergency operation in the night, it takes 3 hours to heat the operating room. Often they perform by pressure lamps. But they do a lot of good work.

The hardy Scots doctor's house wasn't much more comfortable, wrote Audrey:

> Gordon King's house is built on native lines (lathe and plaster) and is quite minute. One tiny sitting room and 2 tiny bedrooms. A place with a basin and a pottery crock (not even a proper thunder-box) forms the bathroom. You can hear absolutely everything that goes on from one room to another and it was bitterly cold – but we enjoyed it as the country is really lovely and we went for some good walks. The only form of heating was a charcoal stove, which Gordon didn't light until the evening (I think he must be impervious to the cold). Max and I sat with our teeth chattering, and the only warm place was bed. So we retired both nights soon after 9.0 and lay shivering until we had warmed ourselves up a bit.

On return to the city, Max and Audrey's most immediate concern was that they had to get married *again* – this time in a civil ceremony conducted by Sir Horace Seymour on February 25. As Audrey put it, writing to her family that day:

> *I am sure you will be pleased to hear that we are now legally married! The Ambassador married us at 12.0 this morning, with Berkeley and Lady Seymour as witnesses. Up to date we have only been 99% legal, so our married life has always had a tang of illegality about it, which I shall now rather miss.*

In truth, Max's request, as a British military officer, to be married by his Ambassador while serving in China had generated a whole file full of high level correspondence between Chungking and London. After marrying the couple on January 8, Canon Allen had sent a copy of the certificate to England, explaining in a letter to Somerset House, the official Registrar:

> *We have no Church of England church or chapel in our refugee quarters in Chungking; and we have therefore no official records which could be preserved here.*

But England would have none of it: on February 14 a Foreign Office official wrote back to Canon Allen:

> *…I am directed by Mr. Secretary Eden to return herewith the certificate of marriage solemnized by you on the 8th January last and to inform you that, while there is no reason to doubt that English Church marriages, solemnized in China are valid as common-law marriages, under English Law, no provision exists for the registration of such marriages in this country apart from any arrangements which may be made by the ecclesiastical authorities themselves.*

Max and Audrey didn't want their vows to go unrecognized back home, but anticipating this rebuttal from the Foreign Secretary, the Ambassador's deputy, Prideaux-Brune, had taken another tack. He had telegraphed the Foreign Office on January 3 to ask whether the Embassy could marry the couple under the Foreign Marriages Act. The issue here was whether Max was serving the Royal Air Force in China, in which case a regulation would prohibit him from marrying there, or whether he was a member of the Embassy staff. Luckily, after a self-important exchange of correspondence between the Foreign Office and the Air Ministry, London ruled on January 20 that Max was obviously in China as a diplomat, clearing the way for a civil wedding. Even in wartime, formalities mattered. Thus the official record of the marriage of the Assistant Air Attaché and an Embassy Secretary on February 25, 1944 was entered on the last yellowing page of a decades-old volume of the British Consul District of Chungking's marriage register, a volume largely filled with the marriages of British missionaries in China. So Max and Audrey were doubly blessed – quite fitting for a marriage in Chungking, which means 'double jubilation' in Chinese.

Another cause for jubilation that month was the long-delayed arrival of Audrey's missing trunk. 'My trunk arrived yesterday!' wrote Audrey on February 15. 'It was flown into China by the RAF and then came on by convoy.' It was heavily encrusted with dust, but everything inside was in perfect condition, and Audrey was thrilled to discover favourite things that she'd completely forgotten about in the nine months since she'd packed them so carefully in London.

Soon, however, she had to set about selling all those precious possessions, since she had resolved to leave Chungking at the same time as Max, despite feeling 'a skunk' for abandoning her boss before her replacement arrived. Violet Seymour had told Audrey's father that 'she is so good at her work here and Jack Hutchison hates the idea of losing her'. But, Audrey rationalized, her husband came first. If the dates worked, she and Max hoped to travel by road as far as Kunming and then fly out over the Hump to India. 'The scenery is supposed to be wonderful from here to Kunming,' Audrey told her family, 'it takes 5 or 6 days but the Chinese drivers are apparently hair-raisingly reckless!'

The dusty trunk and its contents could not travel with them – air freight to Calcutta was far too expensive, but Audrey would at least make a bit of money from selling her possessions in Chungking. It was an unwritten rule in the foreign community that you sold clothes and toiletries when you left since these were in terribly short supply in the Chinese capital. She would replace her things more cheaply in India.

Max and Audrey's departure date and means of travel were still uncertain, but this didn't stop their friends and colleagues from beginning to throw farewell parties. Audrey admitted that she would be really sorry to leave, because she had enjoyed Chungking very much,

At Max's farewell lunch with Chan Chak and Henry Hsu, March 1944

and Max too was wistful – he was leaving the city that had been his home for over two years, a refuge of sorts after the drama of his escape from Hong Kong. Max had stayed in close touch with Admiral Chan Chak and Henry Hsu, both of whom were based in the capital. He was pleased when the British government recognized the Chinese for their roles in Hong Kong and on the escape – in late 1942 Chan was awarded an honorary knighthood, a KBE, and Hsu an OBE. Now that Max was about to leave China, the trio posed for a formal photograph at a farewell lunch party held on March 17, and made sure that they signed each other's copies. It was a poignant occasion bringing together not just Max's escape partners, but also his friend Berkeley, Audrey's boss and the kindly Canon who married them.

Then the ever hospitable Lady Seymour gave a 'small' dance for Max and Audrey at the residence (actually for about 60 guests); the couple were invited out to dinner practically every night in March, and Berkeley, true to form, insisted on giving a final farewell party on March 21 and ten days later taking them to his infamous North-South Club one last time. Eventually, Max and Audrey had clearance to travel, and on April 1 it was time to say goodbye to the inner circle of friends and colleagues who had cheered on their affair and celebrated their wed-

The strange karst outcrops of Guizhou province, 2008

ding – Ambassador and Lady Seymour, the staff of the Embassy and the Military Mission, Max's Chinese counterparts and American journalist friends. Max and Audrey were set to embark on the first great journey of their married life.

— • —

A seven hundred mile road trip would take them away from gritty Chungking and over the mountains of southwest China to Kunming, city of eternal spring. They would travel south along the winding road that had brought the convoy carrying Audrey's trunk to Chungking a few weeks earlier. The route was a northern extension of the Burma Road, which the Chinese had built back in 1938 to transport supplies into China from Burma and India. Since the fall of Burma had forced the closure of the Lashio-Kunming road in 1942, the massive Hump airlift had been China's lifeline. A constant stream of aircraft landed supplies at Kunming – never enough to meet demand, Max knew – and from there convoys of trucks transported goods and war matériel around Free China, using the 'northern extension', a packed dirt road that Max and Audrey would now negotiate.

Audrey had told her family that the road trip 'would be much more fun than flying all the way', but she must have set off with some trepidation for the hardships of the journey ahead. For she and Max left Chungking in possession of a thrilling secret: Audrey was in early pregnancy, expecting their first child. They were determined to make the most of pre-parenthood freedom. They didn't have the luxury of a camera, but each kept a meticulous log of the journey, jotting down distances, times, places and noting stops for refuelling and repairs.

On the morning of Sunday, April 2 Max and Audrey left the Embassy compound for the last time, side by side in the cabin of a dilapidated Ford V-8 pickup truck, which was rather like a bread van, said Audrey. Max's closest colleagues, Gidley Baird and Gilbert Bartholomew, waved them off from Hai Tan Chi dock as they loaded the truck onto the ferry to cross to the south bank of the Yangtze and the road out of the city. The driver, a Chinese called Zou, luckily spoke a bit of English; Audrey would remember 'his narrow face and woollen cap'. The truck's open flatbed carried their pared-down possessions, and the all-important fuel for the long journey: the truck ran on alcohol that was stored in petrol cans. Audrey found that 'it was really quite comfortable, except that the windows had no glass, which was trying when we had cold winds'.

'We started off in somewhat of a haze, after a rather too good final farewell, and felt pretty spent by the time we got to our first stop,' she admitted. But despite the hangovers, the beauty of the scenery was evident. The road to the south climbed quickly into dramatic mountain terrain before plunging into a river valley dotted with villages. Terraced paddy fields turned the hillsides brilliant green. That first stop was at 1:30pm, when Max and Audrey had lunch and refuelled the truck in Qijiang, the county town, before the road climbed higher still. The scenery struck Audrey as quite alpine with firs and jagged peaks, and the air was cooler as they crossed from Sichuan into Guizhou province. After scaling one of many summits, the winding road dropped down into a narrow gorge and as dusk fell they reached Songkan, a small village strung out along a river in the shadow of the mountains. In this picturesque spot, they stopped for the night staying at a Chinese inn. Max was plagued by bed bugs, but the pests didn't like Audrey as much, and she found the simple inn with its traditional wood beds 'not at all bad'. She explained:

The extraordinary thing was that he was bitten fairly regularly whilst I never was, and yet we shared the same bedding. We had a pair of sheets with us, a sleeping bag which I had been given by a man on the ship coming out, and a couple of rugs. The beds consist of planks of wood, and you never think of using the bedding roll provided.

Sanitation was primitive or non-existent:

At this first inn they provided us with a spittoon, which served as sanitation – at the other inns we didn't even have this luxury, and had to go out to the nearest field! That I found the most trying part of the whole business, for although I have become accustomed to thunder boxes, dislike squatting in the open.

And they also had to get used to the local diet:

All along we ate Chinese food, except for a tin or two of bully beef and cheese which we had with us, and had for lunch once or twice.

Max and Audrey left Songkan at 6:45 the next morning for a long day's drive to Guiyang, the capital of Guizhou province 175 miles away. The road climbed sharply out of the valley, and in a couple of hours they reached the head of a mountain pass by means of a giddy 72 hairpin bends – one of the stretches which was notorious with the convoys of army trucks. 'The scenery is absolutely magnificent, and in fact it is supposed to be very much like the Burma Road', wrote Audrey. It was also a particularly good time of year, as all the wild blossom was out and the country was 'absolutely lovely':

As soon as you leave Szechuan (Sichuan) the flowers begin to smell, which seems extraordinary. In Szechuan they are peculiarly devoid of any smell. The tung-oil tree is one of the prettiest. The flowers and leaves are out at the same time – the flower is white with a pinky-brown centre, and from a distance the blossom looks almost pink. We saw wild gardenias, laburnum, rhododendrons, a type of lilac, and various kinds of blossoms.

On the steep descent, they stopped for breakfast and then at lunch-time reached Zunyi, a town best known as the site of the 1935 meeting which established Mao Zedong's leading position in the Communist Party during the Long March. The afternoon drive was through a less fearsome landscape – rolling farm country with rice, green vegetables and red chillies growing in abundance on every square inch of land. Farmers lived in simple half-timbered houses with unadorned wooden shutters and doors. In mid-afternoon, Max and Audrey passed through the market town of Shangji, where peasants from the surrounding villages brought their wares to sell. Then they crossed the Wujiang River at a spectacular, deep gorge; stopped to refuel and change a burst tyre, arriving well after dark in Guiyang.

They spent two nights in the provincial capital as guests of Major Gould, the Guiyang representative of the British Military Mission. He was no doubt an intelligence liaison to the Chinese, and in her postwar recollections Audrey found him 'so sinister with his Chinese friends, and hand shaking from over-indulgence in mao tai'. But she was grateful to him, because in Guiyang she was taken ill (an ominous sign) – faint and in pain – and she gave the Major a pair of nail scissors 'in return for his great kindness'. The town straddled a broad river, with stone quays along its banks that reminded visitors of Paris. But Max and Audrey may not have had much chance to explore. The rest day was used to check over the truck, and pick up more fuel – the cheap alcohol, which was terrible to run on. 'The car stalls at every opportunity', said Audrey.

Early on April 5, Zou coaxed the truck into action again to head further south. But they soon had to stop to change another tyre and later to refuel. The road now wound through a bizarre landscape of karst hills – impossibly steep conical outcrops of limestone rising up from the plateau for no apparent reason. The hills were too sheer to cultivate, but some were used as grave sites. The afternoon brought two discoveries – one more welcome than the other. The pleasant surprise was the Huangguoshou Falls, the largest waterfall in Asia, and as deep as Niagara. Max and Audrey were most likely the only visitors that day, and enjoyed a picnic lunch to the sound of the crashing torrent.

But later in the afternoon the truck broke down again, and they had an enforced stop of an hour and a half to clean the fuel system. By now, the country had become very barren and mountainous. They were in one of the poorest parts of one of China's poorest provinces. Wandering around the village, Audrey saw a tragic sight that haunted her for years:

> *The villages you go through seem pathetically poor, and the dogs lying in the streets are nothing but bones. At one place, an old walled town, the shops had hardly any food in them, and the people were dirtier and poorer looking here than in most places. We had to stop there for over an hour to fix something, and Max and I took a walk around. It made me feel quite sick to see a newly-born, but sometime dead, baby floating in the moat. I suppose it was chucked over the wall as soon as it had been born. But somehow the people looked so wretchedly poor that you could understand them wanting to get rid of it.*

It was a baby girl, Audrey remembered in her postwar recollections of the journey, written in her journal in December 1947.

There was nothing to be done, and they had to press on, reaching the village of Yongning as night fell. This was a particularly desolate coal-mining community, and they couldn't find a place to stay. Max and Audrey threatened the driver that they would have to go onto the next town, but the prospect of the 'long, lonely, supposedly dangerous drive' goaded him into finding a room at a Chinese hotel. Here they had unanticipated company: in the middle of the night, Max and Audrey ventured out to a field (in the absence even of that spittoon provided at their first inn) 'to find the Chinese army had come in and lorries with wakeful soldiers stretched for miles'. Nationalist armies criss-crossed this part of China as campaigns against the Japanese waxed and waned.

On leaving Yongning early the next morning, they surely understood why the driver hadn't wanted to tackle the journey in the dark. The exposed, windy and narrow road clung to the mountainside, and Zou had to negotiate numerous hairpin bends, quite apart from starving dogs lying in the middle of the road, and villagers walking their cows. The dire poverty of the mountainous part of Guizhou was always

Huangguoshou Falls, 2008

evident. Audrey wrote in her journal of seeing 'salt in huge blocks being taken miles and miles by men wheeling squeaky barrows. How many months of the year must those men have been on the road, and what [was] their life?'

Max and Audrey made it to the high-mountain village of Qinglong in time for breakfast. This fortified them for another terrifying stretch of road – where 'you look down from the top of a hill and can actually see 24 hairpin bends below you'. This was another infamous section of the Burma Road extension, winding down the barren face of a mountain with metronomic regularity. Numerous convoys of American and Chinese army trucks trafficked it laboriously.

Having survived the hairpin bends, Max and Audrey enjoyed a break at another waterfall, where they took a swim, then stopped at 2pm for lunch, and arrived at 5:15 at the village of Panxian. There they stayed in another spartan Chinese hotel. The next morning they would pass the highest point on the route at Pingyi – an elevation of 6,800 feet, Max noted in his log – and soon enter Yunnan province.

Their route then descended onto a high, bleak plateau, and after yet another stop to fix a burst tyre (their sixth wheel change), they reached Qujing, Yunnan's second largest town, on the night of April 7. Here they lodged with the Friends Ambulance Unit (FAU), an extraordinary Quaker volunteer force made up mostly of conscientious objectors who drove around Free China delivering medical and food aid. Audrey later remembered them clearly: 'FAU men on charcoal burning trucks, arriving in villages with their faces black from the fumes, and sleeping on top of their loads – they were men to be admired'.

She also never forgot a harrowing experience with the admirable men of the FAU that night in Qujing: after supper, the Quakers called for volunteers 'to take the Chinese dead to the cemetery. Otherwise they would be left in the camp and on the road.' All along the way Audrey had seen men of 'the Chinese army – dead and dying by the road – marching until they fell'. These were soldiers of Chiang's notoriously ill-fed and poorly equipped forces; Mao's Communists persuaded many an impoverished young man to enlist with his side by offering better rations.

So Max and Audrey were relieved to be on the home stretch to Kunming, going through 'that strange, flat country with sudden hills rising from the plain, for no apparent reason – and the Americans we met, who hailed us as the first Europeans they had seen for weeks – and undoubtedly took us for missionaries'. They reached their destination at 1:30pm on April 8, after seven nights on the road and an unforgettable journey of 705 miles.

Audrey's April 19 letter to her family described the welcome interlude in the Yunnanese capital:

We stayed in Kunming for a few days, waiting for an R.A.F. plane to bring us down [to Calcutta]. The weather there is perfect. It stands about 7,000 feet and the sun shines continuously now, although there are high winds. It is surprising how tired you get at that height if you are not used to it. We stayed with a

*very good friend of ours who used to be in Chungking – an old
buddy of mine from the "Cabbage Patch" days. It is quite an attractive town, particularly just outside, where there is a lovely
lake, surrounded by hills. We went for several walks, and saw
some good temples – the most ornate I had seen to date.*

Their host from the Cabbage Patch days was Major AH "Sammy"
Samson, a member of the British Military Mission in Kunming. Like
Chungking, the southern city was overrun with foreigners; it was the
strategic hub for American and British commands and the massive
Hump airlift, not to mention the centre of Walter Fletcher's Operation
Remorse, and the China headquarters of the OSS, America's counter-
part to the SOE. It was more American than the capital, wrote Audrey,
and she blamed the Yanks for the even higher cost of living: 'it is about
twice as expensive as Chungking though, since it is full of Americans.
You see Jeeps running around everywhere.' Sammy and his colleagues,
Lt. Col. Kenny Brand and Captain Laidlaw, took Max and Audrey to the
French Club for dinner; French influence was strong since Kunming
was the northern terminus of a railway line and trade route to the old
French colonies in Indo-China.

Max and Audrey had a few days to see friends and explore Kunming's beautiful lake and its western hills, the Xi Shan. They climbed
to a Daoist temple, which clung to a rock face high above the lake, and
enjoyed a picnic lunch. Perhaps Audrey (who suffered from vertigo)
opted out of continuing along a very narrow path to the Dragon's Gate,
the temple's most famous feature. But she visited another renowned
temple, which she called the Copper Temple and is known in Chinese
as the Golden Temple, Jin Dian.

Then on April 13 it was time to leave China: 'Leave by R.A.F for
Calcutta D.V. [God willing] 9:00' wrote Audrey in her diary. Well she
might have prayed, for the RAF Dakota, piloted by Flt. Lt. Hansen, an
acquaintance of Max's, gave them a scary ride:

*The journey down wasn't so good, as we travelled by R.A.F.
transport – not comfortable – added to which we flew over the
Hump at 21,000 ft., which is no joke without oxygen. We both
sat gasping for breath, thinking our last hour had come. They*

generally fly at about 14,000 ft. but there was a lot of cloud about it seems.

As Max and Audrey knew, only the pilots had an oxygen supply, and passengers just had to hold out in the freezing cold until landing at Dum Dum airfield near Calcutta – where they sometimes felt even worse when they stepped out into the blistering heat – a real trial for Audrey, especially because they arrived during a taxi strike:

> *We were quite glad to get to Calcutta, where we have been staying most comfortably with the Trade Commissioner [Mr. A. Schofield]. The only drawback is that it is rather far out, and we arrived the day of a taxi strike – apparently an American had stabbed a driver, so they were, not surprisingly, protesting! We have spent most of our time hanging on the more-than-somewhat congested trams, walking, and using rickshaws. It is very hot and sticky at the moment, so you can imagine our relief when the strike stopped yesterday.*

Calcutta, a vibrant cultural centre during the war years, offered the diversions that Max and Audrey had each experienced before: lunches and dinners at the Saturday Club, a day at the races, and plentiful shopping. They lunched with their best man Alan Bell, who was in town, and Max introduced his bride to two couples who were old friends of his: Douglas and Monica Henderson, and Chuck and Sylvia Sharp. It was also an occasion for Max to see another prewar friend, Sharp's boss, WL Bond ("Bondy"), the American who managed PanAm's twenty per-cent interest in the Chinese airline, CNAC.

But Audrey must have been worried about her health, because one of her first calls was on Stanley Nairn, the doctor who had treated her sinus trouble on her outbound trip.

Max and Audrey's onward flight to Delhi was cancelled twice, and on April 19 Audrey wrote the only letter she would mail home during the journey. She put a brave face on things:

> *We were supposed to be flying to Delhi to-day (where we have to go to arrange for our onward passage) and got up at*

0445 hrs, and were kept hanging around until nearly 0800 hrs when we were told the plane wouldn't be going to-day after all. So it means the same dreary business again tomorrow morning. Lord knows when we shall be home at this rate! But it is a not unpleasant holiday. I can't tell you what a delightful person Max is to be with, and how much nicer it is than travelling on one's own.

It is only because we had no arrangements made for to-day that I am able to write. We have been terribly busy seeing friends, making arrangements and buying odds and ends of linen. Nothing much, but at least we hope to have a pair of sheets and a bath towel. We can't of course take the things with us, but are sending them by sea – I sincerely hope they arrive.

Finally, after a week in Calcutta, they flew west to Delhi early on April 20, before continuing the next day to Karachi, and checking into the Central Hotel. By Sunday, April 23, however, Audrey was feeling dreadful. A military doctor diagnosed dengue fever and admitted her the next day to the British General Hospital and the care of Dr. Shepheard. Dengue fever is a serious illness, and for Audrey it was disastrous: she lost the child she was carrying – a baby boy. For the entire week she spent in the hospital her diary is blank of entries. Max visited faithfully at 5pm each day, and filled in the lonely hours at the Karachi Boat Club where he could go swimming. The second part of Audrey's dream of being 'a good wife and mother' would not come true just yet.

But she was philosophical, and in a long journal entry written in 1947 at her desk in Hong Kong, she remembered both the joys and the sorrows of that spring. She was haunted by the dark memories – the newborn girl thrown into a moat, the dead and dying Chinese soldiers, corpses being buried by the selfless men of the FAU, emaciated peasants and starving dogs. But she also recalled the curious faces of women and children, the majestic scenery, the fragrant blossom, and the wide, open spaces. She had known freedom on that journey:

That fortnight I hope will always stand out clearly in my memory – for I have never enjoyed anything so much – except perhaps Pei P'ei. I remember thinking that my child should be

131

fearless and feel something of that freedom which those great
expanses of uninhabited country gave me.

Audrey left the Karachi hospital on May 1, but she and Max can't
have felt in the mood for celebrating his thirty-ninth birthday two
days later. Nor had Audrey had a chance to buy her new husband a
present. With characteristic ingenuity, she gave him a banana off their
early morning tea tray, with his name stitched on it in white cotton.
The couple were desperately anxious to get out of Karachi, and with
the greatest difficulty had obtained a last-minute seat for Audrey on a
Sunderland flying boat leaving on 4th (Max had higher priority so his
seat was already assured). But they needed a visa for passage through
Iraq – the consulate was closed, and it was only at the last moment
that the Consul was importuned to make out the visa in his private
house. Studying her expiring passport years later, Audrey remembered
the 'potted palms, fans, Turkish cigarettes' of the courteous but infuriat-
ingly leisurely Iraqi Consul. It was a mad dash in a friend's car to get to
the harbour and 'spanking out to the flying boat in a launch'.

From Karachi to Bahrain, then Cairo and dinner at the Shepheard's
Hotel – Audrey was retracing her outbound journey much sooner than
she'd expected. She and Max saw the Pyramids, and got out to the tiny
island of Djerba, where she was struck by the sight of camels loaded
into dhows and sponges growing profusely. Then it was on to Gibraltar
and a very rough landing, with the flying boat bouncing 30 feet into
the air at each attempt. 'Years later I met some man in Singapore who
remembered watching the exhibition', she would later write.

Audrey's convoy had steered clear of the Mediterranean in 1943, but
the situation was different now. Allied forces were slowly but surely
reclaiming the European continent from its Nazi occupiers. An Ameri-
can-led army was fighting its way up through Italy, which the Germans
had taken over after Mussolini's dismissal in 1943. The Americans liberated Rome in early June and continued a long march north towards
the Alps. On the eastern front, the Russians, at appalling cost, had re-
pelled the Germans from their country, and were forcing a Nazi retreat
through Poland.

After a night and a day in Gibraltar, Max and Audrey began the last
stage of their five-week trek – the Sunderland flew through the night

132

and touched down at an RAF base at Pembroke Dock in Wales early on May 9. They made it to London in time for dinner with Audrey's father and elder sister, Joan – and Audrey's first chance to introduce Max to her family. Frank Watson's health and finances were both fragile, but loyal Joan – now the only unmarried daughter – was a great support. They must both have been thrilled to see Audrey and her new husband.

— • —

Max had spent most of the last 14 years out of Britain, and had not been there at all since he left for Hong Kong in peacetime six years earlier. He found London much changed. Gaping holes and piles of rubble scarred the city. Though bombing of the capital had eased up after 1941, air raids had recently started again. And soon after Max and Audrey's return, a new menace appeared: unmanned V1 'doodlebugs' began to strike southeast England. These, and the silent V2s which followed that autumn, unnerved Londoners who had survived the Blitz with great fortitude. Food rationing, unknown to Max and Audrey in China, was in full force and they couldn't go anywhere without their ration books.

They also couldn't go anywhere without seeing Americans. Britain was the base for a massive logistical exercise to prepare for the liberation of northern Europe. Max and Audrey had seen plenty of American faces in China, but that was nothing compared to the 350,000 Yanks positioned in Britain, alongside British, Canadian, Polish and other forces, in readiness for D-Day.

Max returned to duty ten days after his arrival, but before that there were family and friends to visit and a home to set up. After meeting Audrey's father Frank in London, it was Max's turn to present his wife to *his* father in Bournemouth – William Oxford was, like Frank Watson, a widower. His wife, Mary, had died in 1939 a few months before the outbreak of war. The retired baker proudly kept a volume of press cuttings of his only son's exploits, and a red leather album of photos – the only surviving images of Max's life before he escaped from Hong Kong. From Bournemouth, Max and Audrey took a tour of the West Country to pay their respects to Abuelita, Audrey's maternal grandmother, who was living in the moorland town of Bovey Tracey. They enjoyed a few days exploring Dartmoor and south Devon, before going on to Som-

Portrait of Audrey by Anthony Devas,
London 1945

erset for a happy reunion with Audrey's younger sister. Tottie and her husband Buffy Hebeler, whose wedding Audrey had missed, were living in Langport with a veterinary practice serving local farms. Audrey would return as often as possible over the ensuing months to visit their pleasant country home.

On June 6, the Allies launched their long-anticipated ground offensive to retake northern Europe – the D-Day landings on the beaches of Normandy, which outwitted the German forces who had expected an attack on the more northerly Pas de Calais. The Allied commander, General Dwight Eisenhower, was operating under directions to "enter the continent of Europe, and, in conjunction with the other United Nations, undertake operations aimed at the heart of Germany, and the destruction of her armed forces", no less. In August, a second Allied force landed in southern France, and on August 25 Paris was liberated, with the Free French leader, Charles de Gaulle, accepting the German surrender of the French capital. The fighting that summer and on into 1945 was gruelling, but ultimate victory was no longer in doubt.

Back in London, Max and Audrey had moved into a cosy mews flat in Kensington, near the Natural History Museum, setting up their first English home together. With the war winding down, the RAF assigned Max to staff work in London. Audrey dutifully reported to the Labour Exchange, and was hired by the BBC. She began secretarial work for the broadcasting corporation on Oxford Street on August 3. Her hours were irregular – some shifts involved weekend work – but left her with enough free time to enjoy the return to London life. Max was a member of the RAF Club on Piccadilly, and they would often meet friends there, or at the Café Royal on Regent Street, long a favoured gathering place for London society.

It was at the Café Royal that Audrey reconnected with her great friend, Dorothy Hutchison. She had plenty to tell Dorothy, whose uncle Jack had introduced her to China. And Audrey caught up with her godchildren, Dorothy's son John, and Jinty, one of Helen's twins, now energetic two-year olds.

Walking by the Leicester Galleries one day in October, Max was drawn inside by an exhibition of the paintings of Anthony Devas. The artist, trained at the Slade, was making his name as a portrait painter, and the show included a study of the actor John Gielgud, as well as oils of nudes, landscapes and flowers. Max loved the artist's understated style, and stretched his budget to commission Devas to paint his wife's portrait. She had a dozen sittings at Devas' Chelsea studio, and Max was delighted with the end result. Devas had portrayed Audrey seated, wearing a beige silk dress and a red-enamelled cherry brooch on a gold pin (inherited from her mother, the brooch opened to reveal an exquisite watch). Devas chose a neutral background to offset Audrey's golden-red hair, and he captured her quizzical look perfectly. Max and Audrey became friendly with the gregarious Anthony and his wife Nicolette, sister-in-law of the writer Dylan Thomas.

When the portrait arrived in the New Year, Max proudly showed it off to his two best men. Both Berkeley Gage and his understudy Alan Bell were in town, and came to dinner in January, just a year after Max and Audrey's wedding. Berkeley had completed his Chungking posting the previous summer, and travelled back to England via the United

States, where his wife and family were sitting out the war. He was roped in, as he put it, to join the UK delegation to the Dumbarton Oaks Conference, as "just the man" to cultivate good relations with the Chinese delegates. On his return to London, he was assigned to the American Department of the Foreign Office – an interregnum in one of the desk jobs he loathed, leavened only by a return visit to the US in 1945, this time with the UK delegation to the San Francisco Conference that gave birth to the United Nations.

But happily for Max and Audrey, the irrepressible Berkeley shared the tail end of the war with them and several other old Chungking hands who were back in England. They saw each other often: in November they all met up with Lady Seymour (whose husband was still in China) and Antoni Kokczynski (the Polish government-in-exile's emissary to Chungking) for a lunch at the Carlton Bar, and at New Year Berkeley threw one of his notorious parties at the Liaison Club.

In a tale all too familiar in wartime, Alan Bell had come home to discover that his wife had had a child with another man. He must have been glad of the Oxfords' company that winter, and Audrey later remembered him fondly:

> Alan, with his nutcracker face – exceptionally erect carriage and soft hat with rather a small brim – a heart of gold beneath the grim exterior – never loquacious – a slight smile playing round his narrow mouth. Alan, whom we much later discovered had divorced his wife, who had borne a child most obviously not his, as he was in China and she in England – and the boy carries his name.

Alan was due to go back to Chungking, and his old friends organized a big party at the Galleon Club – the guests included Lady Seymour and Antoni Kokczynski again, as well as Sir Humphrey Prideaux-Brune. The following night's dinner and unveiling of the portrait at Max and Audrey's was Alan's final farewell. His friends waved him off at Airways House the next day, January 16. They never saw him again. Weeks later, Audrey learned from the China bulletin she read in her job at the BBC that Alan had slipped in the dark on those treacherously muddy Chungking steps, and died of a broken neck.

But most of the news that spring of 1945 was brighter. In Europe, the Allies pressed on through France, into the Low Countries and eventually Germany, crossing the German frontier along the Rhine in March. The Russians beat the rest of the Allies in a race to Berlin, and all across Europe Allied armies coming from different directions began to join up. Emaciated prisoners were liberated from Nazi concentration camps, and the public began to comprehend the enormity of the Holocaust. Soon after Hitler's suicide, Germany surrendered. 'Total surrender' noted Audrey in her diary on May 7. VE Day was celebrated on May 8, but there's no indication that Max and Audrey went wild. The end of the war with Japan still seemed far away, and only victory in Asia would bring global peace.

CHAPTER EIGHT

The End of the Madness
Singapore and Hong Kong 1945-46

'Five months today since we had a home together and though I can get on alone better than most people I do want to be with you again permanently my darling. I do love having you to share my joys and sorrows, many more joys when you are about.'
Max in Hong Kong to Audrey in Singapore, March 3, 1946.

After the Allied victory in Europe, Max and Audrey held their breath as the United States led the way to the defeat of Japan. By early 1945 American forces had seized the Philippines and other Japanese-held islands in the Pacific and were bombing Tokyo. But it looked as though the end game would involve a ground assault on Japan's heartland, with many more combat losses. Then on August 15, after America had stunned the world by dropping the first atomic bombs on Hiroshima and Nagasaki, Emperor Hirohito declared his nation's surrender. Audrey joined the cheering crowds outside St. Paul's Cathedral in the City of London. Max rejoiced that his many friends who were prisoners of the Japanese would be liberated, and hoped that he would soon have the chance to help rebuild his beloved Hong Kong.

It was, however, by no means a foregone conclusion that the British could retake their former colony. Roosevelt had not wanted to see the map of the world coloured the red of the British Empire again. But after FDR's death in April 1945, his successor Harry Truman brought a less anti-colonial attitude to the US Presidency. And in the case of Hong Kong, the Americans realized that a friendly sanctuary would be strategically valuable when the inevitable civil war between Nationalists and Communists erupted in China. Business leaders with a stake in the region also lobbied for Hong Kong to revert to the British. The territory would once more be an important entrepôt for trade and an oasis of law and order amid the expected turmoil elsewhere. The biggest question mark was over the attitude of Chiang Kai-shek, and of Hong Kong's Chinese majority, to an attempted British return.

In London, the Colonial Office had been busy making contingency plans for all of its captured possessions. Max's former colleague and escape partner, David MacDougall, took charge of its Hong Kong Planning Unit in September 1944. In the final months of the war he staffed up the unit to have a civil affairs team ready to be rushed into Hong Kong as soon as the colony was liberated. MacDougall (Mac to his friends) was keen to recruit Max as the civil aviation expert on his team, and Max was equally keen to return to his old home. In preparation, he spent three months studying Cantonese at the School of Oriental and African Studies, but he was still a serving RAF officer and the Air Ministry was frustratingly slow to allow his redeployment. In April 1945 Max enlisted the help of his old mentor, Sir Hubert Young, who wrote a glowing testimonial to Viscount Swinton, the Minister in charge of Civil Aviation at the Air Ministry. 'My dear Max', (wrote Mac two months later) 'Cautiously and in the light of bitter experience I write to say that I think that at long last we are on the verge of clearing our lines with the Air Ministry and the Civil Aviation people...Unless there is an earthquake I really cannot see now why you will not get something pretty definite within the next week or so.'

In August, the sudden and shattering end to the war brought the question of what to do with Hong Kong to a climax. The British succeeded in retaking the territory in a series of swift manoeuvres that proved the old adage "Possession is nine-tenths of the law". While Mac and his team got ready in London, a Royal Navy fleet intended for Hong Kong sailed from Sydney under the command of Rear Admiral Cecil Harcourt. The task force set off within hours of Hirohito's surrender broadcast, then waited at the US naval base at Subic Bay in the Philippines while Prime Minister Attlee (Churchill's successor) sought personal clearance from President Truman for the British fleet to move into Hong Kong and receive the Japanese surrender. Truman gave Attlee the go-ahead, with the proviso that there was coordination with Chiang. It was a loss of face for the Chinese leader for his troops not to take the surrender, but he had more pressing business: he wanted to reoccupy as much of his country as possible, including his former capital Nanking, before the expected showdown with the Communists. However he did want to make sure that his Communist rivals didn't get a crack at Hong Kong: he ordered Nationalist armies to march towards the territory. The Communist East River guerrillas (successors to the group who had aided the Christmas Day escape) positioned themselves to block the Nationalists' path.

The British slipped through the middle, benefiting from the divisions within China. While Harcourt waited in Subic Bay, the inmates of Stanley civilian internment camp sprang into action. They were led by Franklin Gimson, a somewhat reserved man who had arrived in Hong Kong on the eve of invasion to take up the post of Colonial Secretary and had spent the years of internment struggling to establish his authority as the senior British official in the camp at Stanley. He privately told his wife that he sometimes found his fellow internees harder to handle than their Japanese guards. But now he acted boldly. Within a week of Japan's defeat, Gimson had himself sworn in as Acting Governor and emerged from Stanley with a small crew of former officials to set up a makeshift government. They established a base in the old French Mission building in Victoria. For a crucial period before the arrival of Harcourt's fleet, Gimson and his weary colleagues upheld a façade of British authority. Ironically, they had to depend heavily on the vanquished Japanese and on the Chungking Gang, a Triad outfit led by a follower of Chan Chak, to keep order in the chaotic city.

On the morning of August 30, fifteen days after Hirohito's surrender, Harcourt's task force of almost 30 vessels arrived off the Stanley peninsula, in sight of the grateful internees, and sailed through the Lei Yue Mun channel into an eerily silent harbour. Chiang quietly stood down his army, which was two days' march away from Hong Kong – just as in 1941, the Nationalist relief force never made it to the territory.

Back in London, Max's posting as Director of Air Services in the new British Military Administration (BMA) was confirmed on September 16. MacDougall would run Hong Kong as Chief Civil Affairs Officer, with the rank of Brigadier, in a short-term military administration commanded by Rear Admiral Harcourt. Mac had flown into the colony on September 7 with a core team of just twenty-eight civil affairs officers – scarcely enough to relieve Gimson and an exhausted crew of about 700 ex-internees who were coping as best they could. Within a month most were repatriated to recuperate from nearly four years of captivity, but in the postwar upheavals there was an acute shortage of transport to bring in fresh administrators such as Max. And there was no question of allocating scarce transportation to wives: still heady with the first flush of marriage, Max and Audrey now faced months of separation.

Max left England on October 3 in the second wave of key personnel for the BMA. With her usual sense of adventure, Audrey decided not to sit around in London, but instead interviewed with the planning unit of another recovered colony for a posting that would take her nearer to her husband. She was hired to work for the propaganda operation of the British Military Administration for Malaya, its Department of Printing and Publicity based in Singapore, and would leave England on October 20. If she couldn't be in Hong Kong, at least she would be on the right continent.

Max wrote his first note to Audrey within hours of kissing her good-bye at Imperial Airways House in London for a short hop to Poole. Waiting in his native Dorset for a BOAC Dakota to take off for more distant shores, at 6:30am he wrote from Sandacres Hotel:

> *My darling,*
>
> *In the cold and dismal light of dawn I have been accompanying the seagulls along the shore of Poole Harbour. I slept badly but will no doubt make up for that in the aircraft – I presume it will be a Dakota with seats. One serious error in packing – where am I to put my blue uniform when I cease to wear it and the khaki drill I may buy in India? I should have thought of that...*
>
> *I miss you dearest Audrey, you are such a beautiful companion to me and I did love the home you made for us in England. Remember you have all my love constantly and I only look forward to the happy day when we shall be re-united...*
>
> *Farewell now and God bless you, my love,*
> *Max*

He was on his way, travelling a route that he had piloted himself in the mid-1930s. Mechanical trouble meant a night stop at 'miserable Istres, near Marseilles, cold and windy with inadequate food and simple bedding'. In Cairo, he telephoned Audrey's friends, the Ross-Browns, before continuing along the route that was also familiar to her, into the heat of the East:

From Cairo we did not rest again for 22 hours, we paused for
tea and petrol at Lydda, Baghdad, Basrah, Sharjah and Jiwani.
I changed into khaki at Cairo and was able to force the blue into
the suitcase. The flying was comfortable all the way but slow
and irritating.

Reaching hot and sweaty Karachi after four days he stayed at the
Carlton Hotel, which was full of officers like him waiting for seats on
planes. 'I have just slept for six hours and felt so miserable on waking
that I drank half my precious supply of Scotch whiskey,' he told Audrey.
The dusty city had unhappy associations with Audrey's illness and mis-
carriage two years earlier.

In Karachi, Max and his 15 fellow passengers waited for their cases to go before a Priority Board for onward transport, and by October 10 he had reached Delhi on an RAF Dakota. 'Dawn has come and
the Dakota is warming up outside', he wrote in another 6:30am letter.
He found Delhi depressing but enjoyed an evening with an old friend
at the Gymkhana Club. Then it was on to Calcutta, where he stayed
with Douglas Henderson ('Monica is in the hills and is having another
baby'), and dined with his other Calcutta buddies, Chuck and Sylvia
Sharp of CNAC. 'I don't like the town as I used,' he told Audrey, 'but it
helps to know a few people'. A highlight of his stopover was hearing
Gracie Fields sing for 5,000 for the Red Cross at his old Calcutta haunt,
the Saturday Club. But he was anxious to get on to Hong Kong, and
luckily the Air Priority Board gave him Priority 2 ('only Generals get
better than that'), since its commander was impressed that Max 'was
the first candidate who had not judged himself more important than
all others, of whom there are some seventy waiting here. He thinks Air
Services will need a representation in Hong Kong.'

The congestion on the route to Hong Kong was so bad that six of
Max's travel companions had been held back in Karachi. But Max's high
priority got him a seat just a couple of days later on another RAF Dakota, heading back to China and a night stop in Kunming before leaving
on the final leg of his journey. Four years earlier he had escaped from
Hong Kong with only the clothes on his back, and he returned with
not much more: he lost his precious dispatch case in Kunming. All his
money was gone, his travellers cheques and his pay book (and, much

to his distress, his favourite poetry collection, *Modern Verse*). When Max touched down at Kai Tak, he had to borrow the fare for the ferry across the harbour from an ex-POW.

— • —

Immediately, places and people triggered memories of the battle and his escape. He was told to go to the Gloucester, the stately hotel that he had last seen at the Christmas Day rendezvous with Chan in 1941. To his surprise, he was assigned a spacious suite, as he told Audrey in his first letter from the Island on October 17:

> *At the hotel smooth lifts took me up to the fifth floor where I have a large room, with enclosed verandah and private bath-room. [Baths would be cold water only for a while.] I had some difficulty in understanding that this apartment was for my sole use. I am supposed to feed in the senior officers mess in the Jacobean room of the Hong Kong Hotel, next door, but the company there looks a little dull. There is an allied officers club on the top floor of the building where drink provided by the navy is at present fairly plentiful and not expensive at 8d for a whiskey.*

Altogether his first impressions of conditions were quite positive. But he was soon confronted with the reality of what friends had endured. The very evening of his arrival he met up with his old intelligence buddies, Charles Boxer and Alf Bennett, at the bar of the Hong Kong Hotel. Boxer and Bennett gave Max a 'great welcome' and they all went on to a 'late and excellent Chinese meal' at the Café de Chine. Charles and Alf had had a grim time since the fall of Hong Kong, held as POWs and harshly treated. Max told Audrey:

> *Both looked well but seemed excitable and restless, they were reluctant to recall the recent past, Charles had ended up in gaol in Canton.*

Soon they were both on their way to America – Charles by sea and Alf by air:

Colonial Secretary David MacDougall, Admiral Chan Chak and
Wing Commander Max Oxford back in Hong Kong after the war

> *Alf Bennett walked off the ship in which he was to go to*
> *America, saying he had had 3½ years of that kind of accom-*
> *modation; next day he left by air. Charles must be more tough*
> *as he stayed on board.*

Charles was doubtless longing to see Mickey and their daughter
Carola – a happy reunion that would take place in Mickey's New York
home and be photographed by *LIFE* magazine. But he had delayed his
departure from Asia for two months after Japan's defeat in order to help
with one more critical task – the process of identifying and trying Japanese war criminals.

Other liberated prisoners were still on the scene amidst the postwar
comings and goings. These included Max's former boss in air services,
Albert Moss, who had emerged from internment to act as transport officer in Gimson's skeleton administration. Max confided to Audrey that
he was anxious for Moss to leave the stage and begin his well-earned

recuperation. The younger man had his long-awaited opportunity to be in charge of a department, and looked forward to the challenges ahead.

The day after his arrival Max set to work at the headquarters of the Civil Affairs Office, had a conference with senior officers and went out to his old airport, Kai Tak, with RAF Wing Commander Dobson. He began to get the lie of the land. Cynicism was already making a comeback:

> I am told by people not in Civil Affairs that there is administrative chaos and some contempt for civilians masquerading as colonels. But the colony is peaceful, there is sufficient food, trams, buses and ferries are running, the water supply is excellent and the Chinese look clean and well dressed. Prices are high and there is little to buy, the first being the logical reaction to the latter. The population is much smaller than pre-war and the streets look empty.

In fact Harcourt and MacDougall had worked miracles in the short weeks since liberation. They had precious little time (or inclination) to write reports to London, but two months after his arrival Mac told the Colonial Office:

> When the fleet sailed in, tens of thousands of Chinese lined the waterfront. A man who was there told me that they didn't remark whether the ships were British, American, Russian or Chinese: all they said was "Now we will eat".

The people of Hong Kong had suffered terribly under Japanese occupation. The early days were bad enough, with widespread brutality and rape inflicted by Japanese troops. Then life under occupation fell into a routine of sorts for those who kept their heads down. But from late 1943 living conditions went downhill rapidly. Unable to feed people, the Japanese forcibly deported hundreds of thousands of Chinese to the mainland, even though conditions there were hardly any better. By 1945 the pre-war population of 1.6 million had dwindled to 600,000. In the final months of the war, food was so scarce that there was a threat of mass starvation. That's why the people of Hong Kong hardly cared who liberated them as long as they could eat again.

Despite the progress of recovery by the time of Max's arrival, fresh supplies of essentials were desperately needed. Writing a personal letter to George Hall, the Secretary of State for the Colonies, on November 11, Admiral Harcourt admitted:

The central problem is to hold the position now attained until supplies reach us in the required flow. No matter how resourceful, we cannot much longer conceal the essential weakness of a situation represented by bare larders, empty godowns and a harbour full of men-of-war instead of merchantmen.

Max soon learned more about the enormous challenges of reconstruction. As well as food shortages, coal, petrol, electricity and public transport were all scarce or non-existent in the final year of the war. And very few private cars had survived the occupation. As Max soon noticed, trees had been torn down from the green hills of the territory, and empty houses stripped of wood floors, doors and anything that would burn, in a desperate search for firewood. To add to people's woes, the Americans had bombed Hong Kong repeatedly to wear down Japanese resistance. Allied publications preferred to gloss over the fact that almost 10,000 Chinese civilians had been killed in the US air attacks.

Much housing was damaged beyond repair, and though Max didn't mind the loss of the ornate Victorian architecture of homes on the Peak, the shortage of accommodation was acute. The *South China Morning Post* summed up the situation at the end of September:

The war has destroyed thousands of flats and houses: the Colony must largely be rebuilt. The departure of the prisoners of war and the internees theoretically reduces the demand: but theirs were among the houses rendered uninhabitable. Moreover, their places are taken by scores of new Navy, Army and Government officials: and, although many of these are living in hotels, the pressure upon the housing accommodation threatens to become overwhelming.

There were also difficult questions of the rights of dispossessed owners, landlords and tenants. Max paid a visit to 1 Robinson Road, and found that his pre-war home had Chinese occupants. The process of repairing private property, like everything else, was held up by the lack of basic supplies, and had hardly begun by the end of the year 'owing to lack of timber, paint and plumbing', wrote Max.

He remained in the comfortable suite at the Gloucester, dropping by at the services club on the ninth floor 'where one usually finds a few acquaintances before dinner', and eating with the stuffy crowd of senior officers at the mess next door. There the food was doubtless more lavish than back in ration-controlled England, with the officers paying extra for 'chicken, duck, fresh fruit and more vegetables'.

In the early weeks of the restoration, officers were not paying for their food and accommodation, but by late October Max expected that 'happy state' to change. His pleasure at having a large suite to himself was also short-lived: in early November he was allocated a roommate – EG Price from the Ministry of War Transport. As more officials arrived, the pressure on accommodation was growing intense.

But Max intended to stay in the Gloucester until he knew whether it would be more convenient for his job to live on the Island or on the Kowloon side. He had arrived with two priorities for the Air Services Department in the new administration. The first was to re-establish a civil air service at Kai Tak. The RAF had commandeered Hong Kong's sole airport, and gave Max 'a tiny corner' for civil aviation, promising (but not delivering for months) two Nissen huts for a terminal. To restore regular air service, he quickly began talks with Bondy, his old pal from CNAC – the American William Langhorne Bond had tenaciously kept China's flagship airline going during the war. Max hoped that CNAC would be given permission to restart service from Hong Kong at once. They faced some resistance from the military, but by November 22 Max had planes flying in the first scheduled service to Chungking and Shanghai.

Max's second priority was to develop plans for a new airport to cater for the expected boom in air travel, working with the RAF to meet military needs for an expanded Hong Kong base. There was little room for expansion at the old airfield tucked under the nine dragon hills of Kowloon. As the *Times* would comment a year later:

Only the American pilots of the CNAC who flew in and out

*night after night when Chungking was largely isolated from the
outside world regarded landings and take-offs at Kai Tak with
equanimity.*

Max knew what they meant. He had arrived from London with a
proposal for a new airport in the western New Territories. There was
certainly plenty of land in this rural area, and Max, with the RAF and
Bond, surveyed a promising site at Ping Shan close to the border with
China. But the Ping Shan plan ran into difficulties from the start. First,
there were budget issues. On November 10, Max wrote to Audrey saying that the Treasury in Whitehall had 'pared Ping Shan airfield to the
bone and it will not be suitable for big commercial aircraft'.

The larger difficulties with the project were political. From the outset
Chinese villagers who would be displaced from their land and homes
protested vigorously. 'The first indication of this dissatisfaction came
when many of the notices to quit were returned by the tenants torn in
half', said an official report. Hundreds of villagers presented petitions to
Admiral Harcourt and the Bishop of Hong Kong, and the Chinese press
reported extensively on the villagers' grievances. The protesters natu-
rally found a sympathetic ear in Chungking. Chiang's administration
was very unhappy that the British seemed to be digging in to stay in the
leased New Territories, and planning to locate aircraft very close to the
border. China's Foreign Minister, Dr Wang Shijie, privately told Chiang
that for the British to be building an air base on the edge of Guangdong
province was 'similar to putting up gun emplacements'. He would try to
get the whole question of the New Territories (whose lease China had
the right to renegotiate) on the agenda for talks with the British.

Harcourt stood firm, while promising compensation to displaced villagers. Work began on a military airfield at Ping Shan, but the bureau-
crats in London dragged their feet on the bigger commercial project.
On November 30, Max wrote that '[I] am constantly engaged in discussions of our £5,000,000 airport project...There is a lot of preliminary
work in progress, blasting of thousands of tons of rock and making
approach roads, but the first sod has not yet been cut.'

One Kuomintang leader who would not be unnerved by the British locating an airfield on the border was Admiral Chan Chak. He was
now back in south China, appointed first postwar mayor of Canton.

Admiral Chan visiting Max's office in the Department of Civil Aviation

Before Max's arrival, MacDougall had gone up to Canton and (in his words) 'had a royal welcome from Chan Chak: he is in a stew though over Chang Fa Kwei (Zhang Fakui) who doesn't like us very much.' Mac had to deal with Hong Kong's neighbours on a host of tricky issues and the hostile General Zhang, 'the effective commander of south China', unfortunately had more political power and influence than the mayor. 'The Admiral's presence in Canton is, however, of great value (wrote MacDougall), and there are few visitors from that city who do not convey from him private messages, quaintly worded, to assure us of his continued efforts to maintain and expand the cooperation essential to mutual prosperity'.

Max was one beneficiary of a warm relationship with the mayor. He reached out to his old friend right after arriving back in Hong Kong. Chan was all in favour of Max's efforts to get an air service up and running, writing in October:

I appreciate greatly your very kind and charming letter of the 22nd present, and I can hardly express my pleasure in hearing

*from you. I am particularly happy to know that you are back
from England and ready to start your good work on commercial
aviation. Again, the happy news of your dear wife has equally
enchanted me. [Max had just heard that she sailed from England in the Mauretania on the October 20.]*

He hoped they would meet soon, and told Max:

*I am of the opinion that Hong Kong and Canton must co-
operate on matters of mutual interest, and that an air service
between the two great cities would be most timely and helpful.*

*I always recall with the greatest joy and satisfaction our
Hong Kong "Escape". Whenever I think of Aberdeen, I think of
you and our friendship which is ever so dear to me.*

Just a month later, the Mayor visited Hong Kong as a guest of Harcourt. Max was delighted that on his second evening Chan 'repudiated
ceremony' and the trio of Mac, Max and Chan dined alone, with the
addition just of Mac's deputy Colonel Thomson. Max gave Chan a book
called *English Saga*, and writing a note of thanks the Mayor said:

*I consider myself very fortunate for being able to dine with
you and the Brigadier. I shall long remember our happy gathering. There was a spontaneity about it, and the simplicity of
friendship was altogether delightful.*

Max was pleased that the bonds forged in adversity were still strong.
He was settling down. In late November he moved his office from noisy,
temporary quarters into the Colonial Secretariat – 'a quiet room with
bougainvillea outside the window and a view of the hills' – and acquired an official car, a magnificent Studebaker.

— • —

On December 3 he got news he'd been waiting for anxiously. He
learned by cable of Audrey's safe arrival in Singapore, and wrote:

Welcome to the China Sea, my love. I felt yesterday that you

had arrived and this morning your cable was waiting in the of-
fice…My ever-loving wife I do look forward to loving you again.
Not that I have stopped and you are a great comfort to me even
at this great distance. Be happy darling Audrey and take great
care of yourself for my sake.

Audrey was mightily relieved to reach Singapore, for she had had a slow and uncomfortable journey. She was left to pack up the South Kensington flat, sell every last possession that couldn't be shipped out in a trunk, and deal with the logistics of an overseas move. Their bicycles, she regretted, went for a song. (Everyone was buying cars.) Missing Max already, she told him about going to see a horror film with an old friend who would be taking over their flat:

When I was out with him darling, I missed you more than I
have at any other time. Subconsciously I kept thinking it was
you I was with and the realization it was not was quite horrible.
I do miss you so desperately and if I don't allow myself to
think of you during the day, I dream about you at night.

Audrey had embarked on the S.S. *Mauretania* on October 20, just after hearing that Max had reached Hong Kong. As on her first voyage to the east, the ship sailed from Liverpool. The Cunard liner was serving as a troopship, and was packed to the gills with 1,500 soldiers (Audrey got accustomed to their wolf whistles) and a small contingent of civilians. She was lucky to be allocated a two-berth cabin, albeit an inside one, and to share with Moyra Youds, an acquaintance from the BBC. They were in a party of ten passengers destined for Singapore – eight women and two men. The ship was officially dry but one of her companions had stashed away four cases of whisky. The ship's store sold real silk stockings (a huge luxury) but these were quickly bought up by the officers, and the women on board 'who really need stockings' didn't get a look in.

There weren't many diversions, despite some attempts to entertain the troops:

Last night all the women were asked to go and dance with

the troops. This was obviously quite an absurd idea, but we went. After two dances in a very confined space, the 1,500 odd men who didn't have partners indicated that they would rather sing, which we then did, sitting on the decks.

After a very rough passage through the Bay of Biscay, the weather in the Mediterranean was lovely. The *Mauretania* squeezed through the Suez Canal into the Red Sea (disappointing Max's sister Margaret who'd hoped the ship would take the longer route around the Cape, and that she would meet her new sister-in-law). For Audrey, the Canal route was full of interest: 'The desert looked magnificent, from a distance – Ismailia looked a most attractive place – green and peaceful.'

But the weather was now extremely hot, and it was hard to find a cool spot on deck or in the cabin. Audrey made friends with a married Australian called Fisher – a very pleasant *platonic* friendship, she hastened to tell Max: 'He is slightly like you, in that he is quiet and not pushing – you would like him I think.' But time passed slowly and everyone was eager to reach Bombay where they would disembark:

We are all looking forward to having a drink in Bombay. We spend <u>hours</u> queuing for cups of tea and cigarettes here. The queues are quite social gatherings and fill in the time, which otherwise hangs heavy.

Certainly this fortnight hadn't had the novelty value of Audrey's earlier sea voyage to Africa. But a week in Bombay was much more fun:

Had a most satisfactory week in Bombay, despite the fact that we were stuck in a hotel of a very low order – The Majestic. The first night a sailor divested himself of both his trousers and underpants in the middle of the dance floor. I was enjoying a quiet drink with my Australian friend at the time, and we were both considerably shaken. The next night we came back about 10 o'clock from Chinese chow, to find Military Police on the door, there having been a free fight. It certainly was a lively spot, and I was very grateful to have a nice escort in Fisher. He took me swimming, we watched cricket, went shopping and out to din-

*ner a couple of times. He is a very nice person, and it is such
a relief to be able to go out with somebody who doesn't try and
make a pass at you. But pleasant though he is, I long for your
company darling. There is so much I miss in other people, which
I find in you.*

Max and Audrey were just two of millions of service people and civilians who were on the move in the aftermath of war – some returning home, and some heading out to new assignments. Wherever their
travels took them they found friends, and Bombay was no exception.
There Audrey saw Jean Hutchison, Dorothy and Helen's older sister,
who was waiting for a passage home after six or seven years in India.
She ran into Ben Ellis, one of her disappointed suitors in Chungking,
also on his way home, and yet more China friends, Captain Peter Eve-
rard and his wife Pamela. Peter was going to Shanghai, and Pamela
was trying to follow him. Even Gwen Priestwood – the escapee from
Stanley camp whom Max entertained in Chungking – was said to be
in Bombay.

After a social week in the teeming city, Audrey and her travel companions crossed India by overnight train to Madras. There they were to
wait for a ship to Singapore, billeted in a Civil Affairs Base Depot at Pal-
lavaram in the green hills outside Madras. This transit camp had served
as an internment camp for Japanese prisoners and still had bars on the
windows and Spartan furnishing, but Audrey was pleased to get a room
to herself in a bungalow full of girls. As at her mess in Chungking, she
craved solitude:

*I seized a single room when we arrived, hoping at last to
achieve some privacy. But the girls are gregarious, and the fact
that I am reading, resting or writing, does not prevent them from
coming in and chatting.*

The worst thing was 'the sanitary arrangements are primitive and
since the rains have just started it entails wading out across the garden'.
Getting to the main building for meals in the regular downpours involved donning a Burberry and walking down the road with a large golf
umbrella, that Audrey was thankful to have packed. Stuck at the camp

for two weeks, Audrey enjoyed the company of her Australian friend Fisher, taking walks in hills which reminded her of China, and going into Madras ('a dreary place') to shop for essentials:

> We hear that shoe polish, soap, cigarettes, matches etc. are very scarce and expensive in Singapore, so I am laying in a store. Have been able to get a bottle of Gordon's gin from the mess here, which I shall keep for when you visit me! Oh my love, how I long to be with you again.

Her last few days at the camp were blighted by toothache – a wisdom tooth flared up with an abscess – but a Madras dentist gave her temporary relief, advising her to wait until Singapore for treatment. On November 25, Audrey and her companions boarded the S.S. Dilwara, a purpose-built troopship with greater comforts than the Mauretania, for the final stage of their six-week journey. (A couple of months earlier, the Dilwara had served as the headquarters ship for the Japanese surrender of Singapore.)

Audrey watched alone from the deck 'the lovely approach through the islands' to Singapore, where the Dilwara docked early on December 1. She and her travel companions were taken to the Raffles Hotel, though the fabled hotel's glory was faded: it was serving as a transit camp and working on army rations. Many of the city's buildings were shabby, Audrey thought, but not too knocked about considering that Singapore, like Hong Kong, had been occupied for nearly four years.

— • —

Audrey and her travel companions wasted no time in reporting for duty at the Cathay Building, an Art Deco gem that was Singapore's tallest landmark, but whose recent past was grisly. During the occupation the Japanese had displayed the severed heads of looters on its railings. Audrey was to be secretary to Colonel JD Dumeresque, the head of the Department of Publicity and Printing, the BMA's propaganda outfit. He didn't have a good reputation; Audrey was immediately suspicious of his 'bedroom eyes', but thought she could hold her own. A week later, she wrote to Max that she felt she had judged her new boss too hastily, and explained how hard they worked:

Am finding the work most interesting and congenial. He [Du-meresque] is Director of Publicity and Printing – this includes broadcasting, film censorship, rice problems (why rice I can't make out), control of the Press and a lot more. He is busy all day long with conferences and visitors, so dictates his letters at night. There are two of us working for him, and we have arranged a rota. We come in from 9-5 for 3 days, and then work from 4pm to 12pm 3 nights – Sundays included. Duty during the day is pleasant but not too onerous – night shift is busier, but satisfactory because he takes us back to his bungalow about 8:00 for a drink and a decent dinner, and then we go back to the office at 9:00 and stay there until 12:00 or even 1am. He then drives one home. He is really very nice to work for – polite and considerate and knows what he is doing – but he makes enemies, possibly because he likes to have a finger in every pie, and because he has rather a high opinion of himself. He worked with MacDougall in Washington, who may be able to tell you something about him.

Though Audrey didn't yet understand the 'rice problem', she would soon realize that shortages of staples were critical to public attitudes towards the BMA. In fending off the predatory Dumeresque the other women were friends and allies, especially Joan Yorke, an announcer who had travelled out with Audrey from England.

After a few days at the Raffles, Audrey moved into one of several modern bungalows, requisitioned by her office, on the attractive Caldecott Hill Estate. She was pleased with her new home. She shared a room with bathroom attached and two verandahs, and hoped to upgrade to a single room soon. Food, Audrey told Max, is the great difficulty. Residents of Caldecott Hill ate in a communal mess:

We are on very meagre rations and have now to supplement them with fruit, eggs and vegetables, and occasionally fresh meat. We have had the usual ghastly mess meetings and I regret to say I have been appointed to the committee. We have both civilians and army messing together (we all feed in one bunga-low), the Army get their rations free but we pay $1.20 a day, so

Audrey's military permit for South East Asia

> *of course there is resentment on the part of civilians to pay even*
> *more for the supplementary foods…Bread is very short, and we*
> *sometimes only get biscuits (instead of bread) but there seems to*
> *be plenty of butter.*

Plentiful butter at least was an improvement on rations in England. As War Office personnel, BMA staff were not allowed to eat outside the mess except at the Raffles or at NAAFI canteens, but fortunately the latter included the Tanglin Club, where the food was well cooked. This old-established country club served the same purpose as the Saturday Club in Calcutta or the Ikoyi Club in Lagos – a relaxed place for the foreign community to meet friends, dine, enjoy a swim or a game of tennis. After a dinner there with a new friend, Peter Yriberry, Audrey commented:

> *Every time I go to Tanglin I see some familiar face – either*
> *from the Mauretania, Pallavaram or the Dilwara, but don't*
> *know the names of most of them. I met one young boy there*

whom I had said "good morning" to on the Dilwara once or twice and he asked me to lunch. He thinks no women should have been allowed out here yet – it leads to too much wining and dining and no serious work. I think he has something there. Everybody seems set on having a good time here and the military are getting as much enjoyment out of their last few months in the Army as they can.

With some cynicism she concluded:

I suppose there are some who really are interested in the fate of Malaya.

Many Malays didn't think so. The British had returned to Malaya with an ill-conceived plan to impose direct rule on the nine states of the Malay peninsula, previously governed as a protectorate. This plan undermined the sovereignty of the states' Sultans, and was coupled with citizenship proposals that benefitted Malaya's substantial Chinese and Indian minorities but were anathema to the ethnic Malay majority. Singapore would be governed as a separate colony. The new constitution was railroaded through, and galvanised Malays to speak with one voice in opposition to the British. At the same time, the nascent Malayan Communist Party (which was Chinese-dominated) stirred up labour unrest and strikes. This, as well as the shortages of food and housing, made the BMA distinctly unpopular, and Audrey sensed the communal tension in Singapore.

Max and Audrey were still some 1,600 miles apart, and the delays in getting news of each other were agonizing. Max didn't receive a letter from Singapore until December 12, though Audrey's cable had told him of her arrival. She in turn had received only a couple of cables from Max during her six-week journey. She savoured a bunch of ten letters that awaited her in Singapore. Every letter was full of longing for their reunion, which might be months away. As Christmas approached, both Max and Audrey dreaded a lonely holiday. Audrey tried hard to get into the festive spirit. She took a party of friends to the Raffles Hotel for an evening that turned out to be rather costly:

*I took Pigge, Yriberry, a couple of girls from the office and an-
other man from the office to Raffles for dinner last night. It is a
transit camp as I told you, but not run by NAAFI and the dinner
set me back $30, which is quite fantastic – the dinner was very
indifferent into the bargain. We danced afterwards and the floor
is appalling, very crowded too. But I had a bottle of whiskey and
one of the girls brought some gin. The whiskey was finished and
I think they all enjoyed the party.*

It was the anniversary of Max's proposal, which she remembered in
a poignant postscript to another letter:

*Two years ago on the 21st I accepted your wonderful pro-
posal. Were you to ask me the same question again every year of
our lives my answer would always be the same.*

Then on December 23 she wrote a heartfelt Christmas letter, which
she hoped would catch the next day's plane and reach her husband
for the 25th:

*I should like to tell you of my love for you, but there are no
words I can find for this. When I am with other people I think of
you and long for your company. When I am alone I think of you
and love you intensely, deeply and unendingly. I remember very
clearly the Christmas we spent two years ago, before we were
married, and know I love you in the same way as I did then, and
have during these two years found so many other things to love.
My life is very empty without you near my darling Max and
though I sometimes in the evening get enjoyment from watching
the fireflies and stars alone on my balcony, it all seems somehow
pointless, because you are not here to share even that with me.*

In Hong Kong, her 'waiting husband' wrote of his longing to possess
his wife again, and hoped that:

*By next [Christmas] we will have a happy home together
and I shall kiss your golden hair and exciting lips. My dear love,*

look after yourself well and come back to me soon.

He hoped that long before the following Christmas they would see each other in Singapore. He was angling to visit on a liaison mission, and this glimmer of a promise tided the separated couple through the Christmas season.

Max was in the mood for a quiet Christmas at Kap Sing, an uninhabited island off Lantau, the largest island in the Hong Kong archipelago. He and an old friend, Lt. Cmdr. Bill Davis, the Deputy Harbour Master, had discovered the tiny island in early November when they were exploring the site of a wreck in the harbour near Castle Peak. (Max got involved in the expedition because he thought the location might work as a base for flying boats.) On a second recce by launch to paint a buoy marking the wreck, Max and Davis found Kap Sing. It was deserted but for a maritime light, a little house built by the Japanese, and an attractive bathing beach. The men planned to make the spot their private hideaway, and invited a third friend to join the exclusive 'Kap Sing Club', as Max wrote on November 17:

> *This attractive country club with excellent sea bathing has now some furniture and three members, Lt Cmdrs Davis and Thompson and myself. I acquired a great quantity of balloon fabric with which to build a sun shelter and yesterday we were nearly airborne trying to erect it in a high wind.*

The friends equipped the shelter with furniture, quantities of tinned food and bottles of beer, and it became an idyllic retreat for *Boy's Own* weekends of camping, swimming and boating. But Max's friends demurred at the suggestion of Christmas on Kap Sing, preferring the lights and music of Hong Kong Island. And 'Davis oddly enough insists that he must go to church.' Max was invited by David MacDougall to a Christmas Eve drinks party, but told Audrey:

> *I stayed at home and drank two whiskeys with you, one each, I hope you enjoyed yours. I felt lonely but you cheered me.*

It was a time for reflection. On Christmas Day, the fourth anniversary of the escape from Aberdeen, Max returned to the port:

> *I went up the Peak by tram, working for the first time after four years, and walked down the other side to Aberdeen where I had a simple lunch at a Chinese eatery house.*

Now he was not fleeing Hong Kong, but rebuilding a life there.

Max had been elected food member of his mess committee, and oversaw the Christmas dinner arrangements with the manager of the Gloucester. It was quite a feast: about seventy people came (not a woman among them) and:

> *We enjoyed turtle soup (genuine), fish, turkey and magnificent ham, plum pudding and ice cream. With this we drank red wine and finished off the evening fairly early on rum punch.*

Max had invited Gerry Wormal, Audrey's friend from Nigeria who had recently been appointed to Hong Kong, but 'Gerry was absent and came in the morning to apologize, said he had had too much to drink at lunch time'. Some of the old colonial ways had come back with a vengeance.

Down in tropical Singapore, Audrey's Christmas was livelier. She and her girlfriends were dreading their mess dinner, but helped to decorate the hall for the Christmas Eve event. The party was better than expected – until a fight started by a drunken Irishman broke it up. The survivors moved over to Audrey's mess and sang songs until 5am 'by which time I was just beginning to get going myself – having remained horribly sober all the evening – and so entertained them with a couple of dances. The can-can was a success.' Though a married woman, she hadn't quite lost her Chungking habit of dancing on tables.

Partying carried on until late into the night on Christmas Day too. Dumeresque invited two fellow Colonels from the office, as well as Audrey, Barbara Birchenough (his other secretary) and Joan Yorke (the announcer) to dinner. At midnight, after an excellent meal (prawn cocktail, stuffed fish, turkey and chocolate mousse, Audrey noted in her diary), they all went on to a new nightclub, the Coconut Grove, for its opening night. Again, there was much singing of old songs with a bunch of Americans (Audrey herself was quite hoarse from the previous night's revelries), and the women weren't home until 4am.

Dumeresque, as Audrey's first instincts had told her, was a man to beware:

> With Dumeresque I have to look after myself! He is very flippant and "sophisticated", kisses us both [Audrey and Barbara] good morning, lightly on the cheek, calls us collectively and singly "darling" tells us both, collectively and singly that he loves us madly. It is all quite amusing. Or is it?

'I should prefer to keep such intimacies for you,' she told Max.

On New Year's Day, she was consoled by a 'beautiful, intimate' letter from Max. Reading it on her verandah watching the sunset, 'my blood turned to water and my strength went from me, as it so often does when you hold me close in your arms'. Writing back, she told her husband:

> And I shall join you to live with you again as your wife as soon as I can. There is nothing else I wish to do. The independence I once enjoyed, the ability to stand alone, I know now were nothing as compared to the joy and happiness I found with you. This love I have for you is the purest feeling I have ever known.

She hoped Max had contrived to visit soon, though he hadn't been able to confirm a date. He was aiming to arrive in Singapore in time for their second wedding anniversary on January 8. Friends at both ends were helping to make this happen, but there were crossed wires. In the end, Max decided not to wait for an official invitation from Singapore, but set off by flying boat on January 7. The RAF Sunderland made it to Singapore in nine hours, and Max landed that evening. Audrey had hoped against hope that he would arrive that day, and fully expected to be speechless and tearful when she greeted him.

We don't know if she was, but we do know that the couple's second honeymoon was blissful. Audrey had arranged for Max to stay at her mess, and for her co-worker Barbara to take the evening shifts so that she would have plenty of free time. She introduced Max to her boss over lunch on January 8, and enjoyed an anniversary dinner that night. On Audrey's day off work, she and Max drove by Jeep to a local beauty spot, the Kota Tinggi Falls. They had time alone, but also a string of social and official events, including visits to the Tanglin Club and dinner with Fraser Crawford, Max's former Chungking colleague.

When Max flew out on January 20, Audrey's room seemed very empty. But she said that his Christmas gift, a string of pearls, 'are a constant joy to me darling and I shall wear them all the time'. Max was equally bereft on returning to his lonely room at the Gloucester Hotel after a long flight. Sitting in the cockpit as the aircraft approached a 'cool and bright Hong Kong' he was struck that the colony seemed barren after the lush vegetation of Singapore.

— • —

During Max's absence another large spanner had been thrown in the works of the Ping Shan airport project. Back in London, the Air Ministry and Ministry of Civil Aviation had had cold feet about the technical suitability of the Ping Shan site, and had decided to send out a joint mission to review alternatives for an international airport. The Air Ministry informed Harcourt of this in a top-secret telegram dated January 10, to which Harcourt replied on January 25, defending the choice of Ping Shan:

> It is not understood why the suitability of the Ping Shan site should be questioned again…Meteorological and topographical aspects may not be ideal but these are common to the whole China Coast. There is no rpt no better site within colony or new territories…Whilst I welcome mission to examine Ping Shan with view to major development, I hope question of alternative site will not rpt not be raised for reasons stated and also in view of political difficulties already reported. Meanwhile airfield construction[s] to meet minimum requirements is continuing.

The Ministry of Civil Aviation had elaborated on the decision to send a high level mission in a letter to Max's liaison in the Colonial Office, WJ Bigg:

...Hong Kong will be so important from the Civil Aviation point of view in the future that we feel we must be completely satisfied that the best site is chosen – hence the forthcoming Mission.

The mission, headed by Air Commodore CC Darley, President of the Airfield Board at the Air Ministry, and including representatives from the Ministry of Civil Aviation and BOAC, arrived in Hong Kong on February 5, and spent ten days in the colony. Max hosted a welcome dinner, shepherded them around, and took part in endless meetings and visits to Ping Shan and alternative sites. The mission's conclusion was a recommendation to ditch Ping Shan and instead build the international airport at Deep Bay: 'Deep Bay will make the better site but will cost more money and take more time.'

Surprisingly, in view of Chinese government sensitivities, the Deep Bay site was even closer to the border – two miles northwest of Ping Shan village – though half the number of villagers would be displaced (900 versus 1800 for the 'full scheme' at Ping Shan).

Max gave his own feedback to Bigg in a letter revealing his frustration:

> *...The civil element of the Mission immediately took a dislike to the southern approaches to Ping Shan and set out to find another site. The one they have chosen [Deep Bay] certainly has better approaches but will cost far more in time and money to turn into an airfield and most of the work put into Ping Shan will be wasted; however, if civil aviation cannot accept the limitations of Ping Shan I suppose another place must be chosen and we will have to tolerate the delay. I hope that the decision, one way or the other, will be arrived at quickly, because if Ping Shan is to be stopped the less damage done to the villagers' land the less hostile they will feel.*

This was a good point. By March 1, work on building a runway at Ping Shan had been suspended. The RAF decided that it could make do with its existing base at Kai Tak for the foreseeable future. A new international airport for Hong Kong would serve only civil needs – and funds would have to be found from non-defence budgets. Throughout 1946 and beyond, there was plenty of public support for a new airport to meet the growing demands of civil aviation and restore Hong Kong's pre-eminence as a centre of international trade. On October 22, 1946 the Hong Kong correspondent of the *Times* wrote an impassioned plea for a decision on the airport proposals. Without a modern airport, he argued, Hong Kong would be sidelined instead of being 'the heart of the network of Far Eastern air services', and would not recover its position as a hub for international trade.

This must have been music to Max's ears. But it did no good. The debates dragged on, but whether ultimately for budgetary reasons, or because of political sensibilities, the Deep Bay airport was never built. It would be fifty years before a new international airport opened in Hong Kong – Chek Lap Kok on the big island of Lantau. For now civil aviation would make do with Kai Tak – with its Nissen huts and terrifying landings.

When Max had written to WJ Bigg at the Colonial Office about the mission's disheartening conclusions, he also referred to his recommendation that, on return to civil rule, air services should be managed from a fully-fledged department, a new Department of Civil Aviation. He privately hoped that he would be appointed its director, but another professional disappointment was in store. Apparently without consulting the Hong Kong administration, the Colonial Office had decided his old boss Albert Moss should cut short his leave in Australia and return to Hong Kong at the end of military rule. 'This will shake me to the core', Max admitted to Audrey. Moss would be in charge again, and Max would be relegated to number two – with all the professional and social consequences that entailed in status-conscious Hong Kong.

But much more importantly Max and Audrey would face the future together. Not long after their January reunion in Singapore, Max heard that the ban on bringing wives to Hong Kong would soon be lifted, and sent Audrey a clipping from the *South China Morning Post* of January 28: the story was headlined 'Colony's Wives'. 'How does it feel to be the wife of a colony?' Max quipped. From March 1, civilians already resident in Hong Kong would get to decide when their wives and children should join them – bearing in mind that housing and transport were still key problems.

Max, of course, wasn't a civilian but still a serving officer in the Military Administration, so might have to wait for return to civil rule and his demobilization. It looked as though both Hong Kong and Singapore/Malaya would revert to civil government on April 1, but Max was impatient for Audrey to join him sooner. To test the water, he applied for an entry permit for her.

Then in March, after a long search, Max solved his housing problem. A Colonel Burgess offered him a six month sublet of his one-bedroom flat at one of the best addresses in Hong Kong – Aigburth Hall on May Road in the popular Mid-Levels, below the fog belt of the Peak and with magnificent views of the harbour. Max wanted Audrey to resign from her job and move up as soon as possible. Audrey was more than ready to quit a job she found increasingly irksome in a colony that was tense with civil unrest. Transport was still a problem and, to get a priority passage, Max suggested that Audrey take a short-term position as a secretary to the incoming Governor, whose identity was still secret. In the event, she was granted permission to enter Hong Kong 'irrespective of job', and the official instruction to the BMA Singapore of March 16 requested 'early departure by air'.

'I am all ready to welcome you, my only love', said Max in the last letter he would need to write for some time, 'and it will be a great moment when you at last reach the port of Hong Kong'. He expected Audrey daily, and finally on March 22 she arrived in grand style – on the Sunderland flying boat of the Maharajah of Jaipur.

CHAPTER NINE

Picking up the Pieces
Hong Kong and Home Leave 1946-48

Audrey in the gardens of Branksome Towers

'There was a time when we felt nothing was too hard, too much trouble, too great a sacrifice – this was all so that we might win a war. Shouldn't we feel all that far more strongly now, to ensure peace?'

Audrey writing in her journal, August 17, 1947.

N ow it was time to turn the May Road flat into a home: there were curtains to choose, servants to hire, and menus to plan. But before Audrey could enter into the swing of being one of the 'Colony's wives' she was needed at Government House. Experienced secretaries were in short supply, and she agreed to help out in the transition. When civil government was restored on May 1, 1946, she found herself working not for a new Governor, but for Sir Mark Young, the man who had had the unenviable task of surrendering the colony in 1941. Though frail from four years of harsh internment, Young was back to show the world that he could pick up where he had left off. He was given a hero's welcome.

The returning Governor and David MacDougall, now Colonial Secretary, had many uncomfortable issues to deal with in the aftermath of a bitter war. Japanese war criminals were convicted in trials held in Hong Kong and China. Suspected collaborators among Hong Kong's Eurasian, Indian and Chinese communities presented a more delicate problem: some prominent pre-war leaders were asked by the British to withdraw from public life, but others, such as the Eurasian Lo Man Kam, were given the benefit of the doubt and played an important role in rebuilding the colony. But for all the difficulties of the recent past, Audrey – like Max – found that Hong Kong sprang back to life remarkably quickly. When she first arrived, the physical devastation was still very evident: no houses beyond their Mid-Levels apartment building on May Road were habitable. She saw 'ruins, deserted gloomy ruins everywhere…it was impossible to go beyond the ground floor in most houses – since there were no staircases.' Overall, seventy percent of European-style residences and twenty percent of tenement buildings were reckoned to be unfit for habitation. Thankfully, recovery was well underway. Months earlier, David MacDougall had persuaded a respected Chinese businessman, Dick Lee, eldest son of the tycoon Lee Hysan, to forge ahead with new construction in Happy Valley. The word went out that 'the Lees are building!' Other Chinese entrepreneurs followed the Lees' example, kick-starting business life and the physical rebuilding of the territory.

Governor Young's return symbolized continuity, but both he and MacDougall knew that change was vital. In a very deliberate break with the past, together they enacted reforms that brought new racial and social integration to stuffy Hong Kong society. The 'Peak ordinance', which prevented Chinese from residing at the smartest addresses in the colony, was repealed in July 1946. The recruitment of cadets, a fast-track entry to the colonial service, was opened up to Chinese applicants and Paul Tsui, who had served the clandestine wartime BAAG, became the first Chinese cadet officer in October 1946. Social welfare was improved. Soon people of all kinds flooded back into Hong Kong – former residents and newcomers who were fleeing the civil war that had, as many had anticipated, broken out in China. From the war's end low point of 600,000, population numbers were up to one million by the time of Audrey's arrival, and by 1947 would rise to two million.

The city was going through a period of political and cultural openness. In addition to scrapping the most obviously racist elements of the old order, Young and MacDougall also tried to introduce a measure of democracy to the colony, as a way of cementing Chinese support for continuing British rule. But for a number of reasons the radical 'Young plan' for constitutional reform ultimately proved to be ahead of its time and was quietly dropped, much to the dismay of liberals such as Max and Audrey. Young retired as governor just a year after his post-war encore, to be replaced by a more conservative leader, Sir Alexander Grantham, who had been governor of Fiji. The 1946 spirit of openness was soon stifled. Economic growth and the prospect of régime change in China became more pressing concerns than democracy.

Audrey tried to make sense of her new environment, as well as bringing order to domestic life. She hired a Chinese couple to serve as cook and 'amah', 26-year old Ng Wing and his wife, Ah Mui, who took up residence in the flat's servants' quarters. Audrey, with her domestic sci-

Ah Wing and his wife Ah Mui
at Branksome Towers

ence training, prided herself on her cooking skills. But in Hong Kong the kitchen was the province of the staff, and Audrey concentrated on drawing up guest lists, menu planning and teaching Ah Wing (as she called him) to make some of her favourite dishes. Max and Audrey grew accustomed to returning home from an early evening cocktail party just in time to host a dinner. Audrey knew she could rely on Ah Wing and his wife to have everything ready.

Audrey bought a leather-bound guest book, and faithfully entered details of every social occasion from the most casual tea party to the grandest Government House dinner. On one side she recorded engagements 'here', with guest lists and menus, and on the facing page the events 'there' with guest lists and locations. There would be more engagements 'there' than 'here' in what would become a full calendar. Periodically Max and Audrey raced to catch up by throwing larger parties than they really liked to host: 'There are *so* many people to whom we owe hospitality now, that I am quite overwhelmed, and since we do not have large cocktail parties, feel I will never get straight', said Audrey in November 1947. Their own entertaining style was homely and they feared they'd be thought stingy hosts. 'At least we do not vie with that rather silly factor of HK society who are out to impress, and give false ideas', wrote Audrey in August 1947. 'It does seem foolish to spend money so lavishly on wines, 4 or 5 courses, liqueurs and chocolates from Lane Crawford. I enjoy simpleness in other peoples' houses; and there must be some genuine persons who enjoy it in ours.'

The Oxfords were also budget-conscious when it came to furnishings. Luckily Audrey enjoyed combing through local Chinese stores in search of a stylish bargain. On one such scavenging trip she found a chess set which exactly matched Max's description of the one he had lost when he escaped in 1941: it had distinctive red and white ivory pieces, stored inside a folding board which was decorated with gold-painted figures. Max was delighted to have it back, and enjoyed many a game with his wife.

But there were also bleak times. A few months after Audrey reached Hong Kong, family tragedy struck when her younger sister, Tottie, who was just 25, fell ill with meningitis. Nothing could be done to save her, and there wasn't time for Audrey to travel to her bedside in faraway England. Tottie died on August 21, 1946. Her grief-struck husband, Buffy Hebeler, was left alone in Somerset with their one-year old son, Christopher, and a fledgling veterinary practice to tend. None of the Watson family was in England – Audrey's father had retired to Peru, where he spent his last years impoverished and in ill health. Her elder sister, Joan, was also in South America, working at the British Embassy in Ecuador. When the awful news of Tottie's death reached Audrey by telegram, Max walked home from his office in the pouring rain to be with her – and stayed with her the rest of the day, she later remembered gratefully.

It was some solace for Max and Audrey to escape for weekends at Kap Sing, the dot of an island off Lantau which Max and his buddies had made their own in the heady days of late 1945. A boatman called Cho San would ferry them to the island, and at Christmas 1947, by which time Kap Sing was off-limits, he took the trouble to call on Max with gifts of a chicken and a bottle of whisky. Audrey later remembered their idyllic weekends:

It was such a perfect place – clean beaches, clear water, rocks and pools – the sea slugs at low tide – the sun setting over Lantau – the junks outlined darkly against the hills – their riding lights when it was dark. Above all, the utterly peaceful silence. Voices would drift up from the junks and sampans as they sailed beneath us in the narrow, swift-flowing channel. The privacy of the whole island, which enabled us to swim without costumes if we felt inclined. And can there be a more delicious sensation than to feel the cool water soothing one's hot skin – the freedom of movement when not hampered by a costume. I remember sitting in the fine sand, under a blue sky and bright sun, watching the cool clear water breaking gently on the shore, the green hills of Lantau and Ma Wan in the background, aware of the friendly silence and thinking that Heaven would be like this. The setting was perfect for the life of complete simplicity and lack of artifice which we enjoyed at those weekends. Journal, July 6, 1950.

— • —

As Audrey settled into the colonial life, she tried to find that same lack of artifice in her friendships too. The woman friend who best met Audrey's authenticity test was Nan Wormal, 'a very real and true person'. Nan was the amusing, slightly scatty and rumpled wife of Gerry Wormal, the colonial administrator who had befriended Audrey on her first voyage out East in 1943. At that time he was stationed in Nigeria, and he spent most of the war years in Africa. But in 1945 he transferred to the Hong Kong Planning Unit at the Colonial Office. This brought him to Hong Kong at the end of 1945, in time for Max to invite him to the Christmas dinner that he was too hung over to attend. In his professional life, Gerry dealt with dry statistics (he became Hong Kong's chief statistician), but his passion was art – he was constantly sketching Hong Kong scenes, or doing oil paintings of junks and other icons of island life. Nan had two children (the elder from a first marriage to a pilot killed in the war) but, with a Chinese amah looking after them, Nan found plenty of time to see Audrey.

One hot July morning in 1947, the friends met for coffee at the American Club, their refuge in the centre of town. Audrey was casting around for a new pursuit, and after coffee she and Nan went shopping:

Water landings at Kai Tak were still common:
Colonial Secretary MacDougall (right) returns from a trip, greeted by
Max and DCA Albert Moss, January 1947

they bought paints for Gerry (who was laid up in hospital) and a thick, hard-backed notebook for Audrey at the modest cost of HK$2.50.

That afternoon Audrey sat at her desk in Aigburth Hall and penned the first entry in a journal that she would write regularly for years, filling seven volumes of cheap, lined notebooks like the first one. Nan and Audrey were sceptical about the idea of a journal, but Max encouraged his wife from the start, telling her she should write only for herself, but with a view to publication...and profit! She made it a daily discipline to write a long entry in her neat handwriting, and she discussed issues large and small. In one breath she would describe the minutiae of daily life, and in the next she would explore her feelings on marriage, social life, war and peace, and the raging civil war in China.

Audrey was scarcely into her writing routine when she and Max managed a move to a new flat. They had found a larger, more permanent Mid-Levels apartment at 12A Branksome Towers on Tregunter Path, conveniently close to the May Road stop on the Peak Tram. They

enjoyed unobstructed views down to the harbour from the building
that was then about four stories high. The Towers backed into the steep
hillside and were set among lush trees and shrubs. Renovations were
in progress when Max and Audrey moved in on July 28, and initially
Audrey was depressed by the state of the place. There was no hot water
(this took four months to install), and she was unsure how to handle
workmen: 'Three men come in to polish floors – lounge around in the
best chairs, smoking. I do the polishing myself – just to show them –
don't know whether they or I lose face.' But with efficient service more
typical of Hong Kong, a tailor promised curtains within a week, lamp-
shades were chosen, and furniture arranged to Max and Audrey's liking. In the summer ceiling fans cooled the apartment, and in the chilly
winter months Max and Audrey stayed warm with a wood-burning fire
in the living room. They moved their few pieces of furniture around
according to the season, making sure that guests would be comfortable.

Auspiciously, the Oxfords' first guests were Admiral Sir Chan Chak
and his wife, Lady Chan, visiting from Canton. Max and Audrey invited
them and their entourage to tea on August 7, causing 'much excitement
in the kitchen' when Audrey told Ah Wing the identity of their distinguished company, which also included Lt. Col. Harry Owen-Hughes
and his wife, Frances. Owen-Hughes was the Cantonese-speaking military liaison officer who had met the Christmas Day escape party along
the route through China, giving the men warm coats and vital funds.
When he had taken the last flight out of Kai Tak that December on a
mission to Chungking, he had left his parents in the colony. Both were
interned in Stanley, and only his mother survived. Now Owen-Hughes
was back in his native Hong Kong to help his mother and rebuild the
family trading company, while Frances split her time between Asia and
England, where their children went to school.

At tea, the Chans much admired Max and Audrey's new flat, and the
Admiral sent a characteristically fulsome thank-you letter: 'We thoroughly enjoyed the abounding graciousness of the party and appreciate
very highly the honour of being your guests.' The Chans were in Hong
Kong on a courtesy call to the new Governor, Sir Alexander Grantham,
and his American wife, Lady Maurine. Max and Audrey were among
the few non-Chinese guests at a dinner to honour the Chans at Government House the previous evening. David MacDougall was there of

course, and Max's friends Dick and Esther Lee, of the Lee Hysan family. Audrey found the Government House dinner slightly odd, but the date had significance:

> *Dinner rather indifferent. Mystery of fruit plates and no fruit. Port went round once and no more. One drink before dinner. Chan Chak rose to leave before a final whiskey – no liqueurs – Lady G. neither drinks nor smokes. After the toast to the King and then the President of China, [I] asked A.D.C and Commander Wong to drink to Abuelita's health, on this her 80th birthday.* Journal, August 8, 1947.

Even if she anticipated more lavish hospitality at Government House, Audrey was conflicted about leading a self-indulgent life, especially compared to her closest family and her own youthful years. It was all relative – Max and Audrey had plenty of friends who could spend more freely than they could. So they were alarmed when Max's monthly accounting for July showed that they had 'topped the [HK]\$1,000 mark – for the second time', a sum equal to over £2,000 in today's money:

> *Yet M[ax] tells me the cost of living allowance has been reduced as prices are lower. This I do not understand – particularly as we have just agreed, foolishly, I suppose, to give the staff a \$10 increase [Ng Wing would write to his employers with a detailed case whenever a rise was needed]. I really do dislike intensely anything to do with money – the memory of those very stringent days at home are often with me, and in comparison we live a most self-indulgent life – no sooner is one bottle of hand-cream finished than I buy another. I smoke without considering the cost – life is certainly very different indeed from those depressing days. [I] have a feeling of security which I always hoped one day to have. And yet, when we do the books am horrified at the amount we spend – and should perhaps remember those dark days more often as self-discipline – for even now my father and sister are always hard up.* Journal, August 14, 1947.

Max and Audrey would regularly send gifts of money to her father, struggling in Peru. Audrey felt strongly that, just two years after the end of a wrenching world war, humanity was losing its way again. Ruminating on a depressing book that she was reading, she reflected:

> We have become avaricious and grasping and out for ourselves – the war may have made its effect on some, but how very few – we are not humbled, we are losing our perspective, worldly things become important again. I think perhaps some people never lost their sense of their own importance, or even stopped bemoaning their earthly losses, and so perhaps never had time to gain what was there to be gained. There was a time when we felt nothing was too hard, too much trouble, too great a sacrifice – this was all so that we might win a war. Shouldn't we feel all that far more strongly now, to ensure peace? Surely no sacrifice should be too great for peace. Perhaps peace is only a negative thing, which cannot be seen and felt the way war is.
> Journal, August 17, 1947.

She was by no means alone in feeling that the end of the struggle led to a loss of purpose in people's lives, and to a return of pettiness. She noticed that survivors of the prison camps, quite understandably, liked to swop notes on camp life – almost vying with each other as to which contingents of prisoners (civilians in Stanley camp, or military in Sham Shui Po) endured the greatest hardships. She may also have detected an attitude, noticed by some other newcomers to Hong Kong, that if you hadn't been through "camp", you didn't really count.

But most of the time both the Chinese and Western residents of Hong Kong were focused on the future. The postwar world offered a cornucopia of opportunities for risk-taking entrepreneurs, such as Max and Audrey's friends Stanley Smith and John Galvin, the Australian duo who had run psychological warfare for the British in China. They became business partners. The pair recognized that there would be huge opportunities in supplying Japan during its reconstruction under General MacArthur's mandate, but access was very restricted. So Smith and Galvin bought the *China Mail*, a nearly defunct newspaper in Hong

Kong, thus acquiring press passes for early entry into the defeated nation. Their company, Scott & English Ltd., won approval as a 'foreign trader' and for two or three years had a profitable monopoly on Australian wool exports to Japan. They also supplied peanuts from China (for much-needed cooking oil), iron ore, coal and tin, re-opening disused Malayan tin mines.

Stanley Smith was based in Hong Kong as the business empire grew, while Galvin travelled constantly. The partners asked Ted Ross, Mac-Dougall's former deputy and a veteran of the Christmas Day escape, who was now on government service in Shanghai, to look after the Japan end of the business. Ross agreed and spent three years in Tokyo before he was laid low with a bout of tuberculosis, from which he recuperated in Australia, eventually returning to Hong Kong to run Smith and Galvin's company.

Smith lived in a splendid house on Repulse Bay, which John Galvin and his wife, Pat, had restored after the war but did not need for themselves. Number 10 South Bay Road had one of Hong Kong's finest views of the South China Sea, its lovely garden leading down to a private beach and the mooring for Stanley's yacht. In 1947 May Wong, who had worked at the Ministry of Information in Chungking and later became Stanley's second wife, joined her former boss in Hong Kong. Audrey remembered enchanting evenings with the couple, who were generous hosts and good friends. On one occasion, wrote Audrey: 'Sitting on the wide porch, we can hear the sea on the beach below. May Wong plays gramophone records for us – the night is cool and the view of the distant islands and the lighted fishing boats in the black water magnificent. Reluctant to leave.'

Smith and Galvin became immensely successful, and so did another pair of entrepreneurs of Max's acquaintance. Australian Sydney de Kantzow and Texan Roy Farrell were ex-air force and CNAC pilots, veterans of flying the Hump. As CNAC chief pilot, Syd de Kantzow flew Max over the Hump and around China on several occasions in the war years, and they would sometimes dine together in Chungking. While Smith and Galvin focused on Japan, de Kantzow and Farrell were among the first Westerners of the postwar era to see the potential of China as a trading partner. Farrell formed an export company, but quickly recognized that it had no means of getting supplies into the turbulent country, and that the real opportunities lay in transportation. He bought a US army surplus Douglas Dakota DC-3, nicknamed *Betsy*, landing her in Shanghai on New Year's Day 1946. Later that year, scrambling to keep up with demand, de Kantzow and Farrell together founded Cathay Pacific Airways in Hong Kong, and *Betsy* won her place in history as the first plane in the fleet of what is now one of the world's leading airlines.

As de Kantzow and Farrell established their base at Kai Tak, Max and 'Uncle Moe' Moss (as the Cathay founders called the DCA) dealt with them frequently. The aviation directors doubtless had to juggle competing demands from Cathay, CNAC, CATC, BOAC and other airlines who wanted to serve the burgeoning Asia market from the increasingly inadequate facilities of the cramped airport. So de Kantzow and Farrell made sure that they remained on good terms with Max, the airport manager. Syd had a sleek yacht, appropriately called *Cathay*, and invited Max and Audrey out on long, boozy days of sailing to outlying islands. Audrey felt she didn't have much in common with the swashbuckling pair, but Max admired their hard work and ambitions for the infant airline.

The fact was that Audrey preferred her husband's company to anyone else's, writing after an October typhoon had passed through:

> *Max will be home late to-night, as B.O.A.C. is arriving (several days late because of the bad weather recently) bearing the Parliamentarians [a visiting delegation], which he must meet if Moss doesn't go. Is it unusual I wonder, to have the same feeling for your husband after nearly four years of married life, as you did when you were engaged? I love Max in many more ways, possibly, now, and yet I retain that same feeling of – not adoration, and not respect – of, I suppose being what is normally called "in love" for which I can think of no better expression. I still look forward to his return each night. I still am moved if I see him unexpectedly – we have had misunderstandings, and have been curt with each other – generally when we are both tired...My life is so complete with him and I enjoy his company more than that of anybody else I know.*
> Journal, October 8, 1947.

Lord Nathan, Minister of Civil Aviation (fifth from left),
visited in September 1947

She was doing some hard thinking about her own role as a colonial wife. Her youthful declaration that her main ambition was to be a good wife and mother had shocked the headmistress of Cheltenham Ladies' College, but Audrey now questioned whether being 'only a complement' to her husband was enough. Perhaps, without the 'mother' part of the equation it wasn't, but Audrey rationalized her situation to herself. Late one night, when Max was thinking about applying for a diplomatic service job as an air attaché, it came to her 'with rather startling clarity' just what being a good wife meant in her case. She got out of bed and wrote the following in her journal:

> It means a life of social entertainment, of leisure, of dressing to please the eye, of freedom from care that one is not doing anything further than being an adjunct. It can be done, and pleasure can be found doing it, however different it is to preconceived ideas, so long as one's husband is proud of an otherwise mean

179

achievement – the socially minded and socially presentable wife. It no doubt does help a man, but I don't think I had ever before realised quite how much. Journal, September 18, 1947.

This would be her guiding principle in years to come. On this occasion, though Audrey stood ready to support Max's ambitions, he decided to stay put as Moss' deputy. In September 1947, Lord Nathan, Minister of Civil Aviation in Attlee's Labour government, visited the colony. Moss and Max showed the Minister the Deep Bay airport site and it looked as though airport development there or improvements at Kai Tak might get the go-ahead. Max thought his Hong Kong job would be full of challenges. But this optimism didn't last long. On October 14 Max noted morosely in his diary: 'Kai Tak building programme abandoned, including dock.' It would be another few years before Kai Tak got a major new runway, and of course another fifty years before the airfield was retired in favour of a spanking new airport on Lantau.

— • —

In the fall of 1947 Max and Audrey were due for a spell of local leave, and decided to visit Shanghai and Fuzhou – a trip to mainland China that would be off-limits after 1949. They flew to Shanghai on a CNAC Skymaster on October 27, a comfortable journey of four hours. In the bustling city they were guests of the Consul General of the Netherlands, Duco Middelburg, and his wife Fanny, staying in their grand wood-panelled flat on the top floor of 91, Haig Court, a nine storey building which reminded Audrey of the 'better London blocks'. The next day they had a reunion with Audrey's Chungking boss, Jack Hutchison: the veteran diplomat had returned to Shanghai as Commercial Counsellor. They met for lunch at the Cathay Hotel on the Bund, overlooking the wide Whangpoa River. Hutchison took Audrey shopping, and she and Max rapidly formed the impression that 'Shanghai is the metropolis and HK the suburb. The shops are so much better here, and it is, of course, so much larger. Terrifying crossing the road. No European drives [him] self. Cars are sent backwards and forwards from the office. Drivers wait whilst one shops.' Audrey was in search of a fur coat for the chilly Hong Kong winters – and chose a handsome one made of skunk, for which Max paid HK$200 in gold.

After a week of seeing friends and shopping in sophisticated Shanghai, Max and Audrey flew on to the former treaty port and provincial capital, Fuzhou, which brought back memories of old China. In 1943 Max had visited the city with Berkeley Gage on their tour of Fujian province. This was before the Japanese re-took the city in 1944, and it was now if anything even more dismal. The airstrip was no more than a ploughed field, noted Audrey, the roads were appalling, the European club was shabby and depressing, as was its sole occupant. This, Audrey reminded herself, was her familiar China: 'Rickshaws, chits, bells rung on arrival home and gates opened. "Gin and chow". Otherwise Foochow (Fuzhou) reminds me of the forgotten splendour of Canton. Big, unkempt, tumbledown houses – and little remains of the old British regime in the East. There are only a handful of businessmen here now, and they cannot even form a bridge four.'

This was indeed the last gasp of Britain in China. But the hilly countryside around the city was beautiful, and Max and Audrey enjoyed a walk through orange groves, guava orchards, and fields of cotton, watching cotton pluckers and weavers at work. The hills were covered with pine and eucalyptus, and from the air the fields were a patchwork of yellow and green, with their crops of sweet potatoes and rice. Still, a week in Fuzhou as guests of the Commissioner of Chinese Maritime Customs was more than enough for Audrey, who'd come down with a bad cold, and she longed for the CNAC flight back to Hong Kong on November 10 – a bumpy journey, as it turned out, on a full C-47. Airsick passengers didn't bother to use paper bags – many just threw up on the floor.

The worldly pleasures of Hong Kong must have seemed quite appealing after this. The holiday season was soon under way. On November 25 Audrey attended the christening of Dick and Esther Lee's son, Christopher, which was followed by 'an excellent tea'. Oxford-educated Dick Lee, who was credited, along with his younger brothers, with the postwar development of Causeway Bay, had inherited a family business whose distant origins were in the opium trade and was a leading figure in Hong Kong society with a distinguished war record. Max and Audrey grew to know him and his wife Esther very well, and always enjoyed their company.

At Thanksgiving, Max and Audrey enjoyed dinner at the American

Club with American friends, the Eicholzers of Standard Oil. The Oxfords were also members of the Club, which at that time was conveniently housed in the Hong Kong and Shanghai Bank headquarters. The next night, it was the annual St Andrew's Ball at the Peninsula, site of the legendary last dance before the Japanese invasion six years earlier. Lady Grantham, the Governor's wife, wore a tiara and Hong Kong's leading Scot, Jack MacGregor, looked magnificent as a chieftain. Max and Audrey didn't get home until 3am after an exhausting evening, with Audrey still hankering after a simpler, less 'unnaturally social' life. Max maintained that it was easy to adapt: 'I must admit that he has a great capacity for doing so. I do adapt myself ultimately, but it takes longer,' confessed Audrey.

She was actually doing rather well. In December the Oxfords hosted two parties to 'get straight' on their entertaining, and accepted numerous festive season engagements. Some of these Audrey enjoyed very much, in particular an evening at Skyhigh, the Peak home of Iris and Reidar Johannessen. Reidar was the Hong Kong head of the Norwegian shipping company, Wallem & Co., and his delightful wife Iris was from Cornwall. The couple had met and married in Hong Kong in 1935, and after the Japanese conquest they had fled via Macau and travelled through China, walking part of the way with their two very young children. They had spent the rest of the war in India, and returned to Hong Kong to rebuild their cherished home and the shipping business. Audrey was dazzled by the candlelit evening:

> *Magnificent house, enhanced by red candles in wrought iron holders, electricity having failed. Beautiful red and white gladioli, burning fire, mirror above fireplace, circular stairway. Such food as I have never seen, and far too much – smoked salmon, ham, excellent pâté, everything of the very best, and expense absolutely no object. Was it the candlelight that made it such an unusual party, or the luxury and abundance? I have never seen the like.* Journal, December 12, 1947.

Reidar adored his beautiful and independent wife – Audrey thought he treated her like a bird who might fly away. She and Audrey were kindred spirits and became firm friends.

Audrey also especially liked the company of the American Consul General and his wife, George and Sue Hopper. Their residence was on Shouson Hill on the south side of the Island, and a party they threw on December 19 was a 'fine start to Christmas'. Max and Audrey themselves hosted a festive dinner for good friends on Christmas Eve – this became an annual tradition: 'The house looks well with our immense tree, log fire and red and white flowers,' wrote Audrey. All the guests were given presents from under the tree, then: 'Turkey and pudding very good and we sit singing until nearly three, throwing log after log on to the fire. The black velvet before dinner was a success,' said Audrey with some pride in her Guinness and champagne cocktail. Somehow Max and Audrey managed to keep up the pace with a highly social Christmas Day: eggnogs before noon at the Robbs, drinks with the Wilsons, lunch with the Potts ('Most guests seem a little jaded,' Audrey noted.) After a siesta, it was on to a games-filled party at Alan Rogers', and a debauched Greek and Roman dress party with French hosts on Mount Cameron, before another 3am bedtime.

Understandably, Max and Audrey spent Boxing Day reading and relaxing. As they often did, they drove to their favourite quiet beach, Chung Hom Wan (West Bay), which was tucked away on the peninsula between Repulse Bay and Stanley. Though nowhere on the Island was very far from town, here Max and Audrey were usually the only people, other than resident Chinese fisher families, enjoying the fine sand and clear water. In those days the relatively undeveloped south side of Hong Kong Island offered a wonderful shifting vista of sea, sky and land. Leaving the beach on another occasion, Audrey was captivated by the sheer beauty of sunset over the South China Sea:

And as the sun sinks we leave and walking up the valley, we look back and the sun has turned the hills pink, a few boats ride at anchor in the bay, and the veil of mist which has been lying on the water between the islands all the afternoon, continues to weave itself in and out of them. Journal, January 31, 1949.

That December of 1947, they saw in the New Year at the annual Hogmanay party thrown by Jardine Matheson at their godown. The Commander-in-Chief conducted the traditional firing of the noonday gun. The Colonial Secretary and loyal Scot, David MacDougall, was with Inez Thompson, a companion he had met in London. Max and Audrey had first been introduced to Inez in October after she had joined Mac in Hong Kong and begun a job with a local newspaper. (Inez lived at first with a shipboard friend, Isobel Turner, in a house owned by John Galvin, but soon Mac's mother arrived in Hong Kong to share the house and afford Inez and Mac respectability, for he was still married to his first wife). That New Year's Eve Mac and Inez came back to Branksome Towers for a drink, leaving at 4am. 'It was an enjoyable evening', said Audrey, undaunted.

Despite what seems now an exhausting social schedule, life wasn't all about revelry. Like many wives, Audrey spent hours as a volunteer for charities. During the holiday season, there was a big drive to collect donations of food to send to Britain – the homeland still had rationing and severe food shortages. So women in the colonies dutifully packed up food parcels to send halfway round the world. Audrey spent many shifts sitting in Lane Crawford, the venerable Hong Kong department store, waiting for donations to trickle in. More rewardingly, perhaps, she became involved with the Society for Protection of Children, or SPC, and their fundraising activities. She didn't much like committees but was a willing hands-on volunteer.

As 1948 dawned, Max and Audrey prepared to go on long leave to the UK via South Africa – one compensation for serving in the colonies was a paid trip home every three or four years. They would be absent from Hong Kong for over nine months – for Max, six months of leave and three months on attachment to the Ministry of Civil Aviation in London. They sub-let 12A Branksome Towers and recommended its capable staff to Terence Sorby, a young high-flier in the administration who eventually became Director of Commerce and Industry. They found a home for their kitten, packed their trunks, and set sail on the *Ruys* on March 31, 1948. At that time, friends marked each other's departures on leave with great fanfare: Max and Audrey enjoyed a round of parties held in their honour. Once they boarded the *Ruys* several friends sent flowers, and others came out from Queen's Pier for a farewell beer. The Oxfords were to share a table with Jack and Diana Armstrong – a congenial couple who would become lasting friends. The ship sailed after dark, with Audrey writing:

*And so here we are at sea, and it is all quite the same as other times – the white paint, the bubbly sea around the ship, walking round the decks, sitting in the bar. But we find things to complain about – no soap, no bath mat, a poor shower, no hot sea water, expensive drinks, no deck chairs – only wicker ones, which make one very stiff. The food is good but in no way superlative. But the cabin is certainly most comfortable and roomy, with plenty of wardrobe space…not many British passengers, we have several Russians…*Journal, March 31, 1948.

China, by now, was in the throes of a devastating civil war as Chiang's Kuomintang battled Mao's Communists, and Audrey left Hong Kong with conflicting feelings about the future. She was pretty sure that the British Empire had reached its zenith (after all, India, the jewel in the crown, was already independent). She hoped above all for a peaceful transition to a new era – even if that meant allowing Communism to prevail in the East. 'We all say we do not want war, and yet today America is considering sending military aid to China in her fight against Communism. This is provoking, causing war. And the motive? Not consideration of the individual, but retention of the capitalist.' 'Am I a Communist?' Audrey asked herself, 'I don't think I have any affiliations to any "party" but peace is worth all sacrifice – even though it be that of the British Empire…The very idea of another war fills me with utter horror…'Audrey's private views were naïve, perhaps, but heartfelt. Plenty of others – better informed than she – did not know what Communist rule would mean for China or its neighbours, or whether the corrupt regime of Chiang Kai-shek was really a better alternative.

— • —

Audrey would keep these thoughts at the back of her mind, but for the rest of the year she would enjoy the embrace of family and friends back home. She filled the second volume of her journal during nine months of constant travel around South Africa and Britain, an extended mid-career sabbatical for Max. There were leisurely interludes but also frequent moves in order to fit in Max's business and all of the relatives and old friends that the expatriate couple wished to see.

One week out of Hong Kong, the *Ruys* docked in Singapore. Max and Audrey wound down from their gregarious Hong Kong life with a date night at the familiar Raffles Hotel, enjoying a dinner of oysters and chicken in the luxuriant garden's cool night air. 'It has been a long time since we had enjoyed an evening like this together,' wrote Audrey. She found that Singapore, like Hong Kong, had improved greatly in the two years since she had worked for the BMA right after the war. She imagined that it would be a very pleasant place to live – but chiefly a 'club life' since Singapore lacked the more northerly colony's wonderful beaches. After a few days, the *Ruys* sailed on to Penang and Mauritius, and on April 25 Max and Audrey disembarked at Durban, on South Africa's eastern coast. Destined for the Cape Town home of Max's elder sister, Margaret, they chose to take a cross-country train in order to see the African landscape – a 39-hour journey across the desolate, arid Karoo and the mountainous, green Cape. They were to spend two and a half months in Cape Town, staying with Margaret and her family.

It was nearly five years since Audrey had come into Max's life, but this was the first opportunity for the sisters-in-law to meet. Margaret, who had emigrated in her twenties to work as a schoolteacher, had found a husband in South Africa and stayed on. She had married Roy McColl, another British émigré, who owned a business selling flooring. The couple had settled down in the leafy suburbs of Cape Town and had two children, Gail who was five and Peter who was three years old. The children took to their new aunt and uncle immediately, and Peter ('a sensitive child') became particularly attached to Audrey. She had a more strained relationship with the forty-five year old Margaret, who plainly adored her brother but seemed unsure of her 'little sister-in-law'. Audrey was cautiously optimistic though, writing at the end of her stay:

> ...I think perhaps Margaret and I can be friends – despite the difference in age and background. I realise that of twelve years adult life, 6 years of mine have been coloured by war. And coloured a vivid, terrible red. Of 25 years adult life, Margaret has known only 6 war years – less than a quarter – and although her husband was fighting in it, our sense of what is important and real is not the same. To her 19 years of convention, I claim

only 6 – so it is not really surprising that our outlooks differ...
Journal, July 14, 1948.

It was a good holiday: Margaret and Roy were generous hosts, despite the stress of an extended stay and Max and Audrey's palpable unease with South Africa's segregated society. They took wonderful side trips from Cape Town, fishing at Hermanus on Walker Bay, visiting beautiful Cape vineyards, admiring Table Mountain, and touring with Margaret and Roy along the rugged coast and into the bush.

Settlers newly arrived from England told Max and Audrey that things were worse in the homeland than they had been three years earlier. So they must be grim indeed, thought Audrey. Spam, the unappealing canned meat, was now a treat and so were sausages. Max and Audrey duly despatched food parcels to family in Britain. Then on the day they sailed for England on the *Durban Castle*, they drove to rural Constantia, outside Cape Town, to pick up two dozen eggs. They would transport this delicate cargo on a fortnight's voyage via Madeira to Southampton – an extraordinary indicator of England's food shortages. Half of the eggs arrived with broken shells – but 'all can be saved' said Audrey. More distressingly, at the very gates of Southampton docks, a porter allowed some pieces of luggage to roll off the trolley, smashing a bottle of the precious whisky that Max and Audrey had nursed all the way from Hong Kong. To add insult to injury, they had just paid costly duty on the bottles. The golden liquid permeated their stash of cigarettes and cigars, and put up the price of the remaining four bottles considerably.

This minor setback aside, Max and Audrey were delighted to land in cool, green England and to be greeted without fanfare by Max's father, William – it was as though they had never left. Father's modest house at 65, St Luke's Road in Bournemouth would be their base for nearly five months, but Max and Audrey spent their treasured time in Britain in almost perpetual motion. By early November Audrey noted that she had made twenty-six moves since August 1 – and Max even more. There were relatives to tend to – Audrey's first priority was to visit her grandmother in Bovey Tracey, arriving on Abuelita's eighty-second birthday on August 6. Audrey was quite overcome with emotion at seeing the family matriarch – 'the same dear, sweet person – smelling of Pond's cold cream, her face as soft and fresh as a peach.' But the residential hotel where she was living on Dartmoor was finding it increasingly difficult to manage the aging Abuelita, and Audrey later helped her to move to a different hotel in Teignmouth on the Devon coast. Max's priority was his widowed father, and after waiting a few days for delivery of a car that Max had bought to ship back to Hong Kong, the pair drove down to meet Audrey in Devon. They took in many of the county's beauty spots on a week's tour before putting Father on a train from Exeter back to Bournemouth.

Max and Audrey motored on to Langport in Somerset, home of their brother-in-law, Buffy. Within months of Tottie's sudden death he had married Sybil, a willowy young horsewoman, who had helped to take care of Christopher when Buffy was so prematurely widowed. Audrey took to Sybil right away, and she became very attached to her nephew Christopher, now an enchanting, curly-headed three year old.

Max and Audrey's views on having children of their own were evolving. There is no hint in Audrey's early writing that she longed to be pregnant again, after miscarrying in India soon after their marriage. She seemed to accept that Max did not like children, and she resented outside pressure to have a family. Even though in South Africa she was troubled by a sense that she led a 'useless' life, she didn't take kindly to her sister-in-law's unsubtle messages about children. But on the *Durban Castle* she had a chance conversation with a Dr Williams who convinced her of the importance of having children if you could. She in turn persuaded the sceptical Max of this: 'If you have children, you do not die – that is what I now think. And if we should have a child, I must never let Max regret it, but it must be a source of pleasure to him – which I feel it really would be.'

Max and Audrey would be child-free for three more years, but perhaps not by choice. They were immensely happy in each other's company – Audrey was sad at even a short separation that followed a memorable trip through the Lake District and Scotland in October. Her philosophy was that compared to a happy home life, 'all else was somehow unimportant', and that joy was to be found in simple things rather than in monetary wealth. She found role models in Sir Hubert and Lady Young, Max's former Governor in Africa and his aviator wife, when visiting their home in Wiltshire in November. The Youngs had retired to a country life in the village of South Wraxhall, near Melksham, gardening and keeping chickens on the side. They gave Max and Audrey a warm welcome, and after a tea of buttered crumpets and fresh cake, Sir Hubert and Max settled down to a game of chess, like old times. Audrey found her way to the kitchen to offer her help with dinner: a housekeeper, aged 75, sat peeling vegetables while Lady Young did most of the real work, and their son Nicholas prepared a tray of drinks.

This informal domestic scene was in sharp contrast to the customs of Sir Horace and Lady Seymour, the former envoy to China and his expansive wife who had given the seal of approval to Max and Audrey's marriage. After leaving the Youngs and visiting the Seymours at Bratton House in Westbury, Audrey commented:

> *Where the Youngs make no pretence of their domestic duties, the Seymours say that unless their guests stay more than 2 days, they keep up a façade – and do not allow the sordid business of the kitchens to be seen! Their house is much more of a mansion than the Youngs', and they live altogether more grandly. But where Lady Young always holds her hands decorously together, and plays with her food until the guests are all quite finished, Lady S. will wave her fork at you to make her point, finish as she wishes, and sit comfortably with her [arms] folded across herself. They are both delightful people, but in rather different ways.* Journal, November 22, 1948.

That autumn Max spent three months on attachment to the Ministry of Civil Aviation, updating his skills with a training course at Bletchley Park, visiting Britain's modernizing airports (Heathrow had now replaced Croydon as London's gateway), giving talks and having briefings at the Ministry. In the course of Max's work, he and Audrey travelled around the Home Counties and spent several weeks in London. There was plenty of opportunity to catch up with old friends: including Audrey's great friend Dorothy and her husband Peter Neild, and their artist friend, Anthony Devas and his wife Nicolette. They were very taken with a new oil by Devas, painted while he was sick in bed with a temperature of 102: ' – wild flowers most delicately done – standing in a window with the breeze ruffling the thin white curtains. The white of the vase, window sill, and curtain so cleverly show the different textures – a piece of black velvet ribbon sets off the whole to perfection. He wants fifty guineas for it.' An expensive purchase, but one that the Oxfords couldn't resist.

There was one other important person to see before Max and Audrey's leave ended: Audrey's elder sister Joan was travelling home from her diplomatic posting in Ecuador on the *Queen Elizabeth*, but the ship was delayed by a dock strike in the United States. It would be heartbreaking to miss her, but happily the liner docked in Liverpool on December 4. Max and Audrey were there to meet Joan, 'looking lovely – smartly dressed, hair wavy and a good colour', said Audrey. They enjoyed a happy ten days taking Joan around the family in the West Country and the Home Counties, a gratifying culmination of a most successful leave:

> *It was wonderful to see all our friends and find that we had not grown apart from them. The country was beautiful – green, mauve and yellow when we arrived, and the bare trees the colour of prunes against pale blue skies when we left. Everybody has been most kind and friendly and we have felt very much at home. Sad though it is to leave those of whom one is so fond, it makes the return to Hong Kong easier, being confident that one will remain a part of this English life.* Journal, December 16, 1948.

So on December 17, Max and Audrey boarded the *Canton* at Southampton for the voyage back East. They took with them the car that Max had bought at the start of their leave – an Austin A40 nicknamed 'Stumpnose' – as well as good wishes and gifts from friends and family. The memories would need to last them until the next home leave in four years' time, but should not called up too often, thought Audrey, 'or else it will be difficult to grow accustomed once more to the life of HK.' The eastbound voyage took exactly a month, with ports of call in Port Said (for a dusty Christmas Day); Aden, at the bottom of the Suez Canal; Bombay (with the distinctive sights and smells of India); Colombo (admiring gems); Penang (for Indian curry with friends); and Singapore. Jack Hutchison and his wife Dora were among the passengers who enlivened the days at sea. The *Canton* sailed into Hong Kong harbour in the pink light of dawn on January 17, 1949. Terence Sorby, Max and Audrey's tenant, and Nan Wormal came on board to meet the returnees. Ah Wing had kept the flat in perfect condition and welcomed them home with 'an excellent goose' for lunch. An invitation from Sue Hopper, wife of the US Consul General, awaited them – plunging Max and Audrey right back into the social round.

CHAPTER TEN

A Small Strange Place
Hong Kong 1949-51

Dinner at Luna Park, 1950

'At least I feel we have lived...I shall always be glad to remember we have drunk champagne freely – eaten exquisite black caviar – a tight icy mass – off a Russian ship.'

Audrey writing in her journal after leaving
Hong Kong, April 12, 1951.

Max and Audrey came back to familiar friends and places, but the world around them was changing; 1949 would be a momentous year in China and Hong Kong. The endgame felt imminent in China's civil war, and there was now little doubt that Mao Zedong's People's Liberation Army (PLA) would defeat Chiang Kai-shek's crumbling Kuomintang régime. After a string of Communist victories in late 1948, in the New Year Mao published an audacious programme for peace. Chiang did not reject its terms outright, but accepted a ceasefire and made a show of removing himself from the picture, leaving Li Zongren as acting president. Around the time that Max and Audrey sailed back into Hong Kong harbour, the Nationalist government retreated south from Nanking to Canton, the mainland city closest to Hong Kong. The important northern port of Tientsin fell to the PLA in mid-January. Max and Audrey's American friends, 'Eich' and Hilda Eicholzer of Standard Oil, got the last plane out and passed through Hong Kong – telling Max and Audrey that they had 'no fears about the Communists'. Dick Frost, another friend in the oil business, stayed on in Tientsin and was completely cut off, according to his wife Pat who was in Hong Kong.

Once the Communists occupied Peking on January 31, they effectively controlled all of northern China, and if their peace terms were not accepted, would surely take the battle south to Shanghai, China's commercial hub, and Nanking, the erstwhile capital higher up the Yangtze River. Friends told Audrey that once China became Communist, Hong Kong would very rapidly follow, but those fears were premature. Most Hong Kong residents were resigned to the prospect of Communist neighbours across the border. Their immediate worry was a new influx of refugees that put enormous pressure on the colony.

As always, unrest in China brought certain benefits to the island on the edge of the vast country. Major Chinese companies from Shanghai moved their operations to Hong Kong, giving the colony a new industrial base that would serve it well in years to come. The European-owned trading houses, or 'hongs' – Jardine Matheson, Butterfield & Swire, J.D. Hutchison, Wheelock Marden, among others – moved their headquarters to Hong Kong, if they had not already done so. Just as British businessmen such as John Keswick of Jardine's, the wartime chief of SOE in China, had anticipated, Hong Kong became of greater strategic importance, both commercially and politically, with the advent of Communist rule.

Max's business, civil aviation, was also booming, experiencing new pressures along with rapid growth. While Max was on leave, DCA Moss had been much involved in a change in ownership at Cathay Pacific Airways (CPA). In late 1947, Moss had to tell its founders, Australian Syd de Kantzow and American Roy Farrell that, for national security reasons, the powers in Whitehall wanted the British-registered airline to have majority British ownership. At the same time, Jock Swire, chairman of John Swire & Sons (parent company of Butterfield & Swire), was thinking of taking the venerable shipping and trading firm 'into Air'. In June 1948 a consortium led by Swire acquired eighty percent of CPA, and later added Roy Farrell's ten percent when he decided to return to his native Texas. Max's friend Syd de Kantzow retained ten percent ownership and a seat on the Board, remaining with the company as operations manager. By 1949 Cathay's fleet had half a dozen DC-3s, and was poised to expand further with the backing of Swire and its valuable experience of catering to Chinese customers, the mainstay of the young airline's business.

There would be difficult days along the way. Not long after Max's return from leave, one of Cathay's DC-3s and its 23 crew and passengers were tragically lost in a fiery crash. Johnnie Paish, an experienced captain flying from Manila with a full load, inexplicably approached Kai Tak in foggy conditions, circled and crashed into the Taikoo (Braemar) reservoir in the hills on the Island side. Max and Moss had the distressing job of inspecting the scene of the crash, and 'watching the charred remains of human bodies being taken out of the wreck', recorded Audrey on February 25. The loss of nineteen passengers (all Chinese) and four crew members was headline news for days.

In a more positive development for Cathay, in May 1949 the airline benefited from a new agreement that divided the Asia region into two service areas. Cathay Pacific secured valuable routes from Hong Kong to Southeast Asia, and Hong Kong Airways (a subsidiary of BOAC at the time) was given more risky routes to cities in China. Meanwhile, intercontinental air travel surged ahead. Max noted in March that Qantas Empire Airways made its first flight from Sydney to Hong Kong with a DC-4. BOAC, the British national carrier, increased its service from London to Hong Kong, and PanAm stepped up flights from the US. Business entertaining became an important part of Max and Audrey's life, with Audrey commenting in April on the success of a party they hosted for Chinese and Western 'air interests'. FY Ho of CNAC delighted Audrey by explaining the symbolism of a Chinese scroll that had been a wedding gift. In December 1948, Ho's airline, CNAC, had relocated its headquarters from Shanghai to Hong Kong and invested in maintenance and warehouse facilities at Kai Tak. The Nationalist Chinese airline was Kai Tak's largest customer, but its presence would soon become a bone of contention with the British authorities.

Whether entertaining for business or pleasure, Audrey knew she was privileged to enjoy the good life in Hong Kong, relatively sheltered from the turmoil in China. As refugees flooded into the colony, one incident brought home to Audrey the contrast between her comfortable expatriate life and the sufferings on her doorstep:

Again a beautiful day. Decide to wash the carpet. It is now out on the coal shed roof – Ah Wing is scrubbing it...This marvellous dry cool weather is most invigorating. The sky is cloudless – blue, shading almost to pink over the hills – the water in the harbour an intense blue and the trees and bushes change colour as they are ruffled by the wind. The silver of the underpart of the leaves flashing as the wind turns them.

We know that there is a war in China – yet how remote and even unsympathetic are we to the sufferings of those caught up in it. We are inclined to dismiss the whole thing from our minds

A garden party at Government House

as being inevitable in such a country. But this afternoon I was forcibly made aware of the effects of this war. I heard a scratch at the front door – this is the way the young flower man often announces himself – so I went to answer it. There stood a woman – a plain, unpretentious woman – her clothes were clean but hardy. She had a zip canvas-covered holdall at her feet and said she had underclothes for sale. I politely said I did not need anything and recommended her to try somewhere else. She just stood there – without saying a word – and then, tragically turned her head to hide the tears that welled from her eyes. She did not sob, just wept. Tears of exhaustion – tears of utter despair. I brought her in. She has 7 children and with her family has come down from Shanghai. There they had a shop, and had built up through their industry a good business. All their sav-

ings appear to have been put into gold dollars – these they were forced to change into the hopeless Chinese national currency. And now she is taking this pathetic bundle of drawn work from door to door...I still feel sick with shame that I did not give her rice or food. I only took a cloth in exchange for $13. I did not help her at all – and there was so much I could have done. Given her more than she asked or food. Poor woman. And she is one of so many. Journal, May 10, 1950.

So many indeed: the wave of refugees from Communism drove the colony's population up to 2.5 million by 1950, over four times its size at the end of the war.

On returning from long leave, Audrey noticed other changes since the early postwar years: new buildings, new faces, and a new uncertainty about social norms. Hating to make an issue out of 'the dress question' but wanting her dinner guests to be comfortable on a hot and humid night in May 1949, she alerted the ladies not to wear long frocks: 'When I first came to Hong Kong we used to change [into long dress and black tie] – women always – men if they had dinner jackets. Now it is sometimes one thing and sometimes another.'

Government House garden parties were still major fixtures on the calendar, and invariably required a new dress. Every time Audrey went to some trouble to put together a striking outfit, with matching shoes and handbag, and was pleased to be complimented by the Governor on one occasion. But: 'As Max says, one is annoyed if not on the list, and yet one has not the slightest desire to attend...' The parties were usually uncomfortable affairs. For the King's Birthday garden party in June 1949, guests walked around in their hundreds in the rain, waiting to go in and be received by a line of dignitaries, including AV Alexander, the visiting UK Defence Minister. Everyone congratulated Arthur Morse, the well-respected chairman of HSBC, on being knighted that day in the King's Birthday honours. For Audrey, the only pleasure was a stroll in Government House's extensive gardens because it was hot and stuffy indoors, and the rations were meagre: 'one cup of tea and one miserable sandwich'.

It was more fun to visit government friends who were stationed in outlying areas. Eddie Teesdale was District Officer for Yuen Long, living with his wife Joy near Castle Peak in his New Territories domain. Their official residence was a large bungalow called 'Dunrose', which had a lovely garden and tennis court. Max and Audrey enjoyed putting their car onto the cross-harbour ferry and driving out to the rural Territories for barbecue lunches and casual games of tennis.

Back at Branksome Towers, Audrey could see the hills of the New Territories – a magical sight on a clear, spring evening:

> *The cicadas thrumming, the sky a deep sapphire blue, with these myriads of lights shining across and on the harbour. The blue slowly deepens until it is quite dark and the lights are even clearer. In these days of neon lighting they are white, green, red, blue, and still the gold of the ordinary domestic light…From the dining room window I can see the hills of the Territories – they divide the window almost in half – the dark sky above and the darker hills outlined below.* Journal, May 22, 1949.

Sights like this made up for gloomier days of dripping humidity and stultifying company. Though Audrey had many good friends, including other colonial service wives, social gatherings could be a bore. On the positive side, some of her women friends went back to Chungking days: Beth Thompson was a favourite. Audrey had attended the simple ceremony when Beth married Pat Sedgwick in the wartime capital. Pat was at the time an attaché at the British Embassy and back in Hong Kong was a senior administrator in the Secretariat. The Sedgwicks, like the Teesdales, had an official residence, and the couples exchanged hospitality often, once in the company of Noel Croucher, veteran Chairman of the Hong Kong Stock Exchange:

> *We dine with Beth and Pat in their vast mansion. It is a nice house and they have extensive "grounds". V. glad to think Beth has such a nice place to live in. Noel Croucher the other guest – he talks incessantly – all little reminiscences of the past, which we find quite amusing and interesting…He is entertaining to watch – he makes some amusing statement and then smiles a bland smile, slightly quizzical – as if he feels you must be a little amazed by the information. One wonders whether he and Si-*

A day out at 'Dunrose', New Territories home of Joy and Eddie Teesdale

monne [his estranged wife], the most talkative of women, talked at the same time, all the time, when they were together. I think perhaps he was silent before her barrage and only talks when alone. Journal, September 13, 1950.

It was the all-government gatherings that Audrey found stifling. One such occasion was a supper party thrown by Terence Sorby, their former tenant and a senior official, on his birthday in January 1950. There were 26 guests, *all* government servants, said Audrey. 'Feel completely overwhelmed by so many – it makes me feel like a school girl somehow, amongst our fellow workers.' On another occasion, she reflected ironically on *why* she found government servants dreary:

[I] believe it is (a) they all know what the other earns and all feel they are poor in comparison with civil firms, (b) they continually play up this poverty in order that they may not be frowned upon as (i) social climbing or (ii) being involved in graft. All of which tends to make them humbly dreary – "Yes, we were lucky, we got it cheap from the Custodian, otherwise of course we could not have afforded it…" "We would like to play golf, but, of course, cannot possibly afford it." "Yes, I should like one, but it will have to wait until next month." "He was Acting – for a few months – so we were able to buy it – otherwise, of course…" "Oh no, we could not possibly keep up with them. Terribly wealthy, aren't they?" They are somehow all afraid of having much, or spending much – presumably in case others wonder where the money comes from! It is rather a cramping attitude. Journal, June 14, 1950.

She and Max had more catholic tastes in the company they kept. Many of their closest friends were not British at all, but Chinese, Eurasian, Australian or American. And rather than being colonial servants, many of them were in the private sector or were foreign diplomats and journalists. 'It is strange', Audrey commented soon after returning from leave, 'how many of our closest friends are Americans'. Max and Audrey revelled in informal weekends at the cosy Shouson Hill home of George and Sue Hopper, the US Consul General and his wife. On one occasion in May 1949, the American journalist Stewart Alsop (brother of Joe Alsop, who Max knew in Chungking) and his English wife joined the party for Sunday lunch. Alsop and Max traded stories of forced landings in dangerous spots: Max's story of coming down in the African jungle was capped by Alsop's tale of parachuting into France during the war, jumping too soon and losing touch with his companions. Audrey would miss the gracious and friendly Sue and her husband when they were recalled to Washington in September 1949.

Max and Audrey's liking for Americans perhaps explained their joining of the American Club – as associate members since full membership was open only to US citizens at that time. On returning from long leave they also became members of a quintessentially British institution, the Ladies' Recreation Club, founded in 1883 by intrepid women who had lobbied the colonial government for a place to take whole-some exercise. The club was conveniently situated just below Brank-some Towers, and offered plentiful tennis courts, a wide terrace to meet friends for tea or cocktails – and, from 1949, a pool! Audrey was there to see it unveiled:

> *...In the pouring rain we go to the LRC for the opening of the swimming pool. So English! Mackintoshes, umbrellas, drips of rain, speeches which cannot be heard – tea and buns.* Journal, April 30, 1949.

Despite the inauspicious opening of the LRC's pool, the clubs were a haven for colonial wives who had long hours to fill while their hus-bands were at work, and the plentiful live-in help kept households running smoothly. Audrey spent many afternoons on the LRC's ten-nis courts, playing both with other women, and at weekends in mixed doubles games with Max.

In contrast to the genteel Englishness of the LRC, in July 1949 Max and Audrey were invited to the opening of the new press club at 15, Kotewall Road. A Mecca for foreign journalists, the Foreign Correspon-dents' Club had been founded in Chungking in 1943, and after spells in Nanking and Shanghai, left China for Hong Kong in 1949, ahead of the Communists. Max and Audrey's Chungking friend Nina Moosa, wife of AP correspondent Spencer Moosa – who was away that week reporting from Canton – met them at the opening party:

> *A party that was different – rather what we expected – hard-drinking correspondents – many glamorous-looking women. An interesting collection of people. The man who was desperately looking for his copy of "The Observer" – his evening ruined by its loss.* Journal, July 16, 1949.

Nina and Spencer Moosa, who had told the world about Max and Audrey's marriage in an AP press release, were part of the network of friendships formed in the war years – a network that was especially strong. A remarkable number of the Christmas Day escape group and of the Chungking crowd were drawn back to Hong Kong. Of course this

Kai Tak airport from the hills of Kowloon, 1950

was where many had connections, expertise, businesses or government jobs, and in some cases homes to salvage. And despite everything that they had endured as survivors of the war in Asia, it was on this familiar terrain that they could take advantage of new opportunities. In addition to the inner circle of friends, many more names from the past crop up regularly in Audrey's guest books and journals. For example, Mike Kendall, Colin McEwan and Monia Talan, the trio of SOE agents who escorted the escape party, were all still in the region. Kendall, the smart Canadian who was central to the organization of the escape, was based in Manila and Hong Kong, working for the Philippines airline PAL, and often seeing Max on business. He and his wife Betty frequently dined with Max and Audrey. Colin McEwan returned to Hong Kong, bringing his wife Elizabeth, and became the colony's director of physical education. The White Russian Monia Talan developed various business interests with his second wife, Tatiana, including a store called Paquerettes where Max and Audrey sometimes shopped. Harry Owen-

Hughes, who attended the Branksome Towers tea party for the Chans, could imagine no other home than his native Hong Kong, though his wife and children spent much of their time in England. SK Yee (Yee Shiu Kee), Chan Chak's erstwhile second-in-command, was another important figure in postwar Hong Kong: he took over a bank in 1947, re-establishing it as the Chinese United Bank, and he and his wife Hannah eventually became generous philanthropists.

— • —

In late April 1949 core members of the Christmas Day escape crew came together for a bittersweet occasion – a farewell dinner for David MacDougall, hosted by Dick and Esther Lee. Admiral Chan came down especially from Canton. Henry Hsu was there, as were Max and Audrey, Hector Chauvin (a wartime intelligence officer who met the escape group in Huizhou) and Ronnie Holmes (who had served with the BAAG in China). Mac, the visionary Colonial Secretary who was widely credited with Hong Kong's rapid recovery after the war, had abruptly resigned his position in February, taking early retirement at the unusually young age of 44. Outwardly, Mac was positive about his departure, as Audrey learned at a large Hong Kong Club cocktail party on March 11: 'MacDougall is delighted at the prospect of an early retirement – he is to marry Inez Thompson when he leaves.' The next day 'MacDougall's resignation – retirement rather – was made public'. Audrey was not alone in being confused about the situation. MacDougall was not yet divorced from his first wife Catherine, though the couple had long been separated. But after Inez joined Mac in Hong Kong in 1947, it seemed that the colonial establishment could not tolerate a situation where the official who deputized for the Governor in his absence had a partner to whom he was not married.

That at least was one story – but Mac's many supporters felt that, in the nervous climate of 1949, the cautious Governor Grantham and his associates had seized on a pretext to push the reformer out. The editor of the *South China Morning Post* wrote privately to Mac expressing dismay that he had been railroaded out of the colony, 'one of the most tragic things that has ever happened'. More publicly, the Chinese press pleaded with the government to keep the popular MacDougall, and hundreds signed a petition.

But the die was cast, and Mac was, after all, looking forward to an escape from public life and to trying his hand at farming in his native Scotland. Mac and Inez were feted with a round of parties, including a small dinner at Max and Audrey's on April 23, before their ship sailed on May 14. 'I could hardly sleep for worrying about them the other night, when they said they had 11 days before they sailed – and in those ghastly 11 days – 11 luncheons, 11 cocktail parties and 11 dinners!' Audrey wrote on May 3. She and Max were angry about gossip – typical of Hong Kong society, sadly – that continued to swirl around MacDougall's departure. After a dinner with Chinese friends on May 25, Audrey asked herself: 'Are all small places like this? It appears so strange. HK is the most beautiful of places – and yet some such ugly thoughts and minds are bred here.'

Of course life wasn't all parties and gossip. It had been four years since the Japanese had surrendered, but in East Asia the fighting had never really stopped, and great power politics had a way of inserting themselves into everyday life. A few nights before Max and Audrey's dinner for Mac and Inez, they had just dropped off to sleep when they were rudely awakened by a phone call from the King's Messenger. The panicked courier told Max that HMS *Amethyst*, a navy frigate, had been sunk on the Yangtze between Shanghai and Nanking, and it was imperative for the messenger to get an RAF plane to Nanking in the morning – his last chance to reach the British Embassy with important papers before the city fell to the Communists, he argued. The *Amethyst* had not actually sunk but had come under heavy fire and run aground, Audrey read in the morning paper on April 21. Her immediate reaction was: 'Even though she [the *Amethyst*] had been cleared by the Nationalists, it does on the surface seem folly to allow a British naval craft to travel up the Yangtze (it happened between Shanghai and Nanking) when it was generally known the Communists were to start their offensive on the Yangtze. Just asking for trouble.' How right she was.

The *Amethyst* incident began just as yet another Communist ultimatum to the Kuomintang to accept a peace agreement was set to expire. In the absence of a settlement, the PLA was poised to cross the Yangtze and take the Nationalist strongholds of Shanghai and Nanking. The British knew that April 21 was the possible zero hour for the Communist advance, but had cleared their ships' movements only with the Nationalists and not with the PLA. Despite the volatile situation, Royal Navy Vice-Admiral Alexander Madden despatched the frigate *Amethyst* 200 miles upriver from Shanghai to relieve *HMS Consort*, a destroyer that had been supplying and guarding the British Embassy in Nanking. As the *Amethyst* entered a stretch of the river known to be a danger zone, PLA artillery opened fire on the neutral vessel, apparently without warning. She was shelled repeatedly, went aground on a mud bank and became a sitting duck. The ship's captain was mortally wounded, and in total 22 men were killed and over 30 wounded. The *Consort*, which sailed to her rescue, was herself attacked with a further loss of life, and two other British ships that made later rescue attempts met a similar fate.

Lt. Commander John Kerans boarded the captain-less frigate on April 22 and assumed command. In negotiations with the PLA, he refused to sign a confession of 'criminally invading Chinese territorial waters', and the ship and crew were held hostage for 100 days before Kerans made a dash downriver at dead of night on July 30. Running a gauntlet of PLA guns, the scarred ship reached the mouth of the Yangtze early on the 31st, and steamed full speed ahead for Hong Kong. Admiral Madden's decision to send the *Amethyst* into a battle zone may have led to a tense and humiliating episode for the British, but Hong Kong gave the survivors a hero's welcome:

> *This is a thrilling day. The Amethyst arrives in HK – and such a welcome. Although it has been pouring with rain since yesterday, this does not damp the ardour with which she is greeted. Through the gloom planes fly over the harbour, to warn us of her arrival. Then this low-lying grey wraith-like ship steams slowly through the grey waters, followed by countless tugs. Every hooter in the harbour goes, fire-crackers are let off, a fire tender sends streams of water up in to the air – as if there were not enough water already – it is very moving and thrilling – the gallant ship back at last after suffering many casualties and being incarcerated amongst the Communists on the Yangtze for so many weeks.* Journal, August 3, 1949.

Sailors were royally entertained in clubs and homes around the colony, telling tales of their ordeal and voicing nothing but praise for the resolute Commander Kerans. One detail struck Audrey: the crew had used anything that came to hand – duffel coats, hammocks – to stuff the shell holes in the sides of their damaged vessel, only to find that at night enterprising Chinese would row out to the ship and steal the materials for their own use.

That spring, the Kuomintang had still not accepted Mao's peace terms, and Shanghai came under Communist control in May after bitter fighting. Airlines flew desperate evacuees to Hong Kong, until Shanghai airport was forced to close on May 21, a date Max noted in his diary. John Gillibrand, son of Patrick Gillibrand, BOAC's operations man in Shanghai, was a small boy living with his family in the city's French quarter. He recalled that a Chinese gang invaded their house, threatening to kill him and rape his mother. The gang leader changed his tune when he realised who the family were, and demanded a ticket out of town – which he did not get, instead being arrested and executed. Other Chinese turned up at the airport with bars of gold, slicing off just the right amount to pay for a seat on a plane.

— • —

Other events that summer of 1949 brought the troubles in China closer to home for Max and Audrey. In the space of less than three months, both Admiral Chan and his wife died most unexpectedly. Max and Audrey learnt in June the distressing news that Lady Chan had died in childbirth. On August 22 the widowed Admiral was in Hong Kong, visiting some of his children who were being educated in the colony. Max attended a lunch at the Nathan Hotel with Chan, Henry and Amy Hsu, Raymond Cheung and, Max noted in his diary, 'Misses C.C., Duncan and Donald'.

The next morning Max waved goodbye to Chan and Hsu at Kai Tak as they took off for Canton. Their flight had been delayed by fog, and while he waited Chan phoned his eldest daughter Paula from Max's office. She remembered the call clearly since it was the last time she heard her father's voice: a week later the indomitable one-legged hero of the Christmas Day escape was dead at only fifty-five. He was taken ill in the night after hosting a seafood dinner, and though ulcers and depression were blamed there was speculation that he was poisoned, possibly by agents of Chiang who suspected that the former mayor of

Canton was about to defect to the Communists. On September 17 Max and Audrey attended a Hong Kong memorial service for Chan: among the ten orphan children were his only sons, twins Donald and Duncan, the two boys who had been at Max's last lunch with his old friend. 'We are much saddened by the appearance of the orphans – dressed in black and white and looking overcome with grief', wrote Audrey in her journal. The British had lost a trusty ally.

Within weeks there was more disturbing news from Canton. On September 9 Max and Audrey read a story of a 'shooting drama' involving Maya Redevitch, the Polish beauty who had been Max's captivating Chungking girlfriend before Audrey arrived on the scene. In 1945 she had married Willard Freeman, an American business associate of General Claire Chennault and Whiting Willauer, founders of the American-Chinese airline, CAT. The couple had recently settled in Canton in a house owned by Willauer. A celebration of the Freemans' wedding anniversary and Maya's thirty-third birthday on September 8 went horribly wrong. Maya's account was that she had gone to bed, leaving her husband and two friends, Leonard Clark and Harold Harris, to continue a night of carousing. She awoke next morning to discover three bloodied bodies: Harris was dead from gunshot wounds, and her husband and Clark were critically wounded. They were rushed to Canton's dilapidated emergency hospital, where (the press reported) both Freeman and Clark asked to see Maya.

It seemed that the three men, all of them the worse for wear, had got into a free-for-all fight when Freeman, in a fit of jealousy, accused Clark of being in love with his pretty blond wife. Shots were fired. Maya was at her husband's bedside when he died of his wounds a few days later. 'We had one hell of a drunken party', admitted the only survivor Leonard Clark in October, when he was charged with manslaughter in the deaths of both his host and Harold Harris, a Shanghai-born Englishman who worked for Freeman. Both the American and Asian press had a field day with the shocking story. The accused Clark was a well-known explorer who had just returned from western China, where he claimed to have discovered a mountain peak taller than Mount Everest. His account of finding 'the highest mountain in the world' appeared in the October 3 issue of LIFE magazine. To add to his allure, Clark had a dashing wartime past as a senior officer in the OSS in China. But, as the *Miami News* pointed out on October 5, though Clark was the sole suspect in a major crime, the Nationalist Chinese court was 'supported by a wavering government that may flee for its own life any time as Communist forces push ever closer to Canton'. And indeed the case was never brought to trial. Clark left China a free man, and went on to explore other remote regions of the world, writing a number of travel books before his death in 1957 at the age of 49.

The distraught Maya packed up in China, a country she had made her home since the 1930s, and in December sailed for America, where her parents-in-law lived. Max and Audrey saw her off from Hong Kong on the *President Wilson*. They had seen a good bit of Maya during her transit through the colony, but refrained from asking what in fact did happen on the night of the shooting. Audrey found Max's old flame to be interesting and intelligent, but clearly disapproved of her strong perfume (which lingered in the room for a full two hours after her departure!) – and quite possibly of her risqué lifestyle. Max and Audrey were left with a lasting reminder of the flamboyant Pole – her gramophone and collection of records – and they gave her a 'gorgeous red handbag' from the Talans' store, Paquerettes.

— • —

Maya and her dramas were perhaps a welcome distraction that autumn. For Max was involved in one of the trickiest issues of his career.

Cramped Kai Tak was stretched to the limit during 1949 as every available plane shuttled diplomats, missionaries, business people and Chinese refugees out of the cities that were falling like dominoes to the Communists. Max noted in his diary that 28,027 passengers went through Kai Tak in April, and in August the figure was over 41,000 – a new record. The *Hong Kong Sunday Herald* reported that more than 3,000 planes took off and landed in August, making Kai Tak the third busiest international airport in the world. And at that point Max was managing with just a single runway (number 13/31), since the other one was being reinforced to accommodate larger aircraft, such as the new PanAm Constellation.

CNAC, the flagship airline of the Nationalist government, carried more passengers to and from Hong Kong than anyone else. Max's longtime friend, the American executive WL Bond, who was the driving

Kai Tak passenger terminal, opened in 1947

Disputed planes grounded at Kai Tak, 1950

force behind CNAC, pointed out that it had done so for more than a decade. By early 1949 the airline had moved its headquarters from Shanghai to Hong Kong, ahead of the Communist advance. On the basis of assurances from DCA Albert Moss, CNAC invested heavily in a full-scale base at Kai Tak, building maintenance workshops and hangars. Moss consulted the Governor before laying out the welcome mat, but apparently the Hong Kong authorities didn't consult Whitehall – or the RAF, who shared Kai Tak with civil aviation. After the fall of Shanghai in May, the security implications of giving refuge to a Nationalist airline – hence making Hong Kong a potential target for the Communists – hit home.

Internal Whitehall memos talked of 'incompetence' in the colony's initial handling of the question. Max and Audrey heard gossip of 'Moss's folly'. Before Whitehall forced the issue, the Governor decided that CNAC must leave, and in June Moss had to write to his biggest customer giving notice to vacate its new installations. Bond was enraged at the reversal of fortune, which he felt was tantamount to a death sentence for his beloved airline. The Chinese Ambassador in London lodged a complaint with the Foreign Secretary, but Whitehall stood firm. To save face, the Chinese were told that CNAC's space was urgently needed by the RAF.

CNAC was not going to give up its investment willingly, and fought the eviction in court. Finally the Hong Kong government proclaimed a state of emergency, and, Max noted on August 16, sent bailiffs to requisition the airline's maintenance base. In response, CNAC suspended all of its flights. Bond and Moss eventually reached a compromise. CNAC would conduct a limited service from Kai Tak, using some of the airport's warehouse space and doing maintenance nearby. But the cordial relations between the DCA, Bond and the local CNAC management must have been soured. The line that the RAF required extra space for 'reinforcements which are vital for the defence of Hong Kong in the event of an emergency' had some validity: with the tense situation in China, the British had decided to reinforce the Hong Kong garrison – they wanted to avoid a repeat of the humiliating invasion of 1941. Royal Navy ships steamed into the colony transporting thousands of additional troops. The aircraft carrier *Ocean* brought a full deck of RAF Spitfires – destined for that precious space at Kai Tak. Hong Kong's own auxiliary defence force was expanded, and Max was appointed the first commander of its air arm. But space for the Spitfires was not the only issue: once-secret files in the archives show that the British government was every bit as concerned about the politics of housing a Nationalist airline as it was about finding space for the RAF.

At this critical juncture, Max stepped into the middle of what was turning into a full-scale international incident. 'Moe' Moss, the long-serving director, left the colony on September 15 for six months' leave in Tasmania, and Max became acting Director of Civil Aviation. Presuming that Moss might retire and not return, the twenty-one aviation companies in Hong Kong threw him a farewell cocktail party, and toasted his contribution to the huge growth in aviation since his arrival in 1930. Calling Kai Tak 'the worst aerodrome in the world', Moss paid tribute to his 'small but efficient' staff for turning it into one of the most important. He asked his hosts to extend the same courtesy and kindness to Max that they had shown him. Max was already well established, but he would need all the help he could get in the difficult months to come.

On October 1, Mao Zedong declared victory in China's civil war, proclaiming the People's Republic of China (PRC) in Peking. Some Chiang loyalists kept up a brave face: SK Yee, now a prominent Hong Kong banker, thought the Nationalists would still make a strong stand. On October 10, the anniversary of the founding of the Republic of China (ROC) in 1911, TW Kwok, the Harvard and Cambridge-educated Nationalist Commissioner in Hong Kong, threw his customary party. It was a very crowded affair, said Audrey, but Communist flags were already flying from some houses on the road leading to the Kwoks', and she had the impression that 'we were drinking the champagne of a dying era with the red threat right on our doorstep'. Kai Tak was busy with passengers fleeing Canton, the Nationalists' latest capital, until its airfield closed on October 13. Remnants of Chiang's government flew to Chungking, and then on to Chengdu, before the final retreat of the ROC to Formosa (Taiwan).

Foreign governments debated if and when to recognize the PRC. Britain, for instance, had withdrawn its Ambassador to China but still had some diplomats in the country, including Audrey's old boss, Jack Hutchison. Most Chinese understood that the Nationalists were a spent

Planes, junks and ferries traffic Hong Kong harbour, 1950

force. In Hong Kong, Col. CY Liu, Managing Director of CNAC, and Col. CL Chen, his counterpart at the other Nationalist-owned airline, the Central Air Transport Corporation (CATC), decided it was time to side with the winning team. On November 9, Liu and Chen, along with nine other Chinese pilots, took off from Kai Tak in planes belonging to CNAC and CATC, cleared for destinations in Nationalist territory. Once out of Hong Kong air traffic control, the fleet of eleven planes changed course and landed in Communist China. The audacious defection took the American partners in CNAC by surprise. Bond and his deputy, Ernie Allison, immediately sent Max a note: 'Hell's A Poppin', may we see you?' The Americans maintained that the aircraft would return soon for maintenance, but of course the planes and their pilots (with one exception) were gone for good. Awkwardly, seventy-one CNAC and CATC-owned planes were still on the ground at Kai Tak.

These 71 civil aircraft, mainly Convairs and DC-4s, became the subject of an international political and legal drama lasting for years. The acting Director of Civil Aviation would be at the centre of it. If the planes fell into the hands of the Communists, Mao could easily take the island of Formosa, the last redoubt of the Nationalists. This at least was an argument made by Whiting Willauer, American partner of General Chennault in Civil Air Transport (CAT), another airline closely iden-tified with the Nationalist cause in China, in a meeting with Chiang Kai-shek in Taipei on November 11. So Willauer offered CAT's services in preventing the aircraft from being seized by the Communists. The Nationalist Civil Aeronautics Administration defensively suspended the planes' registration certificates. On November 16, Max wrote to the two airlines to forbid the de-registered aircraft from flying, and so they remained grounded at Kai Tak. Max was bombarded by questions from reporters from the international and local press. Parliamentary ques-tions were asked in London. The acting DCA became a frequent visitor to Government House for meetings with Governor Grantham, John Nicoll (the Colonial Secretary), and other top officials. Willauer and Nationalist officials called on Max at home, drenched with rain, late in the evening of November 14. They held out the promise of a better Sino-British air agreement, one that would benefit UK airlines flying into the remnants of Nationalist territory. In the same context, Max met George Yeh, the Kuomintang's Foreign Minister, on November 17.

Meanwhile, the Americans Chennault and Willauer engineered the purchase of the Nationalists' interest in CNAC and CATC for their own company, CAT. PanAm sold its twenty percent interest in CNAC to the Nationalists, and that too became part of the deal with CAT. The US gov-ernment quietly supported CAT, since the last thing they wanted was for the planes to go to the PRC. With unusual speed, the US Civil Aeronau-tics Administration (CAA) granted American registration of the stateless planes, and on December 18 Chennault and Willauer announced their purchase. Now all they had to do was take possession of their assets.

That proved to be easier said than done. The Communists argued that the Nationalists had had no right to sell the planes to the Ameri-cans, since the planes belonged to China's government and the PRC had been the government since October 1. The PRC had also registered the planes, so that there were now duelling registrations and owner-ship claims. Both factions took out injunctions to prevent possession by their opponents. As early as December 1, Sir Oliver Franks, Brit-ish Ambassador to Washington, was made aware of the US position.

He reported to the Foreign Office that the State Department, while acknowledging that any legal process could not be influenced, asked whether the Governor could take any extraordinary measure to prevent the planes from falling into the hands of the Communists. But the British – and especially the Governor of Hong Kong, living on China's border – were much more reluctant than the Americans to antagonize the new Communist government. Most of the airline employees were pro-Communist and pretty soon they were guarding the planes at Kai Tak, with the tacit agreement of the Hong Kong authorities.

The situation was tense. Max and Audrey tried to enjoy their traditional Christmas rituals, hosting a party with champagne and charades on Christmas Eve, and seeing Stanley Smith and May Wong to drink eggnogs on Boxing Day. But, Audrey remarked on December 29:

> M[ax] is having a busy time. HK has become an important place in world affairs – and it all swings on the aviation axis – Whiting Willauer and Chennault with their "purchase" of CNAC and CATC planes have made everything most complicated. Journal, December 29, 1949.

Chennault and Willauer called in heavyweight legal advisers: General William 'Wild Bill' Donovan, the founder of America's wartime OSS, and his law partner Richard Heppner, former head of OSS in China. They arrived in Hong Kong on January 3, 1950. Donovan called on Governor Grantham on January 4 to demand the handover of the planes, 'thumping the table, metaphorically if not physically', Grantham recalled in his memoir. Grantham was unmoved by Donovan's threats, and insisted that he could not intervene since the issue of ownership was before the courts. The same day, Max had the awkward task of turning away representatives of the US CAA who arrived at Kai Tak to inspect the grounded planes. Without a CAA certificate of airworthiness, CAT would not be allowed to fly the planes. But Max, with the backing of Hong Kong's Attorney General, denied access for the same reason that the Governor gave – the question of ownership was before the courts. He also declined to withdraw airfield passes from the Communist airline employees who were guarding the planes.

In his suite at the Gloucester Hotel, Donovan and his colleagues held a press conference for American reporters – one that CAT deemed so significant that the proceedings were published verbatim in the airline's newsletter. Max kept a copy: Donovan and Willauer were clearly incensed at what they perceived as "noncooperation" from Hong Kong officials. They argued that most of the planes had been supplied to the Chinese at little cost under the wartime lend-lease arrangements, and really belonged to the people of the United States. Correspondent Tillman Durdin's story in the *New York Times* reported the DCA's refusal to permit a CAA inspection, and ended up saying:

> *Mr. Willauer said the planes were rapidly deteriorating in value and were being subjected to sabotage by pro-Communist airline employees who had access to them and whom Mr. Oxford had declined to deny the right to enter the airfield.*

No wonder that Audrey wrote in her journal:

> *M spends much time with the AG [Attorney General Griffin] and then at 5.30 goes to GH [Government House] for further conferences, and does not get home till 8.0pm. Things are both difficult and serious. All my fears that HK was the pivot of things seem confirmed. Will we stand up against the Americans? They blackmail with their dollars.* Journal, January 4, 1950.

Significantly, at midnight the very next day, the British government accorded diplomatic recognition to the PRC – recognition that the US, of course, would not grant for decades. Audrey wrote on January 6:

> *We expect this, the Twelfth Night, to be the Day of Recognition. Max said on the phone that the other side – presumably the Communists – are now after him. The Nationalist lawyers have already threatened him with contempt of Court for not withdrawing the passes – What a situation! He at least has the backing of our Legal Dept and has become a pawn in a highly diplomatic game – USA versus Great Britain. What will be*

the outcome – only hope we remain firm and do not bow to the blustering bullies. Journal, January 6, 1950.

Max and Audrey had an unexpected encounter with two of the 'blustering bullies' on Sunday January 8, their wedding anniversary. James Warburton, Max's former boss in Chungking, who was now air attaché in Formosa, spent the day with the Oxfords. On the way to a picnic at Big Wave Bay, Warburton, his wife Toni, and Max and Audrey all stopped at the Turtle Cove home of Erik Watts of Hong Kong Airways – yet another old Chungking hand. Willauer and Donovan were visiting, and 'Wild Bill' Donovan studiously avoided the DCA, sitting out in the corridor talking instead to his host. 'He looks a respectable, peaceful man, which he obviously is not', remarked Audrey.

Donovan and Willauer returned to the US empty-handed, and prepared for a long fight. On February 23, Hong Kong's Chief Justice, Sir Leslie Gibson, ruled that the grounded planes belonged to the PRC, but as Audrey noted a few days later, the situation remained complicated and difficult. The US Secretary of State Dean Acheson vigorously protested against the court ruling, and challenged the decision on legal grounds. CAT appealed. Max and his colleagues allowed a shipment of spare parts to leave for the mainland, but adopted stalling tactics to keep the aircraft on the ground. The *Economist* magazine summed up the British dilemma:

> ...*The trouble from the British point of view is that, if the aircraft are kept grounded, the Chinese Communists will attribute it not to any requirements of legal procedure, but entirely to American political pressure, and may work up an anti-British propaganda campaign over it. On the other hand, if nothing is done to meet the American protest, some circles in America may take up the cry that Britain is appeasing Communist China even to the extent of surrendering American property in order to avert an attack on Hong Kong.*
>
> *This unpleasant incident is typical of the very delicate situation which now exists in the China Seas in consequence of the difference between British and American policies towards China...*
> *It is an extraordinary situation, and there is no end to it in sight.*

*Max's HQ at Statue Square and
his Austin A40, 'Stumpnose'*

*The good life: sailing to Macau on
the yacht 'Cathay', 1950*

Max was engaged with correspondence and high-level meetings almost daily, but the situation had escalated way above his pay grade. To underline their displeasure, on April 2 Nationalist agents sneaked into Kai Tak and planted bombs which damaged seven of the aircraft. Peking blamed the government of Hong Kong for not preventing the sabotage. The British Cabinet discussed the issue on April 6. Ministers were between the rock of American threats to suspend aid to the UK and the hard place of Chinese antagonism, and were divided on tactics. Grantham was told to find new ways to keep the planes on the ground while Ministerial level discussions were held with the US. Washington remained implacably opposed to letting the planes go to the PRC, and when the British Cabinet discussed the issue again on April 24, it agreed on a new stalling mechanism – the issue of an Order in Council, which was signed by King George VI on May 10 and had the effect of keeping the aircraft in Hong Kong, pending a decision on the Americans' appeal. Jack Hutchison, who was now Britain's senior diplomat in China, was handed a note in which Peking declared the UK's attitude 'most unfriendly'. However, right to the top level of appeal in the Hong Kong courts (reached in December 1951), the decisions continued to favour the PRC – much to the disgust of powerful American supporters of CAT and its anti-communist stand.

Ultimately, it is likely that President Truman raised the issue personally with Winston Churchill (who was once again in office as Prime Minister) during a visit to Washington in January 1952. In May of that year the Hong Kong Supreme Court granted Chennault and Willauer's request to appeal to the Privy Council in London – a body that, some observers felt, would be much more likely than the Hong Kong judiciary to take account of the political implications of the case. With the onset of the Korean War, and a more assertive attitude from Peking towards Britain, the political dynamics were changing. On July 28, 1952 the Privy Council issued a judgement which finally gave the Americans what they wanted – possession of the seventy-one planes still at Kai Tak. For nearly three years, the planes had both taken up precious space and posed a security risk. It was a Pyrrhic victory for the aircraft were by now in poor condition, having sat for so long in salt air without preservatives. Britain had insisted that the planes should not go to Formosa, and (in an unprecedented use of the US Navy) *USS Cape*

Esperance was sent to fetch the disintegrating aircraft, and take them to the US for reconditioning and sale.

Chennault and Willauer didn't get much reward for their 'sweat and tears' – except that, when CAT faced bankruptcy in 1950, the airline (minus the disputed planes) had been purchased by the CIA for covert operations in Asia. Unbeknownst to Max, from mid-1950 the plaintiffs in the grounded planes case were actually employees of America's spy agency. Maybe Churchill knew this: as he put it succinctly in a note to his Foreign Secretary, Antony Eden: 'Don't let's fall out with the United States for the sake of China'.

— • —

Max read about the Privy Council's judgement not in Hong Kong but at his desk in Kuala Lumpur. For in early 1951 the Oxfords left Hong Kong for Max to take up a new post in Malaya. Hong Kong had not lost its allure, despite the angst of the grounded planes case, but it seemed as though Moss would never retire and for Max promotion beckoned elsewhere.

Life was very full for both Max and Audrey in their last year in the island colony, where they now counted as 'prominent residents'. Their friend Jack Armstrong invited Audrey to write a history of his law firm Deacons, to coincide with its centenary. Audrey accepted with some trepidation (information was sketchy since the firm's records were lost during the war), but she hoped the project would give her the chance to prove herself. She spent hours delving into Hong Kong's legal history – learning it was not always pure, by any means. She finished a draft of the book on the eve of departing Hong Kong for good, and though she knew it was rushed, she was bitterly disappointed in Jack Armstrong's dismissive reaction to her work – and never saw the fee that she had expected.

Other activities were more rewarding. In early 1949 Audrey turned down a full-time job at the British Council – it didn't fit her vision of being a good wife – but in December she agreed to fill in as the Council's librarian for two months, and enjoyed the work and the extra money. Her volunteer work expanded too. She did a regular shift serving beer to troops at the CheerO, a club started to entertain the growing number of enlisted men in the Hong Kong barracks. In August 1950 her customers were sailors off *HMS Belfast*, en route from Korea to England,

and talking freely about the Korean War. With reinforcements to the Hong Kong garrison arriving by the day, there were further efforts to divert the troops. Audrey was on a committee to entertain them at the Ladies' Recreation Club:

> *Main purpose of town visit is to buy bread, butter and sand-wich filling for the troops' tea at the LRC. Here I officiate, with the valuable help of Mrs Robinson, until after 5:0pm. The fel-lows appear to enjoy themselves, swimming and playing tennis. Four cakes are just enough, with the 5lbs of sandwiches. There must have been just under 30 men.* Journal, May 24, 1950.

And sometimes she had to field complaints from irate lady members about the presence of troops in the pool. Audrey's involvement with fundraising for the Society for the Protection of Children (SPC) continued on her return from long leave. In May 1949 she took on a more onerous role, stepping in as Society secretary while a lady was on leave – 'only for three months [it turned into six], but those the hottest of the year. I do not mind sending out notices, but am filled with ap-prehension at the thought of reading out Minutes!' She saw herself as a 'real worker', spending hours on the secretarial duties, mailings, and the SPC flag day, unlike some of the ladies who she felt were more inter-ested in coffee parties and gossip. She visited SPC shelters with Chinese committee members and was disturbed by the case reports:

> *We saw some case reports at the Sai Ying Poon centre. The average monthly income there is $70 – some have "free" ac-commodation – they live on the pavements. Some have several children – perhaps one or two have died – another has been given away. Such appalling conditions so near the exotic luxury of their neighbours...* Journal, August 11, 1949.

Her volunteering continued, but she felt like a released prisoner when she handed back the Secretary's files on November 9, the very day that Max was preoccupied with the defections from Kai Tak.

After the intense period when Max was acting DCA, he and Audrey took a welcome break – though even their holiday was eventful. Moss returned from leave on March 24 1950, and after briefing his boss, Max and Audrey took off on March 30 for a week's sailing trip to Macau. Syd de Kantzow, Max's buddy from Cathay Pacific, lent them his yacht *Cathay* and its helmsman, Ah Chu. They sailed on the elegant gaff-rigged cutter to the tiny island of Cheung Chau for the first night, and then on to Macau, where they had three days to explore the sleepy Portuguese colony. But while in Macau Max was disturbed to learn of the April 2 bombing of the grounded planes – the incident of sabotage that would further complicate the CAT case. Then on sailing away from Macau, they spotted a large, unnamed ship skulking near what Ah Chu called the 'bad men' islands. The vessel changed course and headed towards the *Cathay*, still unidentified. Ah Chu was convinced these were pirates who were known to haunt the area. Max and Audrey sent up two flares, the 'pirate' ship raised a white ensign, but it was only when she was close enough for Max and Audrey to make out fair-haired figures that they could breathe again – it was a naval patrol boat, which then escorted the *Cathay* to anchor at Tai O, a fishing village at the west end of Lantau. Here they spent a rough night, with their 'pirate' close by. They enjoyed a couple more perfect (but blustery) days around the tranquil outlying islands before a brisk sail back to Hong Kong harbour on April 6. There was no rest for Max – he went straight off to see Moss about the sabotage at Kai Tak, and the negative press that the incident had generated.

Spring turned into a steamy summer, but social life continued unabated – Audrey remarked on August 4 that she and Max had been out seven nights in succession. There was a round of parties for Clifford Heathcote-Smith, a departing political adviser, and his wife, Joyce. Max and Audrey threw them a dinner at which Audrey insisted on 'Red Sea Rig' – black tie, but no jackets. VIP visitors continued to descend from London – Sir Hilton Poynton, Under Secretary of State for the Colonies, headed a delegation in July. Max escorted him to inspect the site of the potential Deep Bay airfield – the plans were on life support but not yet completely dead. One Sunday in late July, Max and Audrey's intentions of getting an early night after a day at the beach were shot through by an invitation from Harold Lee, Dick's half-brother. He wanted help entertaining another distinguished visitor, Captain Tom Hussey, personal representative of the film producer, Sir Alexander Korda. Harold and Christina Lee took their guests, an amusing crowd of Chinese and Europeans, to dinner and dancing at the Lido, a seafront restaurant on Repulse Bay – happily the popular venue was air-conditioned and not too crowded, noted Audrey.

A few days later there was a cocktail party for General and Mrs Doolittle: the General had led the morale-boosting 1942 Doolittle Raid, America's first air raid on Japan's home islands. Cocktails were followed by dinner at the Gripps, the wood-panelled restaurant of the Hong Kong Hotel that served as a gathering place for the colony's élite. 'There is a certain atmosphere about the Gripps which is most pleasant – a luxuriant gaiety', Audrey once said. On August 18, Max and Audrey gave a farewell dinner of Chinese food served with mao tai for James Warburton and his wife Toni. The acting Air Vice Marshal had spent the past year as military and air attaché in Formosa, renewing his wartime relationship with Chiang Kai-shek, and was finally sailing home to England.

Max doubtless discussed his own future with his erstwhile boss and mentor. Months earlier Max had applied for a transfer to Malaya, with the prospect of becoming Director of Civil Aviation in Kuala Lumpur. He finally received an official offer in September. Audrey had just turned 34, and revelled in her life with Max: 'He really is such a generous thoughtful fellow...I think in living with Max I have as much as anyone could possibly desire.' To give up a pleasant way of life in Hong Kong for the unknown in Malaya would be hard, Audrey thought. Financially, they might not be noticeably better off; there was a waiting list for housing; and Kuala Lumpur didn't have the sophistication (or beaches) of Hong Kong. But after learning more about the conditions and thinking things over, Max and Audrey decided to seize the chance, and Max accepted the posting. They would leave Hong Kong in the New Year.

Now it was time to savour a final holiday season among their wide circle of friends in the territory that Max had called home since 1938. There were glorious autumn days out yachting on the *Wild Goose* with John Robinson, dinner at the Ritz, dancing at the Peninsula's annual St Andrew's Day ball, and cocktails aboard *HMS Belfast*. In November, Max and Audrey snatched a few days' local leave and took the ferry to Lantau, passing their old sanctuary Kap Sing on the way. They were heading for the Buddhist monastery, Ngong Ping, perched on Lantau's peak. Max and Audrey walked up the mountain at dusk from the coastal village of Tung Chung, with a Chinese woman as their Sherpa:

It is very beautiful walking through these green fields over the cobbled pilgrims' path – as we start to climb our guide and porter slows her pace. All too soon the sun has gone behind the hills and we walk in a brief dusk and then by the light of our lamp. Max now takes the lead bearing the lamp, the porter follows him and I her. We brush past bushes and grass on the narrow steep path, the narrow gap to which we walk widening as we near it. Beyond the gap lies the monastery. The stars take shape and soon the sky is full of them, the Milky Way showing most clearly on this dark night...Eventually we gain the saddle and soon after see the lights of the monastery. We are greeted by an elderly monk with rheumy eyes...The air is heavy with the smell of joss sticks, the clash of cymbals and the beating of gongs. After a long wait we are served with rice and vegetables. The walk had taken us 2½ hours. Journal, October 30, 1950.

Max and Audrey spent three nights in a simple dormitory as guests of the yellow-robed monks, woken each day at dawn by their chanting. The visitors slipped into a routine of reading or walking in the hills, sharing a 6 o'clock supper with the monks, and going to bed by candlelight as the sun sank. They relished the peace, fresh air and good weather, returning to the worldliness of Hong Kong Island for a few more days' holiday spent at the races, walking and sea bathing.

With echoes of the eve of the Japanese invasion, the St Andrew's Day ball at the Peninsula on December 1 was overshadowed by the prospect of the United States entering the war in Korea. Audrey had heard Secretary of State Acheson speaking as though 'we are on the very verge of war'. She still questioned if it wasn't better to live side by side with Communism than to enter another war on foreign soil. She would not escape the issue by moving to Malaya, which was in the grip of its own 'Emergency' as the colony faced Communist insurgents operating from its dense jungles. But for now Audrey was swept up with parties and packing. It was the Oxfords' turn to be feted with a round of farewell

Max and Audrey's final Christmas at Branksome Towers, 1950

events. Audrey especially appreciated that Dick and Esther Lee gave a party in their honour, letting them choose the other guests. It was the best dinner Max and Audrey had ever enjoyed at the Lees' home, with delicious Chinese food, and piano playing after dinner. The guest list was a roll call of distinguished Hong Kongers and friends from the war years, and included Dick's half-brothers, Harold and JS Lee and their wives, Christina and Leatrice, Dr Gordon King and his wife, Ronnie and Marjorie Holmes, Pat and Beth Sedgwick, Harry and Frances Owen-Hughes, the Teesdales, the Talans, the Stricklands, and Hector Chauvin.

Over Christmas Max and Audrey hosted their largest cocktail party ever, packing over thirty guests into their flat. This was followed a few days later by their traditional Christmas Eve dinner for a dozen close friends. Audrey wore a flattering black taffeta dress, and the men were in black tie. Max and Audrey kicked off the evening with their customary black velvet, and served champagne with a dinner of 'hot consommé, cold salmon salad (crisp and refreshing), then the turkey, plum pudding and mince pies. A good dinner. We play charades later in the evening and the whole affair seems to pass off quite well,' wrote Audrey modestly. On Christmas Day they took the Peak Tram up to a buffet lunch with Iris and Reidar Johannessen, who gave Max and Audrey a pair of Norwegian wrought iron candlesticks and pewter salad servers. At the end of a hectic week of festivities, they were at Skyhigh again, first footing after midnight on New Year's Eve.

On January 8, 1951, Max and Audrey spent their own seventh wedding anniversary celebrating the marriage of Stanley Smith and May Wong at the Roof Garden. Many old Chungking friends reunited to toast Stanley and May; Max and Audrey were delighted to see their good friends happily married. But the Branksome Towers apartment began to look bare as the Oxfords sent carpets and curtains for cleaning, and crated up oil paintings, photographs, and papers to ship to England. They parted reluctantly with their two Devas oils – the portrait of Audrey and the wild flowers – deciding that Kuala Lumpur's tropical climate and open houses would not be safe for these treasured possessions, which 'should be enjoyed for generations to come'. The Hong Kong winter turned bitterly cold, but Max and Audrey were cheered by a party given on January 12 by the Kai Tak air traffic controllers and engineers: 'They honour Max by opening several bottles of champagne and drinking his health. I think they realise his true worth,' said Audrey.

Audrey didn't want to forget the beauty of Hong Kong: 'The sun as it strikes the hills in the evenings, turning them pink and hazy, the oblique way its rays hit them so that they lie like folds of material, the green paths and the flowering shrubs and trees, the bauhinia with the lovely perfume.' Nor would she forget friends: there were many bittersweet farewells during the month of January, when Max and Audrey were out practically every night. Audrey's days were filled with the business of moving, interspersed with farewells to her wide circle of women friends. Jane Wen, a Chinese friend, gave a lunch for a group of other Chinese women, which Audrey particularly enjoyed. Suddenly, it was the Oxfords' last night in Hong Kong and Audrey found she had pushed everything to the back of her mind, 'and I will not think of this – our parting with the servants and friends – and Whim [their cat]. Later it will catch me all unawares.'

On January 29, the suitcases were packed, a final lunch enjoyed with the Sedgwicks at the American Club, and it was down to Queen's Pier to board a cargo ship bound for Singapore, two of only eight passengers. The faithful Ah Wing, his wife Ah Mui and their son were at the pier to wave them off. Friends and colleagues came down to the ship or sent flowers. 'We sail at 5:0pm and sit on deck taking a last look at "the doomed island" as M gloomily puts it.'

Audrey herself took a more balanced view. She drew a bold line under the Hong Kong years in her guest book, writing below it: 'The End of a Very Good Era'. There would be little entertaining from the confines of the Oxfords' first home in Kuala Lumpur – a faded room at the Station Hotel. But, Audrey reflected that spring:

> At least I feel we have lived – and I am glad we did leave HK or the danger of believing this was the real life might have proved too great. Here we are nearer the simple life that is within our means. I shall always be glad to remember we have drunk champagne freely – eaten exquisite black caviar – a tight icy mass – off a Russian ship – not many enjoy this luxury these days. Have attended suppers where every exotic food was to be had – given in our own home excellent meals with good wines. Frequently dressed for dinners in all one's finery and not been over-dressed. Sat at tables glittering with candles, crystal and silver. All extremely pleasant and good to have enjoyed – but as Max so sagely said some weeks ago, he has probably drunk his final bottle of port. From here I see a truer, equally good life. I think we both look forward to a house in England with our own garden and fruit trees – a few ducks and geese and a cow. This I should like best of all – and the gaiety and glamour and luxury of our lives in HK will be very remote. But how nice to have known it. Journal, April 12, 1951.

Epilogue

Max, Frances and Emma, Kuala Lumpur, 1957

Audrey would eventually fulfil her dream of a house in England with a garden and fruit trees – she would even acquire a pair of geese and a hive of bees, though, regrettably, neither ducks nor a cow. But when Max and Audrey reached tropical Malaya these pleasures were still some way in the future

After leaving Hong Kong they were to spend nine more years in Asia, with Max capping off his colonial service career as the Federation of Malaya's Director of Civil Aviation. It was a challenging period: Malaya was in the throes of a Communist insurgency, whose beginning in 1948 was marked by the murder of several British and Chinese rubber planters. While Max and Audrey lodged at the dingy Station Hotel waiting for housing, Audrey became accustomed to the sight of armoured private cars on the streets of the capital and soldiers bringing their rifles into the hotel dining room. The country was under a state of emergency. The Malayan Communist Party had been outlawed, but guerrillas based in jungle camps continued to terrorize villagers, rubber planters and tin miners in isolated areas. In October 1951, British and Malays alike were deeply shocked when bandits assassinated Sir Henry Gurney, the High Commissioner, in an ambush on a mountain road.

Against this unnerving backdrop, life was of necessity more constrained than it had been in Hong Kong. But there was also a nicer reason to focus on the simpler, less social life that Audrey had anticipated. For in November 1951 Max and Audrey finally became parents when I was born at Kuala Lumpur's Bungsar Hospital. Fortunately they could bring me home to an airy house on Circular Road, having just moved out of the Station Hotel. In April 1952, I was taken to Singapore to be christened in St Andrew's Cathedral in the presence of my godmother Iris Johannessen and her husband, Reidar. That summer, I had my first taste of long-distance travel, flying via Rome to England, where I met my Oxford grandfather, my cousin Christopher and other relations. When I was almost three, my sister Frances was born, and in 1955 we travelled by ship to South Africa, for an extended visit to our aunt Margaret and cousins in Cape Town.

Back in Kuala Lumpur, we moved into a newly renovated house on Hose Road, where we had relief from Malaya's relentless heat and humidity from a single air conditioning unit, strategically placed in the study. Frances and I swam at the Lake Club, and we attended the Alice

Smith School, learning to spell exotic words such as 'bougainvillea'. Gurney's successor, General Sir Gerald Templer, gradually brought the insurgency under control, in a rare victory over Communist forces in Asia. Then we were freer to explore Malaya – the hill stations at Fraser's Hill and the Cameron Highlands, the beaches of Malacca, the East Coast and Pangkor Island.

My father travelled frequently around his network of airfields and beyond, bringing back souvenirs from Indonesia, Thailand and other destinations. Modern airliners cut hours off the flying time between continents – in 1953 BOAC's Constellation took Max from Singapore to London in 36 hours, and by the end of the decade an advanced Comet, the first jetliner, made the journey in just 24 hours. In 1956, Max oversaw the construction of a new terminal building and the inauguration of Kuala Lumpur as an international airport. This was a year before Merdeka, or independence, 'so that right from the start our independent country was furnished with an essential adjunct to its new status', wrote the Minister of Transport thanking Max for his service. The new government invited Max to remain in his post through the transition, until he retired in 1960 at the grand old age of fifty-five. The Queen honoured him with the OBE – Officer of the Order of the British Empire – for services to civil aviation.

On home leave three years earlier, Max and Audrey had set out to look for a country cottage for summer holidays in England. Instead they found a mid-eighteenth century Georgian town house in Topsham, a historic town on the Exe estuary in Devon. Draughty old houses on narrow, cobbled streets were not fashionable at the time, but Max and Audrey fell in love with Poplar House, a spacious property with a long walled garden. Our family moved there full-time in 1960, and Poplar House was our home for twenty-four years. Frances and I were educated at the Maynard School in the nearby city of Exeter – a rigorous school for girls, but one where we had a happier time than our mother had had at Cheltenham Ladies' College.

Max and Audrey adapted well to life back in the old country. For some time Audrey had longed to settle down in temperate England. She was thrilled to run her own home and garden after years of handling staff and living in government accommodation. One of her first purchases was a dishwasher – still a rarity in 1960. She gave free rein to her

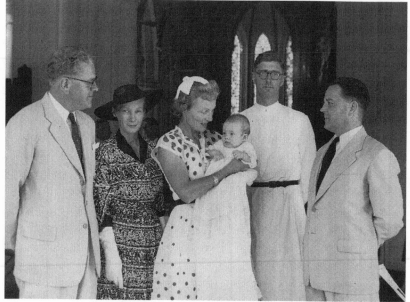

*Reidar Johannessen, Audrey, Iris Johannessen (holding baby Emma),
Archdeacon Woods and Max, Singapore, 1952*

passion for cooking, immersing herself in the recipes of Elizabeth David and Constance Spry, and cultivated unusual herbs and vegetables.
Max, too, became an expert gardener, especially after we expanded
our property with the purchase of an adjacent orchard. To celebrate
my mother's fiftieth birthday, we had a grass tennis court laid on the
land. In Kuala Lumpur Max had taken up carpentry as a hobby, and he
continued to craft inventive pieces of furniture. He also took up wine-
making, using fruit from the orchard, and home-brewing – the kitchen
would often smell strongly of hops.

Max had worked since he was seventeen years old, and he decided to
enjoy retirement and his young family rather than find a post-colonial
service career. But he took on one final assignment: in 1962-63 he spent
six months as interim Director of Civil Aviation in Fiji. We envied his
time in the South Pacific as we coped in Devon with the coldest English
winter in many years. At the end of his posting, my mother joined him
for a richly deserved holiday in her native South America and in the Ca-

ribbean – a chance to fulfil a dream of visiting the Inca ruins at Machu Picchu, and to see two sets of friends from China: Berkeley Gage (then Ambassador to Lima), and Stanley and May Smith (who had retired to the Bahamas). Our family holidays were to less far-flung destinations – typically we went camping in mid-Wales, and occasionally we splashed out on skiing trips to the Alps.

My father took great pleasure in sailing a day boat on the River Exe, teaching my sister and me how to navigate its tricky tidal waters. After we had left home for university, he would often sail alone, heading downriver for the day and coming back on the flood tide. One summer's day in 1980, he had just returned to his mooring when he collapsed and died of a heart attack. He was just seventy-five. By that time, Frances and I were both married and working in London. Audrey sensibly decided to sell Poplar House and join us to be close to her first grandchild, Fran's daughter, Alida. She created a new and welcoming home near Richmond in southwest London, but sadly succumbed to cancer in 1988, at the age of seventy-two.

In Devon Max and Audrey had had an eclectic circle of friends, and a particular talent for making friends with people much younger than themselves. In the early 1970s they met David and Sarah Robinson, then a newly married couple who sailed with my sister. We invited David to speak at a memorial service that we held for Max and Audrey in 1989, and he captured what it was like to know them, not as parents but as friends. He recalled summer weekends at our Topsham home:

> *Visits by Sarah and me included tennis played barefoot on the grass court, under the influence of Bjorn Borg. This would be followed by sailing if the tide was right and afterwards a BBQ in the evening. Audrey would produce a wooden trolley bearing marinated meat, bread rolls, chutneys and fruit. Max found bottles of apple juice, beer and vine leaf wine. We would sit out under the apple tree, talking of politics, Max's experiences in Kurdish territory, our own progress through life or possibly Max's interest in poetry (he told me he tried to read some every day).*
>
> *The Oxford household in Topsham was a place of delight and enthusiasm. A place to share interests and questions and a place*

to plan journeys. When Sarah and I planned our journey on the Trans Siberian train to New Zealand in 1972, it was in the Oxford household that we formalised our plans and generated the effort to resign our jobs and go. It was to the Oxfords that we sent back reports on our experiences and progress. And it was here that we took pleasure in returning months later to recount our adventures.

— • —

Max and Audrey of course understood what it was like to quit a job and set off on an adventure to the other side of the world. But they were undoubtedly better listeners to David and Sarah's stories than I, in my teens and twenties, was to theirs. I knew something of my parents' improbable meeting in the mountains of Sichuan province, of their marriage in Chungking in 1944, of my father's service in Iraq and Africa, and his Christmas Day escape from the fallen colony of Hong Kong. I had memories of childhood road trips around Britain, being dragged off to visit cosmopolitan friends from the days of Empire: retired colonial service officials; ex-intelligence officers including Charles Boxer and his fearless American wife, *New Yorker* writer Emily Hahn; enterprising businessmen and successful lawyers.

These visits were to a certain extent occasions for reminiscences, but mostly my family lived life in the present tense. After school, I left home for a spell in France, and then university at Oxford for a degree in Modern Languages. Soon I had the usual preoccupations of twenty-somethings – friends, partners, career – and did not spend much time quizzing either of my parents about their past. My boyfriend (soon husband), Mike Elliott, was better at this: he showed his aptitude for journalism by drawing out Max's tales over a glass of beer on weekends in Topsham. Max entertained us with war stories of his brushes with death in Africa and Asia, but much was still unexplored. Audrey, who was more of an extrovert, encouraged her husband to write about his life, and she added stories of her own – of her childhood in Chile, of secret wartime work in London, and of being courted by that debonair air attaché in Chungking.

But it was only once my own daughters, Roxana and Gina, were in their teens that I really began to explore their grandparents' early lives.

Poplar House, Topsham, 1959

The quest began in 2004, when I had the opportunity to live in Asia for the first time since childhood – Mike had been assigned from New York to Hong Kong as editor of *Time* magazine's international editions. Whenever I could get to England, I delved into boxes and trunks full of my parents' papers and memorabilia, amazed at the care with which they had chronicled their lives. My sister and I had stashed the collection, unexamined, in the attic of a holiday house built in Topsham, on the land with the orchard and tennis court.

In the Devon attic I unearthed a long, narrow tin trunk of my father's

Max and Audrey were guests of Stanley and May Smith, Nassau, 1963

from his days as a pilot: it was designed for storing aeronautical maps. 'M.N. Oxford RAF' was stencilled in white paint on the lid, and at some point in his travels a blue and white label 'Not Wanted on Voyage' had been plastered on the side. In the tin trunk Max had meticulously kept all his appointment diaries dating back to 1942 – his earlier possessions were lost to the Japanese, except for a few mementoes retrieved from his father. There were manila folders of important letters, ledgers, notebooks, and expired passports, as well as a collection of flying maps to navigate some of the world's remotest regions. Another trunk held Max's RAF blue serge dress uniform, complete with feathered helmet and ceremonial sword, and an array of medals – including his OBE.

My mother had left a battered brown leather attaché case: this was stuffed full of letters tied neatly into bundles. There were dozens she had written from China to her family in England; and there were scores of the long missives exchanged by my parents when they were separated for six months at the end of the war. Most were hand-written on flimsy, war-issue airmail paper – blue paper so thin that when my mother chose to type, the keys often punched through the page. The collection came from a string of faraway places: Cairo, Calcutta, Chungking, Singapore, and Hong Kong.

Then there was a small antique wooden chest, crammed with seven volumes of journals written in my mother's flowing hand, recording her feelings about the events – large and small – of her life, interspersed with poignant recollections of the war years. She had also kept pocket-sized appointment diaries, address books, passports, and leather-bound guest books, detailing a social life so busy that my head spun.

Equipped with this treasure trove, and some other important clues, I began to piece together the puzzle of Max and Audrey's lives. It's taken a good deal of detective work to try to fill in the gaps. Some mysteries of Max and Audrey's past remain unsolved, and maybe that is how they would want it.

But I feel that my parents saved their letters and journals for a reason – so that we, in the next generations, would understand what was important to them and have a glimpse into a way of life that, for better or worse, we have lost. I have certainly been enormously enriched by what I've learned: by talking to survivors of their generation, to relatives, to colleagues and friends, by digging into faded files in public and private archives in the UK and Hong Kong, and by educating myself about the history of mid-twentieth century war and empire in Asia.

— • —

The most rewarding part of my twenty-first century journey has been to explore the places that were important to my parents six or seven decades ago: Hong Kong, China, India, Singapore and Malaysia. Although all of these Asian countries have developed at a pace that would astound Max and Audrey, spreading prosperity and transforming cityscapes out of all recognition, time and again I have been astonished to discover irrepressible remnants of the past, buildings that have survived redevelopment all around, sites of historic importance that have been restored for future generations, colonial-era clubs that have found a new role in Asia's vibrant modern society, religious and cultural traditions that seem timeless, and extraordinary landscapes, enjoyed now by vastly more people, but essentially as scenic as Audrey described them in her writing.

While living in Hong Kong in 2004-06, I got to know the territory that was Max's home before and after the war, the scene of the desperate battle against the Japanese and of the Christmas Day escape. One winter's day, Hong Kong historian Philip Snow, David MacDougall's eldest daughter, Ann Partridge, and I met up in Aberdeen and clambered over rocks on the inhospitable shore of Ap Lei Chau, the small island Max and MacDougall had washed up on after swimming from the disabled launch. Another day, Mike and I hiked to the daunting summit of Ap Lei Chau, and looked down onto the shore from which Max and the other swimmers were eventually rescued. Later, during a visit by my sister, we took a sampan ride around the island, trying to figure out exactly where the men had come ashore and how they had met up with the Motor Torpedo Boats that took them to the coast of China. It wasn't easy; the topography of Aberdeen and its off-lying islands has changed significantly since 1941, with landfill and construction of high-rise buildings permanently altering the landscape.

So I scoured Hong Kong's public records for prewar aerial photos of the area. I read other accounts of the escape, some published soon after the war, some unpublished, some written up in official reports held in Britain's National Archives. The stories complemented each other in important respects but there were also intriguing discrepancies; in the fog of war, no one person could have seen the complete picture.

Fortunately, while I pieced together the story from Hong Kong, other descendants of the escape party had begun to research it too, and one had created a website. Over time some of us met and swapped notes. From a global web of connections, we founded a group called HERO, the Hong Kong Escape Re-enactment Organisation. At Christmas 2009, we brought together in Hong Kong nearly 100 relatives of the 68 men who survived the 1941 escape, and retraced the men's walk from the coast of mainland China to Huizhou. We also opened a special exhibition, *Escape from Hong Kong: The Road to Waichow*, at the Hong Kong Museum of Coastal Defence, which attracted over 400,000 visitors in a run of over three years.

By 2009, my research had taken me to China half a dozen times. The gritty city of Chongqing in China's mountainous hinterland is not a place where many foreign tourists linger – it is best known as a boarding point for cruises down the Yangtze River. But Chiang Kai-shek's wartime capital was the natural destination for my first trip to the mainland in February 2005. The modern municipality of 33 million people covers an area about the size of Austria. Its climate is still dismal – a humid furnace in the summer, cold and damp in the winter – with horrendous air pollution to boot. Han Suyin's description from *Destination Chungking*, written in 1942, remains apt: "Grey in the evening mists, Chungking is like the pointed prow of a ship, thrusting downstream between the Kialing (Jialing) and Yangtze Rivers."

The heart of the old city is tucked into this precipitous peninsula. During two stays in Chongqing, Sun Ying, a professor of English who acted as my researcher, interpreter and guide, helped me to peel away the layers of the modern city and unearth traces of its wartime past. Though Ying was heavily pregnant on my first visit, she was quite tireless in her enthusiasm for my project. Her husband, Jiang, an architect specializing in conservation, was an ideal extra resource.

Sun Ying and I had each done some homework prior to my first arrival. Armed with a few grainy photos from my father's album, and descriptions in my mother's letters and contemporary memoirs, we explored the city's oldest quarters and its surrounding hills. We discovered many of the places that were important in Max and Audrey's Chungking. A decaying neighbourhood rising up a hill above the Yangtze, for example, had a narrow street still known as Lingshi Xiang, or Consulate Alley. This was where the Allied Powers housed their diplomats when Chiang Kai-shek retreated to Chungking in 1938. The missions made do with overcrowded temporary quarters, upgrading small Consulates to Embassy status, adding Nissen huts, and renting extra space from local landlords.

Nearby, we stumbled on ruins of the old French Embassy and an adjoining Catholic Abbey, which had been used as a hospital during Japanese bombing raids. The former British Embassy, where Audrey had worked, was so obscure that it eluded us in 2005. But on a return trip with Mike in 2008, we found it tucked away below Consulate Alley, a stately but dilapidated building whose garden (the 'Cabbage Patch') tumbled down the hillside. It was now a social centre for the elderly. Nearby, we discovered a grey brick building, almost derelict, that was unmistakably the Office of the Air Attaché depicted in my father's only roll of photos from China.

Equally redolent of old Chungking, we found an ancient stairway of broad granite steps leading down to a dock, called Chuqimen, on the north bank of the swirling Yangtze. At Chuqimen dock I pictured Audrey's commute by sampan across the wide river, and her struggle to walk up the hundreds of slick steps to the hilltop Embassy. Today, these stairways are still packed with the stalls of vendors and the relentless traffic of bang bang men – skinny, muscular porters who earn a meagre living by carrying huge loads strung from bamboo poles across their shoulders.

Luckily, we did not have to cross the Yangtze by sampan to explore the south bank. There is now a road bridge across the river, and only perpetual traffic to contend with. I could envisage the area where Audrey lodged in an Embassy mess: many of the larger mansions along the south shore (where the first Westerners to trade along the Yangtze built their residences) are being restored in a belated effort to preserve them.

In a park high above the Jialing, Chongqing's other river, we visited the tiled-roof Chinese villa (*Feige*) that became the British Ambassador's residence after the Embassy was damaged by a bomb, and was the venue for Lady Seymour's announcement of Max and Audrey's engagement. Now open to the public, it was notable as the site of a banquet given by Chiang Kai-shek for his rival Mao Zedong in 1945. Nearby, also overlooking the Jialing, General Stilwell, the American commander who served as chief of staff to Chiang, operated from an airy residence, now restored and open as a museum. Then, set among forests of pine in the rolling hills to the south of the city at Huangshan, we visited the country retreat of the Generalissimo and his wife, Madame Chiang. This too has been restored, a sign of increasing recognition of the Nationalist role in the victory over Japan.

When I returned to Chongqing in 2008 with Mike, we had a new mission. After a few days in the city, we were to take a 700-mile drive south to Kunming in Yunnan Province, retracing the route that Max and Audrey had driven in an alcohol-fuelled truck in 1944, as they left China on the long journey home to England. We had allowed four days for a journey that had taken them a full week, with six tyre changes, numerous breakdowns and refuelling stops en route. Sun Ying agreed to accompany us, and she recruited an excellent driver, Mr. Huang, with a minivan. Our journey was a revelation – choosing old roads whenever possible, we witnessed magnificent scenery, dire poverty in rural areas, and sprawling, anonymous cities which were small towns in my parents' day. We drove an infamous stretch of the hairpin-bend road built during the war to transport supplies around Chiang's China.

We ended up in Kunming, enjoying the beauty of that lakeside city as my parents had before us. But then our paths diverged: they had flown out of China on an RAF transport plane over 'the Hump' into India. Mike and I, taking advantage of twenty-first century amenities, treated ourselves to a few days at the Banyan Tree in Ringha, a sumptuous resort in the mountains of northern Yunnan, before leaving for Beijing and a nonstop flight back to New York.

— • —

As I sat on the balcony of our Tibetan-style villa in Yunnan, enjoying breathtaking views of mountains dusted with snow, I reflected on why my parents' story captivated me – beyond the curiosity that we all share about where we come from – and why I have wanted to tell it for a wider audience.

In part, it is because their story evokes a distant world in the waning days of Empire – a world of piloting small planes, of sea voyages and flying boats, of taking six-month-long 'home leaves', of receiving urgent news by telegram, and learning the merely important by letter; a world before most married women had careers, and one in which couples 'dressed' for dinner even if they were eating alone at home. And in part, it is because Max and Audrey lived in 'interesting times', as the Chinese curse has it: surviving world war, witnessing the impact of civil war in China and the triumph of the Communist forces, watching Britain's colonies become independent nations.

Beyond this, it is because my parents' story gives us an insight into feelings that are deeply familiar: the perpetual human emotions of love, joy, grief and fear; the importance of friendship, the longing for security in an uncertain world, the struggle for success, and the role of fate in determining the course of an individual's life. Though neither came from a background of privilege, both seized opportunities throughout their lives, and my father – with my mother's steadfast support – reached for the sky in his chosen profession. Their lives exemplified the paradox that war brings opportunity as well as horror and misery – it takes people out of their comfort zone, requiring men and women alike to summon up their inner strength and resourcefulness.

Max and Audrey both suffered hardship and heartbreak in the war. They lost friends who died much too young. They knew they were lucky to have lived when others, with similar experiences, did not. But there was more to them than good fortune. They were, as the Chinese would say, doubly blessed – not just to have lived, but to have known how to live well. That knowledge is a great gift to those who came after.

Topsham, Devon
July, 2013.

Acknowledgements

It is customary in acknowledgements to build up to a crescendo of thanks to the author's nearest and dearest. But this has been a family effort, and I want to thank my family first. My husband, Mike Elliott, is an inspiration and support in everything. He is also the indefatigable editor of *At Least We Lived*. Back in 1997, Mike was the first to bring Audrey's journals to light, when he published an extract in a special issue of *Newsweek* to mark the Hong Kong handover. His enthusiasm for this project has never wavered.

At Least We Lived is dedicated to our wonderful daughters, Roxana and Gina. They have graduated from high school and collected three degrees between them in the time that I've taken to complete this book. They have helped me in countless ways, they have kept me grounded and indulged my preoccupations and absences. In 2009, they willingly gave up a traditional Christmas to travel to Hong Kong and China to commemorate their grandfather's wartime escape, entering into the spirit of HERO and making new friends among their generation of descendants of the Christmas Day breakout.

My sister Frances has encouraged this venture from the start, putting her trust in me to tell our parents' story, and waiting patiently for the end product. In 2005, she visited me in Hong Kong and we went on to tour Malaysia together, a memorable return to the country of our birth. I am grateful to our three first cousins: Gail Jonsson and Peter McColl in South Africa, for sharing photos and stories of Max, as well as his crucial escape letter written to their mother, Margaret; and Christopher Hebeler in the US, for sharing correspondence about his mother, Audrey's sister Tottie.

HERO has become an extended family, and I am hugely grateful to its members for sharing knowledge of the Christmas Day escape, and the unforgettable experience of retracing the footsteps of our forefathers. I am especially grateful to fellow founding members of the executive committee: Donald Chan, Duncan Chan (the twin sons of Admiral

Chan, now both sadly passed away), David Hide, Richard Hide (sons of Buddy Hide), Russell Joyce (grandson of Les Barker), Alison McEwan (daughter of Colin McEwan), and Sheena Recaldin (daughter of David MacDougall). Special thanks go to Richard Hide for creating the website, www.hongkongescape.org, and to Tim Luard, for his book, *Escape from Hong Kong*, which adds much rich detail to our knowledge. Many other HERO members have generously shared memories and materials with me, including Paula Chan, Anita Li, Helen Hyatt, Ann Partridge, and Warwick Ross. Rosa Yau and her colleagues at the Hong Kong Museum of Coastal Defence have been a pleasure to work with on the special exhibition, *Escape from Hong Kong: The Road to Waichow*.

In China, it was a joy to work with Sun Ying, my guide and interpreter in Chongqing and on the road to Kunming, and I could not have managed without her skilful help. The staff of the British Consulate-General in Chongqing were also enormously helpful during my visits to the region.

Numerous conversations with contemporaries of my parents and other interviewees have enriched my understanding of Max and Audrey's lives, and I am especially indebted to the following: Mary Harris (Jack Hutchison's daughter), John Gillibrand, Eric Ho, Margaret Jackson, Anne Marden, Dorothy Neild (née Hutchison, my late godmother), Judy Snowdon (Franklin Gimson's daughter), Michael Sullivan, Alastair Todd, Carola Boxer Vecchio, Joan Watson (my late aunt), Miles Wormal (Gerry and Nan Wormal's son), and Ingrid Wheeler (the daughter of my late godmother, Iris Johannessen).

For their expertise and assistance on the history of Hong Kong and China, my heartfelt thanks go to Tony Banham, Geoffrey Emerson, Vaudine England, Jonathan Fenby, May Holdsworth, Alain Le Pichon, Christopher Munn, Elizabeth Ride, Steve Vines and Jason Wordie. I'm deeply indebted to Philip Snow for his sage counsel from the early stages of the project, and for his invaluable comments on the book's final draft.

Friends on three continents have cheered and encouraged me along the way. Special thanks go to Zoher and Shi-ying Abdoolcarim, Melissa Brown and Mark Clifford, Ronnie Chan, Ling and Simon Elegant, Robyn Meredith, Lucy Reed and Michael Glennon for their help and generous hospitality on my return visits to Asia. In England, many friends have made me welcome during research trips: Mandy Alcock, Lucy Booth and Mark Addison, John and Angela Gillibrand, Myra Green, Heather Holden-Brown, Sue and Graeme Leith, Jenny Lo, Sarah and David Robinson, Debbie Sharp and Michael Norman. Annie and Robert Sarfati entertained me at their country home in France while I made final edits. I'm especially grateful to Diana Fortescue and Lisa Buchan for their friendship and support: we have enjoyed innumerable conversations about our common interests in our families' history in Asia.

In the United States, I am thankful for the unflagging interest of friends including Monie Begley, Peter Brown, Pam Davis and Gary Schpero, Peter Godwin (who offered a constructive critique of an early draft), Marcia Masten, Marianne Szegedy-Maszak (who helped to polish my prose), Andrea Willey, and Carlotta and Wendell Willkie. Friends from my book groups in Bronxville and Washington have been a great support (you know who you are!). Viji George and Paul Grand Pré, with whom I worked at Concordia College in Bronxville from 2009-11, generously gave me the flexibility to take time away to write.

I am tremendously grateful to the incomparable Cecelia Wong for her imaginative design of the book and its cover.

Finally, thanks are due to the ever-helpful librarians and staff of the National Archives at Kew, Rhodes House at Oxford, the Churchill Archives at Cambridge, the Imperial War Museum in London, Hong Kong University Library, the Hong Kong Public Record Office, and the National Air and Space Museum in Washington. Close to home, I have benefited from the excellent collection and quiet study areas of the Georgetown University Library, where I have probably logged up more hours than my daughters, Georgetown alumnae both.

Notes

Much of *At Least We Lived* is based on the personal papers of my parents, Audrey Watson and Max Oxford. These include some 30 letters that Audrey wrote from China to her family in England from 1943-44, and an almost daily correspondence between Max in Hong Kong and Audrey in Singapore in the months immediately after the war, October 1945 to April 1946. I also draw extensively on seven volumes of a journal that Audrey began to write in July 1947, and kept up until 1959. Max and Audrey carefully filed away other significant papers, and a complete set of their appointment diaries for the years 1942 onwards: these have often helped me to cross-check details of people, places and events mentioned in the letters and journals.

In seeking to put Max and Audrey's story in context, I am hugely indebted to the published and unpublished works, archival sources and individuals listed in the bibliography and acknowledgements. The errors of course are mine alone. The notes to each chapter (given with page references) aim to indicate sources for key facts and quotes, and to add some details that didn't belong in the main narrative.

Chinese names of people and places are generally rendered in the standard modern romanization (*pinyin*), but I have kept a few well-established traditional forms such as Chiang Kai-shek (Jiang Jieshi), Chungking (Chongqing) and Canton (Guangzhou).

CHAPTER ONE

8　*The Incomati:* The threat of German submarine attacks was very real: on July 18, 1943, only weeks after Audrey's voyage, the *Incomati* was sunk in a U-boat attack south of Lagos (www.uboat.net).

11　*Sharjah airstrip:* The RAF camp is commemorated in Al Mahatta Museum, which is housed in Sharjah's first airport building, one that resembles a desert fortress and is now in the centre of a thriving town.

12　*Watson family history:* Sources for Audrey's family history include an unpublished memoir by her father, Francis Watson, entitled *The White*

Gold of Chile or Memories of the Nitrate Industry in Chile 1904-1914;
Henry Meiggs: Yankee Pizarro by Watt Stewart, and an annotated family
tree and diaries from Joan Watson.

14   *A succession of rented homes in South Kensington*: the Watsons' addresses
included 16 Neville Street, 21 Evelyn Gardens, 22 Cresswell Place
(a book-filled house owned by Agatha Christie), and 17 Drayton
Court on Drayton Gardens.

15   *Farnborough house:* Audrey shared with Dorothy and Helen Hutchison
a house called Harborough, on Waverley Road, Farnborough.

16   *Audrey's employment with the SOE:* Audrey's personnel record was
released by the National Archives, HS9/1561/7.

18   *Sinking of HMS Thetis:* Audrey's friend, Lt. Frederick G Woods, was
grilled at the official enquiry into the disastrous sinking of the
submarine on her maiden voyage. *The Times, How the Thetis was
Flooded,* July 6, 1939.

19   *Hump airlift:* Firsthand descriptions of 'flying the Hump' include Major
Gen. Grimsdale in his unpublished memoir, p72, and WL Bond in
Leary, *The Dragon's Wings,* pp162-3.

21   *Over three years of operating an airlift:* Figures for total losses of
aircraft and personnel differ, but one source, the PRC publication
Hump Air Transport, p80, states that in three years and three months
514 planes and 1,500 pilots were lost on the 'Hump Route', also
known as the 'Death Route'.

CHAPTER TWO

23   *Hutchison family history:* Sources include my godmother Dorothy Neild
(née Hutchison) and her cousin, Mary Harris (née Hutchison),
daughter of Jack Hutchison. I found Mary in Leesburg, Virginia in
2005: she had married an American named Huntingdon Harris, whom
she met in Africa, and had lived in the United States ever since the war.

24   *Chiang Kai-shek's Chungking:* For the history of the Nationalist
capital and its leading personalities I am indebted to excellent
biographies including Fenby on the Generalissimo, Li and Pakula
on Mme. Chiang, Tuchman on Stilwell and Winchester on Needham.
Descriptions of everyday life for foreigners in wartime Chungking
are elusive, and few are from the perspective of Western women. I
draw on Audrey's letters and other contemporary accounts including
reports by Air Attachés Warburton and Bartholomew, and memoirs by
Gage, Grimsdale, Hahn, Han and Peck.

24   *Nearly 12,000 civilians had been killed in the raids:* this figure is from
Wartime Capital: Chongqing Today.

30   *Diplomatic community, the British Ambassador's residence:* sources include

Berkeley Gage's memoir and Sir Hubert and Lady Seymour's papers.

33 *Extraordinarily high cost of living:* many commented on this, including Grimsdale in his memoir, pp88-9.

36 *The North-South Club:* Gage, p113.

37 *Chungking had industrialized fast:* details from *Wartime Capital: Chongqing Today.*

CHAPTER THREE

43 *Madame Chiang's tea party:* The Chiangs' former estate at Huangshan is preserved with many original furnishings and is open to the public. On a visit in 2005, a framed *Time* magazine cover of Mme. Chiang hung in the sitting room of the villa where Audrey met the Chinese leaders.

44 *Wendell Willkie in China:* Fenby *Generalissimo,* pp389-92; Li, pp182-86.

44 *Mme Chiang in the US:* Fenby *Generalissimo,* pp393-96; Li, pp193-237.

44 *Henry Luce, Theodore White and China:* Fenby *Generalissimo,* pp365-66 and pp398-99.

49 *Max's cocktails in Kowloon:* Emily Hahn described Max's 1940 party in *China to Me.*

50 *45 Kadoorie Avenue:* Kadoorie Avenue is still a street of single-family houses, an oasis amid the high-rise flats more common in Kowloon today. Number 45 sits on a quiet cul-de-sac – looking very much as it did in Max's photos, but now with a mature garden, and occupants more likely to be corporate leaders or media celebrities than modestly-paid government officials.

54 *Max's story:* The main sources for the Oxford family history and Max's early life are an unfinished memoir that he wrote in retirement, his RAF service record, and albums of photos and press clippings kept by his father.

59 *Sir Hubert Young:* biographical details from *Oxford Dictionary of National Biography,* 2004.

61 *Press reports of an airman missing in the African jungle: Daily Sketch,* June 14, 1933, *Southampton Echo,* June 13, 14, 15, 1933.

61 *Imperial Airways:* the history of the British Empire's airline is told in *Imperial Airways: The Birth of the British Airline Industry 1914-1940,* by Robert Bluffield.

62 *Kai Tak:* sources for the history of Hong Kong's first airport include *Wings over Hong Kong: A Tribute to Kai Tak: An Aviation History 1891-1998,* and the Hong Kong Civil Aviation Department.

64 *Ernest Hemingway:* the American writer visited Hong Kong in early

1941, as recounted by Moreira in *Hemingway on the China Front: His WWII Spy Mission with Martha Gellhorn*. David MacDougall described a lunch party (a 'great event') that he hosted for Hemingway to meet Agnes Smedley, Emily Hahn and two leading Chinese. Letter to his wife, Catherine MacDougall, February 27, 1941. MacDougall papers, Rhodes House.

CHAPTER FOUR

68 *Staff officer for air intelligence:* Max's official title was air liaison to the Far East Command Centre.

68 *Hong Kong, China and the Sino-Japanese war:* For the twentieth-century history of Hong Kong, China and the conflict with Japan, I am especially grateful to Philip Snow's *The Fall of Hong Kong*, to Jonathan Fenby's *Generalissimo* and his *Modern China*.

69 *Hong Kong neutrality:* 'The colony coasted into the 1940s with its serenity unimpaired.' Snow, p34.

69 *Charles gave Max a hard time, Mickey recalled:* Hahn, *China to Me*, pp160-61.

69 *Mickey spent her first night back in Hong Kong with Charles and Max:* Hahn, *China to Me*, pp201-02.

70 *Sir Mark Young:* biographical details from *Oxford Dictionary of National Biography*, 2004.

72 *Priestwood would later write:* Gwen Priestwood described Hong Kong's last dance in her memoir, *Through Japanese Barbed Wire*, p7.

72 *Carola Boxer:* Carola treasured a letter that her father wrote at her birth to 'my child', comparing his feelings to those of the poet Robert Burns for his 'love-begotten daughter'. Interview with Carola Boxer Vecchio, 2012.

72 *'It's come. War.':* Charles and Mickey's eve-of-battle, Hahn, *China to Me*, pp257-58.

73 *The Battle for Hong Kong:* My account of the eighteen-day battle for the colony draws on histories by Snow, Banham, Lindsay and others, as well as an informative booklet, *The Battle for Hong Kong: A Battlefield Tour*, by Major Helen Wildman and Ivan Wildman.

73 *Max's account of the battle:* from his letter to his sister, Margaret, written 'on the East River', January 3, 1942. Other firsthand accounts include David MacDougall (letter to Catherine), Ted Ross (letter to his mother), Gwen Priestwood, Emily Hahn, Phyllis Harrop and Iris Johannessen.

73 *The Pan Am Clipper which was about to take off:* Wings over Hong Kong, p102.

73 'It was one of those flawless December mornings': MacDougall, letter to Catherine from Chungking, January 17, 1942. MacDougall papers, Rhodes House.

74 'Little information to give them': Banham, p45.

76 David MacDougall...slept in his own bed for the first week: MacDougall letter to Catherine.

77 Charles Boxer wounded: Mickey was distraught when she heard the news, and spent the next weeks torn between caring for her baby and her lover. Charles was eventually held as a POW; Mickey famously avoided internment, and stayed on in Hong Kong for nearly two years, smuggling supplies to Boxer and supporting him as best she could, Hahn China to Me and Hong Kong Holiday.

78 Max took Boxer's place at daily liaison meetings: Max's letter to Margaret; Chan Chak Full Report on how I assisted in the war against Japan in Hong Kong and led British military men out of the encirclement. Memoir. Translation courtesy of Tim Luard.

79 Governor's cable, December 23: Young cable for Secretary of State. NA, FO 371/27752.

CHAPTER FIVE

82 8,000 exhausted men...against around 20,000 Japanese: Luard, p74.

82 The Christmas Day escape: Max's account of the escape is from his letter to Margaret, his official report, and articles in the South African and British press. I consulted many other firsthand accounts, including those by fellow escapees MacDougall, Ross, Guest, Chan, Montague, Gandy, Kennedy and Hide; as well as press articles and published accounts. See also my blog on HERO's adventures at Christmas 2009 at www.destinationchongqing.blogspot.com.

83 Desperate thrust through the enemy blockading line: Chan Chak broadcast speech of March 20, 1942, translated and sent to War Office by Brig. Grimsdale, WO 208/381.

83 Max 'unflappable': Letter from Captain Iain MacGregor, ADC to General Maltby, to Oliver Lindsay, Mar 28 1977. Lindsay papers, IWM. When Max reached Chungking on January 15, 1942 he found a letter from MacGregor's father enquiring about his son, and replied by telegram and a letter of Jan 20 to tell the anxious family that 'Iain was well up to Christmas afternoon' when Max had last seen him. Maltby papers, IWM.

85 'It was a suicidal thing to do': MacDougall letter to Catherine, Jan 17, 1942.

89 'Fortunately the moon was not yet up': David Legge quoted in The Hidden Years, Hong Kong 1941-45 by John Luff.

93 *The 'odds and sods' group:* Luard, p144, quoting Gandy's diary.

93 *'Owing to the masterly scouting and screening of Mr. Leung's guerrillas':* Montague report to Admiralty, ADM 199/357.

97 *Methodist Mission, hospitality and phone call:* Luard, pp205-07.

CHAPTER SIX

100 *'Dressed in an odd mixture of naval, civilian and Chinese clothing':* The Times, 'from our special correspondent, Chungking, January 16', published January 17, 1942.

101 *Chuck Sharp:* biographical details from *China's Wings* by Gregory Crouch.

101 *Jialing House:* Hong Kong residents Iris Johannessen and her family reached Chungking in late July, 1942 after a difficult journey across China, and she said that Jialing House was 'the only European-style hotel in the city'. *Iris: A Diary,* p208.

101 *John Keswick:* SOE set up a China branch under the direction of Keswick after the fall of Hong Kong, Snow p191; Yu, *OSS in China,* p20. Quote from Whitfield, *Hong Kong, Empire and the Anglo-American Alliance at War, 1941-45.*

101 *The Americans really ran the show:* Whitfield and Thorne, among others, discuss Anglo-American relations.

103 *The Flying Tigers:* a small museum, opposite the Stilwell museum in Chongqing, commemorates the daredevil Flying Tigers.

104 *Operation Remorse:* Cruickshank, p216-20; Bickers: *The business of a secret war: Operation 'Remorse' and SOE Salesmanship in Wartime China;* Robert Ryan: *A Very British Coup, The Sunday Times,* Jan 22, 2006.

104 *John Galvin and FE Bureau of Ministry of Information:* Ramakrishna, p72. Relations between Galvin and Stanley Smith, David MacDougall and Ted Ross: conversations with Warwick Ross and Sheena Recaldin.

104 *Stanley Smith:* 'an Australian publicity expert' who was put in charge of the Ministry of Information in China. Erik Watts became Press Attaché. Seymour report June 4, 1942, FO 371/31679.

105 *'Thus at breakfast-time we could read the news':* Gage, p108.

105 *Max and Berkeley Gage's trip to Fujian:* Max's diary; Gage memoir.

106 *Maya Redevitch:* Emily Hahn wrote about the captivating Polish linguist who worked for the Chinese government in *China to Me,* spelling the last name 'Roidevitch', p116-18.

107 *'The Max Oxford-Audrey Watson affair is progressing well':* Lady Seymour letters to Sir Horace Seymour, December 3 and 22, 1942. Seymour papers, Churchill Archives.

111 *15 Fan Niu Hang:* the old building was still standing in 2005—sadly dilapidated and overdue for demolition. A forest of ugly apartment buildings had long since blocked the view to the river.

112 *'You can be perfectly confident that Audrey is completely happy':* Violet Seymour letter to Frank Watson, January 8, 1944. Oxford family collection.

CHAPTER SEVEN

119 *File full of correspondence:* The correspondence about the Oxford marriage is preserved in the National Archives (FO 372/3864), along with the register of marriages of the British Consul District of Chungking (FO 681/33).

121 *Chan, Hsu and Oxford photograph:* the March 17 photo survived in both the Chan and the Oxford families, one of the very few portraits of that period in Max's life.

123 *Logs of the journey:* With these logs in hand, along with Audrey's letters and journals, my husband and I retraced my parents' drive some sixty-four years later. My account is at www.destinationchongqing.blogspot.com.

127 *24-hairpin bend road:* This stretch of road was later 'lost' to all but the locals, but is now preserved as a historic by-way. In 2008, our fearless driver insisted on taking us down the 24-zig dirt road, though now a highway bypasses it.

128 *Friends Ambulance Unit:* Michael Sullivan, who would marry a Chinese biologist and become the pre-eminent scholar on twentieth century Chinese art, was a volunteer from England. I was fortunate to meet him in Oxford in 2008 and again in 2012. On his travels as a relief volunteer, he took extraordinary photos of bomb damage in Chungking and of the Chinese countryside, a collection held in the archives of the Chongqing City Museum.

It so happened that Prof. Sullivan had a connection to the Christmas Day escape: he and his wife, Khoan, for some years looked after Bruce, a spaniel that came along on the escape, and which appeared in the group photo taken in Huizhou.

135 *A cosy mews flat in Kensington:* Max and Audrey's London home was at 7 Cornwall Mews South, SW7.

135 *Anthony Devas:* The artist became my godfather, and I was named after his daughter Emma. Anthony died of a stroke in 1958 at the young age of forty-seven. He had been elected to the Royal Academy in 1953, and shortly before his death he had painted the Queen, a commission for the Royal Artillery Company. His portrait of Audrey has travelled the world with me, as it did with Max and Audrey.

CHAPTER EIGHT

139 *The British restoration and postwar administration of Hong Kong:* historical background principally from Snow, *The Fall of Hong Kong* and Tsang, *A Modern History of Hong Kong* and *Democracy Shelved.*

139 *An oasis of law* and *order:* John Keswick, taipan of Jardine Matheson, whom Max had known in Chungking, advised the Colonial Office as early as 1943 that 'until the East has settled down, to relinquish this last haven of security would be greatly detrimental to British trade'. Snow, pp190-1.

140 *'Cautiously and in the light of bitter experience':* MacDougall letter to Max, June 5, 1945. Oxford family collection.

141 *Franklin Gimson:* conversation with his daughter, Judy Snowdon, December 2011.

145 *A happy reunion…in Mickey's New York home:* Charles Boxer's reunion with Emily Hahn and Carola was captured in an iconic photo in LIFE magazine of Nov 22, 1945. The couple whose affair had shocked prewar society soon wed and enjoyed a long, if still unconventional, relationship. They divided their time between England and America until Mickey's death in 1997. She was the *New Yorker's* longest-serving writer. Charles died in 2000 at the age of 96, and was known as the world's pre-eminent scholar of Portuguese colonial history.

146 *'Now we will eat':* MacDougall to Gent, Colonial Office, Nov 7, 1945, CO 591/20.

147 *Empty godowns:* Harcourt letter to Hall, November 11, 1945, CO 129/592/6.

147 *Very few private cars:* Alastair Todd, Hong Kong colonial service, interview 2006.

147 *'The colony must largely be rebuilt':* SCMP & HK Telegraph, Sept 30, 1945.

148 *WL Bond:* the story of 'Bondy' and CNAC is well told in *China's Wings* by Gregory Crouch.

148 *'Only the American pilots of the CNAC':* The Times, October 1946.

149 *Ping Shan airfield project:* documents from CO 537/1427.

149 *'Similar to putting up gun emplacements':* Snow, p270.

150 *'A royal welcome from Chan Chak':* MacDougall to Gent, Nov 7 1945, CO 591/20.

151 *'I always recall with the greatest joy and satisfaction our Hong Kong Escape':* Chan letter to Max, October 29, 1945. Oxford family collection.

151 *'There was a spontaneity':* Chan letter to Max, Nov 26, 1945. Oxford family collection.

158   *The British had returned to Malaya:* the political situation in Malaya and
      Singapore is discussed in *A Short History of Malaysia* by Harry Miller.

160   *Kap Sing:* Today Kap Sing can be spotted from the road bridge to
      Lantau, but is off-limits to visitors, still the site of a strategic
      lighthouse.

163   *Mission to review airport plans:* documents from CO 537/1427.

163   *Ministry of Civil Aviation letter to WJ Bigg:* January 14, 1946.

164   *'Deep Bay will make the better site':* Mission report, February 26, 1946.

164   *The RAF would make do with Kai Tak:* Eventually the RAF built a small
      military airfield at Shek Kong in the New Territories.

CHAPTER NINE

168   *Suspected collaborators:* Farrell, p130.

168   *70% of European-style residences...unfit for habitation:* Grantham, p103.

169   *'The Lees are building!':* Snow, p284.

169   *First Chinese cadet officer:* Farrell, p134.

169   *Ng Wing and Ah Mui:* The 'excellent' Ah Wing (as Audrey called him)
      remained with Max and Audrey throughout their Hong Kong years,
      and stayed in touch by letter for the rest of his life. I was fortunate to
      meet him and his son on a visit to Hong Kong in 1995.

173   *Branksome Towers:* the 1940s block has long since been replaced by a
      high rise apartment building of the same name.

174   *Harry and Frances Owen-Hughes:* conversation with their daughter,
      Helen Hyatt, July 2012.

174   *Thank-you letter from Admiral Chan:* Chan to Max, Aug 14, 1947.
      Oxford family collection.

176   *If you hadn't been through "camp", you didn't really count:* Interview
      with Anne Marden, May 2006. She arrived in Hong Kong as a
      young bride in September 1947, after marrying John Marden of the
      Wheelock Marden trading firm.

176   *Stanley Smith newspaper purchase:* This account is from 'the Stanley
      Smith Story' in www.churchie.com.au, the website of a Queensland
      school that Smith attended and later donated to; and his obituary,
      South China Morning Post, July 29, 1968.

177   *DeKantzow and Farrell, founders of Cathay Pacific:* Farrell obituary, *The
      Independent,* January 8, 1996; the history of Cathay Pacific is told in
      Beyond Lion Rock by Gavin Young.

182   *Iris Johannessen:* Iris later agreed to be my godmother, and attended my
      christening in Singapore Cathedral. She lived until the age of ninety-

nine. Her beloved Reidar died in Jamaica in 1969, and Iris later married Burke Knapp, an American official of the World Bank. She told her life story in a privately published memoir, *Iris: A Diary.*

CHAPTER TEN

194   *European-owned hongs moved to Hong Kong:* Carroll, p134.

194   *Civil aviation was booming: Wings over Kai Tak.*

194   *Cathay Pacific Airways expansion and sale to Swire:* Young, *Beyond Lion Rock.*

197   *Hong Kong population at 2.5 million by 1950:* Snow, p317.

197   *Visits to the Teesdales in the New Territories:* On one occasion, Audrey commissioned a nearby pottery works to make a small bust of Max, and took a liking to a pottery sculpture of chess players, which was chipped and very cheap. 'It depicts a man and a woman seated at a log, playing chess. I have seldom seen such power portrayed in pottery...' said Audrey in a journal entry of Sept 17, 1950.

200   *The LRC and the FCC:* Both clubs remain mainstays of Hong Kong society, now with much more diverse memberships. The LRC sits on its original site, a very valuable piece of Mid-Levels property, with much-expanded facilities. The FCC moved to the historic Ice House building on Lower Albert Road in 1982.

203   *SK Yee:* postwar career from *Dictionary of Hong Kong Biography.*

203   *SCMP editor's letter to MacDougall:* letter from Stewart to MacDougall, February 3, 1949. MacDougall papers, Rhodes House.

204   *David MacDougall's legacy:* There are no streets or trails in Hong Kong named after the first postwar Colonial Secretary, but historians agree that he was one of the most significant and far-sighted colonial administrators of his generation. Max and Audrey would miss him and Inez, but remained lifelong friends.

204   *The Amethyst Incident:* the incident is recounted in *Hostage on the Yangtze* by Malcolm Murfett, and by Fenby, *Modern China*, p346.

206   *Gillibrand family in Shanghai:* Conversation with John Gillibrand, June 2012.

206   *Chan Chak's last phone call with his eldest daughter:* Conversation with Paula Chan, December 2009.

207   *Maya Redevitch:* Press reports of the shooting drama included *The Miami News,* Oct 5, 1949.

208   *Kai Tak capacity and runways in 1949: Hong Kong Sunday Herald,* Sept 4, 1949.

210   *CNAC eviction from Kai Tak:* documents are from FO 371/75924 and 75925.

210   *Hong Kong authorities didn't consult Whitehall:* FS Tomlinson memo, Aug 5, 1949. FO 371/75924.

210   *A death sentence for his beloved airline:* Bond, p375.

210   *CNAC's space was urgently needed by the RAF:* Memo to Minister of State, Aug 12, 1949. FO 371/75925.

210   *CNAC would conduct a limited service from Kai Tak:* Leary *Dragon's Wings,* p219.

210   *'Reinforcements which are vital for the defence of Hong Kong in the event of an emergency':* Hong Kong government press release, Aug 19, 1949.

211   *Max was asked be the first commander of its air arm:* Max was officially gazetted as commander of the HK Auxiliary Air Force in June 1949.

211   *Moss farewell cocktail party: South China Morning Post,* Sept 3, 1949.

212   *Defection of CNAC and CATC pilots:* PQ Nov 21, 1949. FO 371/75935.

212   *The grounded planes dispute:* documents are mainly from FO 371/93126, CO 537/5628, 5629 and 5633, and CAB 21/3270/2882. The prolonged international dispute is discussed in articles by Victor Kaufman (*The US, Britain and the CAT Controversy*), William Leary (*Aircraft and Anti-Communists*), and Steve Tsang (*Strategy for Survival*), as well as in law journals.

213   *Willauer meeting with Chiang in Taipei:* Leary article.

213   *Sir Oliver Franks report to Foreign Office:* Telegram no. 5618 of Dec 1, 1949. CAB 21/3270.

214   *Donovan meeting with Grantham: Via Ports,* p162.

215   *CAT newsletter: CAT Bulletin,* Feb 15, 1950.

215   *Donovan and Willauer press conference:* When Max's name came up for a second time, American journalist Seymour Topping (then with AP) asked: 'What is Oxford's official position?' and was told: 'He is Acting Director of Civil Aviation, Government of Hong Kong.'

215   *Tillman Durdin's story: New York Times,* Jan 5, 1950.

216   *The Economist magazine summed up the British dilemma: Economist,* March 4, 1950.

218   *It is likely that President Truman raised the issue personally with Winston Churchill:* Kaufman article, p108.

219   *Chennault and Willauer didn't get much reward for their 'sweat and tears':* Willauer per Leary in *Perilous Missions,* p205.

219   *'Don't let's fall out with the United States for the sake of China':* Churchill, as quoted in Kaufman article, p112.

Bibliography

Published Works

Alden, Dauril. *Charles R. Boxer: An Uncommon Life*. Lisboa: Fundação Oriente, 2001.

Banham, Tony. *Not the Slightest Chance: the Defence of Hong Kong, 1941*. Vancouver: UBC, 2003.

Bayly, C. A., and T. N. Harper. *Forgotten Armies: The Fall of British Asia, 1941-1945*. Cambridge, MA: Belknap of Harvard UP, 2005.

Bickers, Robert. "The Business of a Secret War: Operation 'Remorse' and SOE Salesmanship in Wartime China." *Intelligence and National Security* 16.4 (2001): 11-36.

Bluffield, Robert. *Imperial Airways: The Birth of the British Airline Industry 1914-1940*. Hersham: Ian Allan, 2009.

Carroll, John M. *A Concise History of Hong Kong*. Lanham: Rowman & Littlefield, 2007.

Chongqing Association for Cultural Exchanges with Foreign Countries. *Wartime Capital: Chongqing Today*. Chengdu: Sichuan People's Publishing House, 1991.

Colonial Secretariat. *Hong Kong Civil Service List for 1949*. Hong Kong: Govt. Printers & Publishers, 1949.

Crouch, Gregory. *China's Wings: War, Intrigue, Romance, and Adventure in the Middle Kingdom during the Golden Age of Flight*. New York: Bantam, 2012.

Cruickshank, Charles. *SOE in the Far East*. Oxford: Oxford UP, 1983.

Cuthbertson, Ken. *Nobody Said Not to Go: The Life, Loves, and Adventures of Emily Hahn*. New York: Faber and Faber, 1998.

Elphick, Peter. *Far Eastern File: The Intelligence War in the Far East, 1930-1945*. London: Hodder & Stoughton, 1997.

Endacott, G. B., and Alan Birch. *Hong Kong Eclipse*. Hong Kong: Oxford UP, 1978.

England, Vaudine. *The Quest of Noel Croucher: Hong Kong's Quiet Philanthropist*. Hong Kong: Hong Kong UP, 1998. Print.

Fenby, Jonathan. *Generalissimo: Chiang Kai-shek and the China He Lost*. London: Free, 2003.

Fenby, Jonathan. *Modern China: The Fall and Rise of a Great Power, 1850 to the Present*. New York: Ecco, 2008.

Fromkin, David. *A Peace to End All Peace: The Fall of the Ottoman Empire and the Creation of the Modern Middle East.* New York: H. Holt, 2001.

Gage, Berkeley. *It's Been a Marvellous Party!: The Personal and Diplomatic Reminiscences of Berkeley Gage.* London: B. Gage, 1989.

Grantham, Alexander. *Via Ports: From Hong Kong to Hong Kong.* Hong Kong: Hong Kong UP, 1965.

Guest, Freddie. *Escape from the Bloodied Sun.* London: Jarrolds, 1956.

Hahn, Emily. *China to Me.* Garden City, NY: Doubleday, Doran &, 1944.

Hahn, Emily. *Hong Kong Holiday.* Garden City, NY: Doubleday, 1946.

Hahn, Emily. *The Soong Sisters.* New York: Doubleday, Doran &, 1941.

Han, Suyin. *Destination Chungking.* London: Jonathan Cape, 1942.

Harrop, Phyllis. *Hong Kong Incident.* London: Eyre & Spottiswoode, 1943.

Hazzard, Shirley. *The Great Fire.* New York: Farrar, Straus and Giroux, 2003.

Herzstein, Robert E. *Henry R. Luce, Time, and the American Crusade in Asia.* Cambridge: Cambridge UP, 2005.

Hewitt, Anthony. *To Freedom through China: Escaping from Japanese-occupied Hong Kong 1942.* Barnsley: Pen & Sword Military, 2004.

Holdsworth, May, and Christopher Munn. *Dictionary of Hong Kong Biography.* Hong Kong: Hong Kong UP, 2012.

Johannessen, Iris. *Iris: A Diary.* Privately published.

Kaufman, Victor S. "The United States, Britain and the CAT Controversy." *Journal of Contemporary History* 40.1 (2005): 95-113. JSTOR. Web.

Kennedy, Alexander. *'Hong Kong' Full Circle 1939-45.* London: Privately Published, 1969.

Ko, Tim Keung, and Jason Wordie. *Ruins of War: A Guide to Hong Kong's Battlefields and Wartime Sitess.* Hong Kong: Joint Pub (HK), 1996.

Leary, William M. "Aircraft and Anti-Communism: CAT in Action, 1949-52." *The China Quarterly* 52.Oct-Dec (1972): 654-69. JSTOR. Web.

Leary, William M. *The Dragon's Wings: the China National Aviation Corporation and the Development of Commercial Aviation in China.* University of Georgia, 1976.

Leary, William M. *Perilous Missions: Civil Air Transport and CIA Covert Operations in Asia.* University, Ala.: University of Alabama, 1984.

Li, Laura Tyson. *Madame Chiang Kai-Shek: China's Eternal First Lady.* New York: Atlantic Monthly, 2006.

Lindsay, Oliver, and John R. Harris. *The Battle for Hong Kong 1941-1945: Hostage to Fortune.* Hong Kong: Hong Kong UP, 2005.

Lindsay, Oliver. *At the Going down of the Sun: Hong Kong and South-East Asia, 1941-1945.* London: Hamilton, 1981.

Luard, Tim. *Escape from Hong Kong: Admiral Chan Chak's Christmas Day Dash, 1941*. Hong Kong: Hong Kong UP, 2012.

Luff, John. *The Hidden Years, Hong Kong 1941-45*. Hong Kong: South China Morning Post, 1967.

Moreira, Peter. *Hemingway on the China Front: His WWII Spy Mission with Martha Gellhorn*. Washington, D.C.: Potomac, 2006.

Murfett, Malcolm H. *Hostage on the Yangtze: Britain, China, and the Amethyst Crisis of 1949*. Annapolis, MD: Naval Institute, 1991.

Pakula, Hannah. *The Last Empress: Madame Chiang Kai-Shek and the Birth of Modern China*. New York: Simon & Schuster, 2009.

Payne, Robert. *Chungking Diary*. London, Toronto: W. Heinemann, 1945.

Peck, Graham. *Two Kinds of Time*. Boston: Houghton Mifflin, 1950.

Priestwood, Gwen. *Through Japanese Barbed Wire*. London: Harrap, 1944.

Ramakrishna, Kumar. *Emergency Propaganda: The Winning of Malayan Hearts and Minds, 1948-1958*. Richmond: Curzon, 2002.

Snow, Philip. *The Fall of Hong Kong: Britain, China, and the Japanese Occupation*. New Haven: Yale UP, 2003.

State Council Information Office of the PRC. *Hump Air Transport*. China Intercontinental Press.

Stericker, John, and Veronica Stericker. *Hong Kong in Picture and Story*. Hong Kong: n.p., 1953.

Stericker, John. *A Tear for the Dragon*. London: Barker, 1958.

Stewart, Watt. *Henry Meiggs: Yankee Pizarro*. Durham, NC: Duke UP, 1946.

Stokes, Edward. *Hedda Morrison's Hong Kong: Photographs & Impressions 1946-47* Hong Kong: Hong Kong UP, 2005.

Thorne, Christopher G. *Allies of a Kind: The United States, Britain, and the War against Japan, 1941-1945*. New York: Oxford UP, 1978.

Tsang, Steve. "Strategy for Survival: The Cold War and Hong Kong's Policy towards Kuomintang and Chinese Communist Activities in the 1950s." *Journal of Imperial and Commonwealth History* 25.2 (n.d.): 294-317. JSTOR. Web.

Tsang, Steve Yui-Sang. *Democracy Shelved: Great Britain, China, and Attempts at Constitutional Reform in Hong Kong, 1945-1952*. Hong Kong: Oxford UP, 1988.

Tsang, Steve Yui-Sang. *A Modern History of Hong Kong*. London: I.B. Tauris, 2004.

Tuchman, Barbara W. *Stilwell and the American Experience in China*. New York, NY: Macmillan, 1970.

Waters, Dan and McEwan, Alison (eds). Colin McEwan's Diary: The Battle for Hong Kong and the Escape into China. *Journal of the Royal Asiatic*

Society Hong Kong Branch, Vol. 45, 2005.

Whelan, Russell. *The Flying Tigers; the Story of the American Volunteer Group.* New York: Viking, 1942.

White, Theodore H., and Annalee Jacoby. *Thunder out of China.* New York: William Sloane Associates, 1946.

Whitfield, Andrew J. *Hong Kong, Empire and the Anglo-American Alliance at War: 1941-1945.* Hong Kong: HKU, 2001.

Willkie, Wendell L. *One World.* New York, NY: Simon and Schuster, 1943.

Willmott, H. P. *The Second World War in the Far East.* Ed. John Keegan. London: Cassell, 1999.

Winchester, Simon. *The Man Who Loved China: The Fantastic Story of the Eccentric Scientist Who Unlocked the Mysteries of the Middle Kingdom.* New York, NY: Harper, 2008.

Wings over Hong Kong: A Tribute to Kai Tak: An Aviation History 1891-1998. Hong Kong: Odyssey, 1998.

Young, Gavin. *Beyond Lion Rock: The Story of Cathay Pacific Airways.* London: Hutchinson, 1988.

Yu, Maochun. *The Dragon's War: Allied Operations and the Fate of China, 1937-1947.* Annapolis, MD: Naval Institute, 2006.

Yu, Maochun. *OSS in China: Prelude to Cold War.* New Haven: Yale UP, 1996.

Unpublished Papers

Bartholomew, Gilbert. Reports of the Air Attaché Chungking. NA, AIR 40/1361-2.

Gandy, Horace. Lt. Com. GH Gandy RN, Report of *Operation by 2nd MTB Flotilla at Hong Kong 8-26 December 1941,* March 8, 1942. NA, ADM 267/131.

Grimsdale, Gordon. *Thunder in the East,* unpublished memoir of Major General GE Grimsdale, 1947. IWM Documents Section: 8521.

Hide, PO Stephen (Buddy). Account on www.hongkongescape.org, posted by Richard Hide (accessed in 2004 on www.hamstat.demon.co.uk).

Montague, Hugh. Com HM Montague RN, Report of *Proceedings of Party which Escaped from Hong Kong to China.* NA, ADM 199/357.

Oxford, Audrey.
Correspondence, diaries and journals. Family collection.

Oxford, Max.
Correspondence, memoir and diaries. Family collection, including:
Letter to his sister Margaret, January 3, 1942.
Report to Air Ministry on escape from Hong Kong, undated.

MacDougall, David.
    Correspondence and papers. Rhodes House.
    Interview by Dr. Steve Tsang, February 26, 1987. Transcript. Rhodes House.
    Reports and official letters. NA.
Ross, CE (Ted). Letter to his mother, January 1942. Ross family collection.
Seymour, Sir Hubert and Lady Violet. Correspondence, Seymour papers, Churchill Archives.
Warburton, James. Reports of the Air Attaché Chungking, AIR 40/1361-2.
Watson, Francis. *The White Gold of Chile or Memories of the Nitrate Industry in Chile 1904-1914.*
Watson, Joan. Notes on Watson family tree; diary for 1936-40.

Archives

Bodleian Libraries (Rhodes House Collection), University of Oxford.
Churchill Archives, Churchill College, University of Cambridge.
Hong Kong Public Record Office, Carl Smith Collection.
Hong Kong University, Special Collections; Ride Collection.
Imperial War Museum, London (IWM).
National Archives, Kew, London (NA). Series AIR, ADM, CAB, CO, FO, WO.
National Air and Space Museum, Washington DC.